To Give or Not To Give?

RETHINKING DEPENDENCY,
RESTORING GENEROSITY,
AND REDEFINING SUSTAINABILITY

JOHN ROWELL

D1303180

Authentic

ATLANTA · LONDON · HYDERABAD

Authentic Publishing
We welcome your questions and comments.

USA	PO Box 444, 285 Lynnwood Ave, Tyrone, GA, 30290
	www.authenticbooks.com
UK	9 Holdom Avenue, Bletchley, Milton Keynes, Bucks, MK1 1QR, UK
	www.authenticmedia.co.uk
India	Logos Bhavan, Medchal Road, Jeedimetla Village, Secunderabad
	500 055, A.P.

To Give or Not To Give?
ISBN-13: 978-1-932805-86-4
ISBN-10: 1-932805-86-9

Copyright © 2006 by John Rowell

10 09 08 07 / 6 5 4 3 2 1

Published in 2007 by Authentic

Unless otherwise indicated, Scripture quotations are taken from the NEW AMERICAN STANDARD BIBLE ®. Copyright © The Lockman Foundation 1960, 1962, 1963, 1968, 1971, 1972, 1973, 1975, 1977, 1995. Used by permission.

Scripture marked NIV is taken from the HOLY BIBLE, NEW INTERNATIONAL VERSION®. NIV®. Copyright © 1973, 1978, 1984 by International Bible Society. Used by permission of Zondervan Publishing House. All rights reserved.

Library of Congress Cataloging-in-Publication Data

Rowell, John, 1951-
    To give or not to give? : rethinking dependency, restoring generosity, and redefining sustainability / John Rowell.
        p. cm.
    Includes bibliographical references and index.
    ISBN-13: 978-1-932805-86-4 (pbk. : alk. paper)
    ISBN-10: 1-932805-86-9 (pbk. : alk. paper)
    1. Missions. 2. Distributive justice--Religious aspects--Christianity. 3. Wealth--Religious aspects--Christianity. 4. Christianity and culture. 5. East and West. I. Title.

BV2063.R59 2007
266--dc22
                              2006032553

Cover design: Paul Lewis
Interior design: Angela Lewis
Editorial team: Andy Sloan, KJ Larson

Printed in the United States of America

John Rowell is to be thanked for tackling one of the most intractable challenges facing the post-Constantinian missionary enterprise from the West. His book is the best that I have seen on the subject of dependency. *To Give or Not to Give?* deserves to become required reading for church leaders and mission committees, mission policy makers and missionaries, missiologists and missionaries-in-training.

JONATHAN J. BONK
Executive Director, Overseas Ministries Study Center
Editor, *International Bulletin of Missionary Research*

This book is a ringing call for Christians living in affluent nations to reject the seductive rationalizations that harden their hearts against sacrificial economic partnerships with poor Christians. Urgent, compelling, biblical.

RONALD J. SIDER
Author of *Rich Christians in an Age of Hunger*
and President of Evangelicals for Social Action

I praise God for this more sensible, biblical, and down-to-earth challenge concerning money and mission. Though this is a long book and not an easy read, I pray many people will take the time, as I have, to read it and find a more grace-awakened approach to this important issue.

GEORGE VERWER
Founder, Operation Mobilization

I thank God for John Rowell. God has given him an unusual and remarkable spiritual ability to look at the old and to come up with new and unorthodox insights. You may not adopt all of them, but I believe that this is a book that every international and local church missions leader would do well to prayerfully read.

DR. PAUL CEDAR
Chairman, Mission America Coalition

Rowell is provocative in a way that kingdom of God thinkers always are. His perspective will challenge you, trouble you, and leave you rethinking your convictions. But *To Give or Not to Give?* goes beyond asking provocative questions to providing provocative answers. This is a must-read for anyone desiring to effectively give and work in twenty-first century missions. Food for the Hungry International is making this book mandatory reading for our top leadership.

RANDY HOAG
Former President, Food for the Hungry International
Director, Vision of Community Fellowship

John Rowell has provided a great service to the global church. He challenges us to examine how we are to live out oneness in Christ by touching the most sensitive nerve in our body—our pocketbook. His biblical insights coupled with personal experience in Bosnia has lead him to explore an alternative route towards interdependence within the body of Christ. Be forewarned that this book will smash some historical sacred cows of Christian mission.

GARY EDMONDS
President, Breakthrough Partners

In *To Give or Not to Give?* John Rowell takes on long-standing premises that have guided the fiscal aspects of world missions for more than a century. His book shares a new and, I believe, a more biblical approach to funding world evangelism. The reading and digesting of this book will add a new dimension to global outreach—a dimension that could revolutionize the way we do world missions.

DR. KENNETH M. MEYER
Chancellor, Trinity International University, Deerfield, IL

In *To Give or Not to Give?* John Rowell challenges our minds to rethink and our hearts to recommit to meeting worldwide needs that are seemingly "greater than ever." He compels the reader to consider making investments that demonstrate a more biblical approach to stewardship and a more benevolent approach to extravagant generosity—and all this within a strong framework of genuine accountability. Read at your own risk, though, knowing that you will be challenged and likely changed in a way that will increase your commitment to impact the world through tangible expressions of love, compassion, salt, and light.

GREG CAPIN, CPA
Partner, Capin Crouse, LLP, Atlanta, GA

As a former CMA missionary for twenty-five years and denominational mission executive for five more, I have observed the pendulum swinging back from policies discouraging financial assistance to national churches to a more pragmatic approach consistent with principles of partnership and compassion. John Rowell's scholarly work will assist mission agencies and churches to bring this topic boldly back on the table and provide the verbal tools to enter into effective dialogue. *To Give or Not to Give?* is a must-read for anyone responsible for the distribution of mission finances.

JOHN A. HARVEY
Senior Pastor, First Alliance Church, Toccoa, GA

John Rowell's treatise is a welcome call for twenty-first century leaders to overcome the drawbacks of dependency by urging us toward true partnership and healthy expressions of mutual support. He connects both with a profound argument for a return to simple generosity and a spirit of covenant commitment. I am convinced his perspective is missiologically sound and theologically based—a practical approach to advancing world missions that we can all learn from. I have watched the principles expressed in *To Give or Not to Give?* work in practice since we began partnering with John Rowell fifteen years ago. Based on my experience, it is easy to commend his challenges to church and mission leaders everywhere.

DAMIR SPOLJARIC
President, The Evangelical Church of Croatia

John Rowell's contribution to missions and evangelism soars to places where church and mission leaders often fear to fly. When there he asks tough and honest questions with a genuine passion for truth, yet with no ax to grind and no hidden agenda. Beware that Rowell unveils how some Western and church-instituted expressions of Jesus often do damage to God's message. As a result, Rowell's words will bring enough needed turbulence to your soul to require reading it with your seat belt fastened!

BENJAMIN HOMAN
President and CEO, Food for the Hungry, Inc.

Just when you thought it was safe to dismiss Western funding of emerging churches as "welfare dependency," John Rowell revisits the problem in *To Give or Not to Give?* His answer—"Give!"—emerges from his study of Scripture and his experience as a church planter in Bosnia. Rowell writes that, with discernment, Western donors can give "with no strings attached" to foreign churches in order to invest in discipling without dominating or ruining the relationship. Readers will also be challenged to consider living "a wartime lifestyle" in order to move massive amounts of funding to the poor peoples of the world.

BOB BLINCOE
US Director, Frontiers

This is a timely challenge to the accepted limits of Western generosity that compels us all to change our minds and give more freely as a way of life! This book will wonderfully enrich your understanding of how to share financially with peoples from poorer cultures in the twenty-first century.

GEORGE MILEY
International Director, Antioch Network

Every once in a while a book comes along that challenges Christian leaders to review their commonly held beliefs with a new biblical evaluation. By encouraging radical generosity in a world where over one billion are living in abject poverty, Rowell confronts our selfishness, our greed, and our tendency to obscure these sins by our insistence that poorer churches be "self-supporting." This discomforting appeal deserves to be taken seriously—even by those who disagree with some of Rowell's conclusions.

PAUL BORTHWICK
Development Associates International

In *To Give or Not to Give?* John Rowell challenges the global Christian community to stretch financially for the sake of countries which are in need of outside resources. In encouraging mutual partnerships, Rowell helps us see how the kingdom of God can be advanced in today's world, where inattention to countries in dire need too often prevails. This book challenges us all to wake up and to become better stewards of kingdom resources.

KARMELO KRESONJA
President, Evangelical Church of Bosnia Herzegovina

Woven through these pages you will find the heart of a deeply passionate follower, the rootedness of a disciplined mind, and the questions of a twenty-first century reformer. Whether you agree with John or not, his questions and insight cannot be ignored. This book has more challenge per sentence than anything I've read in the last ten years. I find the implications of this resurrected conversation to be personally disturbing, missionally explosive, and perhaps a missing ingredient holding back the answer to our prayer—that God's kingdom would come on earth as it is in heaven.

CAROL DAVIS
President, Leaf-Line Initiatives

CONTENTS

DEDICATION

This book is dedicated to two couples who have consistently chosen to
give, knowing that they have received special material blessing in this
life in order to pass that blessing on to others. I am only one of many
people touched by their extravagant generosity!

May God keep increasing the store of seed available to

ROGER AND ANN STULL

so that they can keep sowing globally for the sake
of the kingdom of heaven.

And may the benefit of heavenly treasure stored up during long and
productive lives spent serving the Lord, the body of Christ, and
those in need around the world be received in full by

PAUL E. AND BARBARA CRAFTON

two godly people who made it their business to invest in eternity
before going home to be with the Lord in 2005.

ACKNOWLEDGMENTS

Special thanks are due to several people who have helped me get this book into print. First and foremost my deepest debt of gratitude is owed to my wife of thirty-six years. Ginger invested as much of her life along the way as I did mine, giving up untold hours of our "discretionary time," allowing me to research, discuss and write about these issues. The project reflects my passion but also her practical wisdom. We birthed the end result together. Thanks to her for reading, reflecting, and listening to my ideas far beyond the limits of her interest in the subject!

I am also grateful to Dani Jacobson, Laura Lyerly, and Heather Thomas, colleagues within my mission organization, who took time from their official duties to type and retype the manuscript. Their service was a labor of love for the kingdom and a special gift to me personally.

This project was conceived because of my experience working with pastors and lay leaders in the Bosnian Church Planting Fellowship and the Evangelical Church of Bosnia Herzegovina. May God bless the brothers and sisters on both sides of the ocean who provoked me to think more deeply and who helped shape my convictions about biblical generosity.

Dr. Peter Kuzmic and Dr. Timothy Tennent provided an academic setting for my initial inquiry into the themes included in this book. They also mentored me through the Doctor of Ministry program at Gordon Conwell Theological Seminary. By going far beyond the professorial service their positions obliged them to offer, their personal examples and professional encouragement have deepened my walk with God. Both these men and the seminary have been generous in the extreme!

A word of thanks is also due to Kris and Lura Mineau who extended extravagant hospitality to me during my resident studies in Massachusetts. They opened their home and their hearts readily as Jesus said men and women of peace are apt to do.

Finally, I am grateful to the staff of Authentic Media, especially to my editor, Andrew Sloan, for making my effort a better book in the end. For all these people and more, I am humbly grateful. Praise the Lord for good and godly friends who choose to give as a way of life!

Transformative Generosity for Global Missions in a New Millennium

Command those who are rich . . . to do good, to be rich in good deeds, and to be generous and willing to share. In this way they will lay up treasure for themselves as a firm foundation for the coming age, so that they may take hold of the life that is truly life. (1 Timothy 6:17–19 NIV)

The world has enough for everyone's need, but not for everyone's greed. (Mahatma Gandhi)

Since God gives to all, and gives through each, cooperation can replace competition, and the gifts can circulate. (Miroslav Volf, *Free of Charge*, 108)

One of the most fundamental questions for Christians in the materially affluent West is how they use their wealth in order to advance God's redemptive work in our world of spiritual lostness and physical poverty. All of us, and especially those living in materialistically oriented societies, need to be constantly reminded that the Bible is full of warnings against the dangers of wealth and that Jesus makes it explicitly clear that we cannot serve both God and Mammon.

Money in itself is morally ambivalent; instead of liberating it can enslave human beings, including its owners. In our semi-hedonistic cultures it is frequently (ab)used to promote evil and ultimately destroy life. And yet it has an enormous potential to be used for good, wholesome, and life-advancing purposes. All human life, individually and in community, seems to be substantially conditioned by the possession and use of money and material wealth. No question: money is power!

The crucial question, however, is how we use it. What is its role in our lives and our communities? Are we wise owners and generous stewards, or are we insecure hoarders and selfish consumers? Do we realize that money is not the supreme value but only a providentially provided means for a greater and common good? Do we recognize that although money and possessions may be a sign of God's blessing, they are not necessarily a badge of our human virtue?

Can we credibly witness for Christ and his kingdom in a world of poverty, pain, and injustice if we cannot clearly profess our faith in the power of the living God over the idols of materialism and the rule of mammon? Can we with integrity confess our faith in the living Christ as our Lord if our self-sufficient lifestyles deny our humble reliance on him—for we have abandoned the way of the cross, of self-denial, and of trusting dependence on him and his provisional faithfulness?

Historically, Christian churches have best advanced missionary objectives when they were so spiritually motivated and organizationally structured that they were able to enlist sacrificial giving and voluntary service. This is the ethos of the New Testament church and of great spiritual movements of both renewal and revival. The modern-day Western (especially American) preoccupation with money, buildings, and programs is foreign to the New Testament, which may be a very serious sign of a compromised Christianity that has been captivated by a secular, materialistic cash-register culture. Preoccupation with budgets, marketing techniques, and frantic search for numerically measurable results can easily degenerate into ministries marked by materialistic patterns without spiritual power.

The holy task of world evangelization at the beginning of a new century—if it is to be done in Christ's way and for God's glory—will require from all of us less competition and more cooperation, less self-sufficiency and more self-denial, less ambition to lead and more willingness to serve, less of a drive to dominate and more of the desire to develop. It is time for the worldwide church of Jesus Christ to learn how to move from the secular patterns of competition and independence toward the full-fledged biblical way of complementarity and interdependence in both life and practice.

The noteworthy volume you are holding in your hands points us with conviction and clarity in that desired direction. John Rowell has written a biblically based, experientially tested, and missiologically groundbreaking book that deserves to become a globally challenging manifesto for Christian stewardship in the twenty-first century. It calls Christians to the kind of generosity that is both an expression of our faith in God and of our love for those in need. My hope is that it will at least stimulate a much-needed discussion and—why not?—a candid and constructive debate of the kind that Ron Sider's classic bestseller, *Rich Christians in an Age of Hunger,* did some thirty years ago and in mission circles Jonathan Bonk's *Missions and Money* some fifteen years later. Both of these celebrated books have been termed controversial by defenders of the status quo, and yet their numerous printings and wide-ranging impact witness to the fact that they have successfully addressed burning problems and challenges in the lives of Western Christians and missionaries respectfully.

Rowell follows in their footsteps, for he has empirically detected what Bonk's subtitle aptly summarizes: *Affluence as a Western*

Missionary Problem. The issues in these prophetic books as well as in *To Give or Not to Give?* are primarily ethical. They pertain to the very integrity of believers' lives and practice, and they address the discrepancy between word and deed in Christian behavior. Rowell, therefore, challenges not only our thinking about matters of money, but calls us to a change of attitudes and to new patterns of giving. The book calls us to genuine repentance in the sensitive area of materialism and to unselfish generosity as an expression of Christian love and strategic participation in the enhancement of God's cause in our broken world. He reminds us not only of the large scale and complexity of the needs of humanity but also of the availability of divinely provided resources to meet these needs. More significantly, he makes innovative and brave strategic proposals on how to match the two.

John Rowell is internationally known as a successful church planter and mission strategist. His earlier book, *Magnify Your Vision for the Small Church,* has been widely read; and, more importantly, its principles have been successfully applied by many mission-minded pastors. There, as well as here, he is analytically and prophetically challenging. Many of his ideas require further reflection and some demand immediate corrective action. Overall, however, Rowell calls for a major rethinking about the way missions are traditionally done, making a bold proposal for what we moderns like to call "a change of paradigm." He makes a strong moral case for greater (distributive) justice in global missions.

In this he does not stand alone.

The most important and enduring outcome of the celebrated 1974 International Congress on World Evangelization was the *Lausanne Covenant.* This sound and globally influential document (mission-centered "statement of faith") of continuing significance, after pointing to the urgency of effective world evangelization, states: "The goal should be, by all available means and at the earliest possible time, that every person will have the opportunity to hear, understand, and receive the good news. We cannot hope to attain this goal without sacrifice. All of us are shocked by the poverty of millions and disturbed by the injustices which cause it. Those of us who live in affluent circumstances accept our duty to develop a simple life-style in order to contribute more generously to both relief and evangelism."

This recognition and appeal have awakened many Christian consciences and led to a new search for viable and credible lifestyles in our world of abject poverty and economic disparities. Although there are in our Western self-reliant and consumerist cultures many hurdles and temptations on the way, this indispensable search for authenticity and effectiveness continues. It is a process in which we need voices like Rowell's. We also need to recover and study again the considerable wisdom and balance of the wholistic missiology of the Lausanne movement as articulated in the Lausanne Occasional Papers, treasures also known as LOP-documents. For the subject matter under consideration, of special relevance are "An Evangelical Commitment to Simple Life-style," "The Grand Rapids Report on Evangelism and Social Responsibility," and "The Willowbank Report on Gospel and Culture."

The last one has a pertinent paragraph on "Power Structures and Mission." After a reference to the poverty of the masses in the Third World, it states that "their plight is due in part to an economic system which is controlled mostly by North Atlantic countries" (today we would probably add "and multinational companies which drive the forces of globalization"). The document then prophetically calls for solidarity with the poor and the denunciation of injustice "in the name of the Lord who is the God of justice as well as of justification." Reminding its readers of the concern about syncretism in the younger Third World churches, the document then addresses the often neglected fact that "Western churches fall prey to the same sin. Indeed, perhaps the most insidious sin of syncretism in the world today is the attempt to mix a privatized gospel of personal forgiveness with a worldly (even demonic) attitude to wealth and power. . . . So we who belong to, or come from, the West will examine ourselves and seek to purge ourselves of Western-style syncretism." *To Give or Not to Give?* can, among other things, serve as a most helpful instrument in this dual process of examination and purification.

In conclusion, Rowell's book has enormous transformative potential—pedagogically, spiritually, and missiologically. It provokes us to rethink the old categories of dependency and independency from a fresh biblical perspective and calls for a new awareness of global interdependence and mutual responsibility in the body of Christ. Some will be tempted to resist its bold questioning of their privileged positions and unscriptural attitudes of superiority and will be quick to rationalize their prosperity and related entitlements. And yet one would hope and pray that the book will be widely read and openly discussed in evangelical mission circles and that in that process many will be led away from what is often justifiably perceived as a neocolonial mindset and practice and move toward a more biblical view of mutuality and sharing at the same "Father's table": recognizing, under the lordship of Christ, that in spite of geographical distances, cultural differences, and political divisions there is in our world only one gospel and only one body—the church of those redeemed by grace and therefore ruled by generosity of love and not by differentiations of law.

This book affirms these fundamental theological truths and spiritual commitments by inviting those sitting at opposite sides of the Father's global table to an honest family conversation, so that "speaking the truth in love, we will in all things grow up into him who is the Head, that is, Christ. From him the whole body, joined and held together by every supporting ligament, grows and builds itself up in love, as each part does its work" (Ephesians 4:15–16 NIV)—to the everlasting glory of God our Father.

Dr. Peter Kuzmic

President of the Evangelical Theological Faculty, Osijek, Croatia, Eva B. and Paul E. Toms Distinguished Professor of World Missions and European Studies, Gordon Conwell Theological Seminary, South Hamilton, Massachusetts

Dealing with Global Need and Western Greed

Reading *To Give or Not to Give?* makes for edgy, stretching stuff. Most who purchase it will be tempted to skip to the end, to the bottom line, to try to find how the prevalent managerial mission systems can make the latest adjustment. But Rowell does not let us do that.

He rightly challenges our existing missionary attitudes about money, our resource distribution systems, and our lifestyle choices—on and off the field. He has well documented his work in history, working from secular and Christian sources alike—quoting from the World Bank, the United Nations, and US foreign policy material, as well as drawing from Jonathan Bonk and Bryant Myers—two leaders to whom Rowell is deeply indebted. But above all he attempts to root his argument in Scripture—not an easy task.

His audience is probably to be found primarily among leaders in the United States, but the core issues of the book are equally applicable to both the Global North and the Global South. The challenge of how to fund Christian global mission is, after all, not a task belonging only to the West, nor to the wealthier nations, wherever they may be found. Significantly, in just about every "poor" nation, there are believers to whom God has entrusted enormous wealth. So Rowell offers a challenge as to how we should make righteous use of riches entrusted to followers of Jesus all over the world. National leaders will do well to read this book too!

How does Rowell help us? The "ABCs of wise giving patterns" he has adapted from Marvin Olasky for missions application are alone worth the price of the book. But Rowell doesn't write as a theoretician. He approaches his task as a rooted practitioner. His church grappled with these issues in Bosnia Herzegovina, a war-torn context that served as his prime schoolroom, allowing him a practical place in which to develop his convictions. Ministry in Bosnia led to the insights included here on the value of covenantal relationships and their impact on managing material resources in missions. These are principles that Rowell has rooted in the biblical text and tested over fifteen years while working in long-term relationships with Balkan brothers and sisters.

In the language that we have used in the WEA Mission Commission, Rowell is a reflective practitioner, representing those "… women and men of both action and study; rooted in the Word of God and the church of Christ; passionately obedient to the fullness of the Great Commandment and Great Commission; globalized in their perspective, yet faithful citizens of their own cultures" (*Global Missiology for the 21st Century: The Iguassu Dialogue,* ed. William D. Taylor [Grand Rapids: Baker, 2000], 1).

Skeptics may wonder how realistic Rowell's proposal for "A Missionary Marshall Plan for the Twenty-First Century" will prove to be. How effective might we expect his key principles to serve the body of Christ as they are worked out in other cultures and nations beyond Bosnia? I don't presume to know the answer, but I am convinced that it's time to explore new paths in dealing with the press of global need and the practical reality of Western greed. The kinds of reform Rowell points us toward are, in my view, worth trying as we Westerners endeavor to become more effective colleague-partners for national leaders who deserve and are eager to exercise more influence in twenty-first century missions. We must go far beyond merely the Three Selfs into the next two—self-theologizing and self-missiologizing.

It is well to remember that new pathways always demand that we accept the prospect of risking failure in order to make better progress in any realm of human endeavor—whether our aim is going to the moon, or exploring medical breakthroughs, or taking the gospel to the remaining unreached peoples of the world. The challenge of *To Give or Not to Give?* confronts us with the choice of adopting a pioneer spirit in mission again as we aim toward the God-ordained goal of reaching the world for Christ. But the pioneering principle is here applied not to how or where we are to reach others with the gospel, but how we are to resource that task.

This book is a legitimate attempt to face this old beast in an effort to find a better way to fund the mission enterprise. Rowell must be thanked for bearding the lion in his den. Now the hard part comes for all of us who will make application of the insights this book offers.

William D. Taylor

Executive Director, Mission Commission,
World Evangelical Alliance

Few Western missionaries engaged in taking the gospel to unreached peoples can easily escape the discomfort of managing immensely disparate wealth while living and working among the world's most desperately poor. This is due in part to the pervasiveness of global poverty. Comparative levels of deprivation and the appropriate measurements for poverty levels vary over time and from one context to another. We nonetheless need to have a general understanding of what it means to be poor as we begin to consider legitimate Christian responses to lending material assistance to impoverished peoples in the many deprived mission contexts around the world.

A general consensus is building in the twenty-first century as to how to define poverty. The concept, however, is not as simple to grasp as may be imagined initially. For example, there are three kinds of poverty generally recognized among government leaders and development professionals today. *Absolute poverty* is a reflection of acute material deprivation resulting from an absence of resources basic to survival. Those who are "absolutely poor" lack adequate access to food, safe drinking water, sanitation facilities, health care, shelter, and personal safety. People in this category are unable to reasonably keep body and soul together.

Relative poverty addresses the inequities experienced by those who are not in life-threatening circumstances but who are routinely denied adequate income or other financial resources sufficient to secure access to "the amenities, standards, services, and activities which are common or customary in (a given) society."[1] This reflection of poverty is a measure of comparative privation, a sense of lack dramatized by relationships between individuals, various groups within society, or between nations of disproportionate means. Those who "have not" feel their loss more acutely because they are surrounded by those who "have."

Social exclusion is a third sort of poverty that has less to do with material wealth and more to do with the interplay of contextual and societal realities like discrimination, unemployment, poor housing, high crime rates, epidemic conditions, or lack of access to education and the development of vocational skills. Nobel Prize-winning economist Amartya Sen helped popularize this third assessment of poverty, which involves what he calls "capability deprivation": a social bankruptcy counted in terms of the loss of personal choices, individual freedoms, and the capacity to live without shame in society.[2] *To Give or Not to Give?* touches in some measure on all three aspects of poverty, but the focus of our attention will be primarily placed on poverty induced by a lack of material resources—the concern of the first two categories.

Joseph Vincent Remenyi, a vastly experienced Australian development expert and educator, offers a working definition of poverty that helps us grasp the magnitude of the problems presented by absolute and relative deprivation. He says, "To be poor means that one belongs to a household which has access to a total annual income less than one half the national average."[3] This is the definition used by the European Commission and other national and international governments and relief agencies. According to this definition, it is estimated that 60 percent of all households throughout the world, and perhaps as many as 75 percent of all human beings, are poor.[4] The World Bank reports that 1.2 billion

1   Peter Townsend, *Poverty in the United Kingdom: A Survey of Household Resources and Standards of Living* (Harmondsworth, UK: Penguin Books, 1979), 31.

2   A. K. Sen, *Development as Freedom* (New York: Anchor Books, 1999), 20.

3   Joseph V. Remenyi, *Where Credit Is Due: Income Generating Programs for the Poor in Developing Countries* (London: Intermediate Technology Productions, 1991), 3.

4   J. Andrew Kirk, *What Is Mission? Theological Explorations* (Minneapolis: Augsburg Fortress, 2000), 97.

of the world's poorest people try to survive on just one dollar a day.[5] Poverty is, therefore, a nagging reality for the vast majority of people in the world, and certainly so among most of the unreached cultures where Western missionaries are focusing their strategic attention in the twenty-first century.

Despite the stresses involved with the reality of living with tremendous riches (at least in relative terms), Western missionaries all too often respond to their financial dilemma by finding sound theological and practical reasons for perpetuating economic advantage. Curiously enough, we manage to convince ourselves that we are somehow acting in the best interests of impoverished people by keeping what is ours, even as we observe their incredible needs. The usual missiological defense for assuming a posture that guarantees the material imbalances of the status quo lies in the conviction that indigenous people and their churches should be *self-supporting* and that giving material assistance from outside sources creates unhealthy *dependency*.

Simply put, I believe that the long-established and widely accepted missiological principles that emphasize Western concerns about dependency are sometimes being applied today to serve selfish ends rather than moving us toward a search for more sacrificial means to meet the immense spiritual and material needs existing among the world's most unreached and impoverished people groups.

To Give or Not to Give?

It seems to me that in arguing against giving when we are capable of relieving at least some aspects of abject poverty we may hit our intended target of reducing dependency in pioneer situations but miss the intention of our Lord as it relates to our own responsibilities for financial stewardship according to biblical principles. So what is one to do? Answers do not come easily, especially in a context where many believe the mat-

---

5 Ronald J. Sider, *The Scandal of the Evangelical Conscience: Why Are Christians Living Just Like the Rest of the World?* (Grand Rapids: Baker, 2005), 20.

ter is settled by long-standing principles and accepted precedents. I am concerned that we are too easily comforted by our convictions and that we find it too convenient to avoid reassessing them. The missiological dilemma created by a disparity of wealth should make us uncomfortable with traditional rationalizations that defend our tendency to hold back our relative riches when our poorer brothers and sisters have serious and often life-threatening needs. If I may presume to parody Shakespeare's well-known words reflecting Hamlet's inner turmoil in a different setting, our solution for dealing with this financial dilemma might be expressed in these terms:

> To give or not to give: that is the question! Whether it is nobler in mind to part with a portion of the means and surpluses of outrageous fortune, or to take up arms against a sea of troubles that flow from sharing wealth and by opposing simple generosity to end them. To buy: to keep; always more; and when we keep to say we end the heartache and the thousand natural shocks that wealth is heir to: 'tis a protection devoutly to be wished. Our neighbors' lot is better off if we determine just to buy: to keep; and thus to spare our friends the pressures that material blessing has brought on us. But what of their need and their chance to dream? Aye, there's the rub.[6]

I am not convinced that anything is solved if we simply choose to buy and keep to ourselves what we deem to be ours. But in the interest of guarding against dependency, that is the routinely recommended response. I find few missiologists willing to strongly challenge the now well-established presuppositions against giving readily, following instead the simple missiological paradigms that presumably answer definitively the inevitable economic questions Western workers face when

---

6 Shakespeare's original version of Hamlet's soliloquy is worded as follows: "To be, or not to be: that is the question: Whether 'tis nobler in mind to suffer the slings and arrows of outrageous fortune, or to take arms against a sea of troubles, and by opposing end them. To die: to sleep; no more; and by a sleep to say we end the heart-ache, and the thousand natural shocks that flesh is heir to. 'Tis a consummation devoutly to be wish'd. To die, to sleep; To Sleep? Perchance to dream! Aye there's the rub."

they confront the world's poor. That errors have been made in the use of money on the world's mission fields is indisputable. I do not argue that we should not learn from past mistakes and minimize them in the future. But I do assert that following a convenient formula that secures our wealth while offering little relief to the plight of the poor is an ineffective answer to our dilemma. As Chuck Bennett has pointed out, "To refuse to share our resources with overseas brethren because there have been abuses is like saying we should outlaw marriage because some husbands beat their wives. The problem is real but the solution is too simplistic. I am convinced that it is possible to 'help without hurting.'"[7]

We would do well to recognize that, all too often, Western concerns alone are allowed to rule the discussion of dependency dynamics. The complicating factors that we Western missionaries add to the problem are usually overlooked when nationals are left out of the debate over financial issues. After all, indigenous leaders have thoughts on these issues too. Even in past mission consultations shaped specifically to address the dependency issue forthrightly, it seems to me that most of the potentially powerful punches, the ones that might hit us squarely and get our attention in forceful ways, have too often been pulled. My hope is that this book will correct this error. My readers will need, therefore, to brace themselves and be prepared to take a few carefully placed blows intentionally targeted to strike at the heart of traditional perspectives on this subject. I hope to stretch them beyond the comfort zones defined by current missiological convictions on this subject.

The Genesis of My Own Discomfort

Thankfully, not all Western missiologists are equally guilty of trying to protect themselves from the painful blows that could be thrown by our

---

7   Chuck Bennett and Glenn Schwartz, "Two Christian Leaders Discuss Dependency," *Mission Frontiers: The Bulletin of the U.S. Center for World Mission*, Pasadena, CA (January–February 1997): 25. Available at http://www.missionfrontiers.org/1997/0102/jf9712.htm.

poorer partners. Dr. Jonathan J. Bonk's short book, *Missions and Money: Affluence as a Western Missionary Problem,* is an excellent example of a reflection that lets the fur fly wherever it will. His honest treatment of the issues is a refreshing exception to the general rule by which Westerners duck punches they would do better to endure. Reading Bonk's challenge to Western missionaries is a singularly uncomfortable experience. He yields no quarter, drives home his point hard, and lands his well-placed blows with consistent effect so that the reader is pushed, like an over-matched prizefighter, into an ideological corner. Being pressed against the ropes, Bonk's victims are pummeled until there is nothing left to do but cry "No more!"—hoping the beating will end.

But it doesn't! The inescapable logic of Bonk's examination of the problem of money for those who minister the gospel among the poor hangs around, like the Ghost of Christmas Past, to haunt one's thoughts and to taunt one's previously unchallenged convictions. As the director of a mission focused on ministry in Bosnia-Herzegovina (Bosnia), a context once characterized by considerable prosperity and now hindered by a postwar economy locked in the brokenness of self-inflicted bankruptcy, I was undone by his book. I owe to Dr. Bonk the impetus for this effort to challenge the widely accepted missiological paradigms touching on dollars and dependency.

After reading *Missions and Money,* I had to find a way to relieve the lingering discomfort he so effectively stirred in my mind and heart. So I read more broadly, took time for long meditation and careful reflection, and then picked up my pen. This statement of my own renewed thoughts on what it means to do the right thing with Western wealth in twenty-first century missions is my attempt to decrease the pressure Bonk's work put on my own system. I have hopes, obviously, that my thoughts might somehow impact my own readers in an equally profound way. Dr. Bonk's perspectives are referenced in chapters 9 and 10 in a section focused on the downsides flowing from upscale missionary lifestyle choices.

I am also indebted to World Vision executive, Bryant L. Myers, and his book, *Walking with the Poor: Principles and Practices of Transformational Development.* His comprehensive reflection on modern development theory is too detailed to capture fully in the pages that follow, but his insights helped me think about possible responses to the angst born while falling under Bonk's merciless barrage. Myer's concept of "transformational development" is a journey of cross-cultural ministry designed to accomplish three goals: helping the world's unreached and impoverished people recover their *true identity* as human beings and as children of God; helping them in the discovery of their *true destiny* (Myers would say *vocation*) as stewards of the gifts and calling God has endowed them with in order to make them a blessing to the rest of the world; and helping them experience *true unity*, or reconciliation, with God, with self, with others, and with their environment. Seen from this perspective, Myers' challenge is a call to a new and more comprehensive approach to "doing mission," not just to doing more effective development work.

As church planters and evangelists, traditional missionaries can easily focus on a narrowly defined (though eternally important) goal of converting individuals and gathering new believers into Christian communities. Myers urges us to reach further toward a larger vision of impacting an entire culture by introducing hope for a "better future." That better future is one where the society comes to experience the full effect of the kingdom of God—the dynamic reign and rule of Jesus Christ and the presence of the *shalom* that only he can engender. "The gospel is not a message of personal salvation *from* the world, but a message of *a world transfigured, right down to its basic structures*. Even creation itself groans for God's plan of redemption to be manifest in nature, which is . . . still suffering from sure effects of the fall."[8]

If we reduce the gospel solely to encouraging people to name the name of Christ as Lord, individuals may get saved but their social order will remain unaffected. E. Stanley Jones called this a "crippled

---

8   Bryant L. Myers, *Walking with the Poor: Principles and Practices of Transformational Development* (Maryknoll, NY: Orbis Books, 1999), 49 (italics in the original).

Christianity with a crippled result."[9] Crippled Christianity is the result of a condensed sense of the gospel—a version too small to capture the vision God has in mind for the transformation of nations. It points people to heaven and leaves their cultures to hell. Thus, vast areas of life remain untouched by kingdom influence, unredeemed by Christ's sacrifice, and unchallenged by the light Christians were reborn to bring into the world. Into the void come philosophies, empty deceptions, human traditions, and other seductive schemes the devil promotes against the knowledge of God (see 2 Corinthians 10:3–5; Colossians 2:8).

A "gospel-driven" approach to bringing relief to the poor and the lost begins with the bold recognition that there is no hope for a better future if we place our trust in science and technology, in free markets and the impact of global capitalism, or in power politics and military might. Neither modernization, nor materialism, nor militarization is able to produce the future promised by God to his redeemed people. Only the reign of Christ can produce the dynamics of the kingdom, and that reign is appropriately the aim of all theologically sound efforts in mission and in development. Many traditional approaches to development are secular at the core, even when pursued by Christians—leaving out an intentionally spiritual dimension. Similarly, many approaches to mission are void of any development component—leaving out concern for social realities. Both of these weaknesses need to be remedied.

Ben Homan, president of Food for the Hungry (US), also challenged my perspectives in the context of our relationship as members of the board of directors of his organization. His insights into doing justice and loving mercy and walking humbly with God are the foundation stones for a biblical vision of community that offers a means to approach ending spiritual and physical hunger in the world. His emphasis on "Micah Initiatives" helped me see light at the end of the tunnel. In my interactions with him I came to realize that, following the footsteps of far too many Western missionaries, I had neatly separated the evangelistic

---

9   E. Stanley Jones, *The Unshakable Kingdom and the Unchanging Person* (Nashville: Abingdon, 1972), 30.

mandate and the social mandate in a way that hindered my sense of what holistic ministry should involve.

I had somehow developed a practical commitment to world missions (a passionate concern for those lost in a spiritual sense) without developing a corollary commitment to confront global poverty (a passionate commitment to those who lack in a material sense). I write this treatise with a humble heart, trying to lay a foundation that might allow me to bring forth lasting fruit in keeping with my own genuine repentance. The essence of my newfound conviction is that it is not enough to send "missionaries" to the unreached peoples of the world. Since most of the truly unreached represent those who are also the most profoundly poor, living in the world's least developed societies, we must send workers who are at once missionaries and what Myers has termed "transformational development professionals."

Transformational development professionals are workers who are committed to advancing the kingdom of God holistically. They are committed to a process that is decidedly Christian and that must incorporate both care for genuine physical needs and the faithful proclamation of a clear evangelical witness for Christ, aimed ultimately at making possible a better future—one informed by God's revealed plan for the redemption of all people in all nations. Neither role (that is, neither evangelism coupled with missionary church planting nor development accompanied by humanitarian intervention) is adequate when pursued alone.

The Financial Connection

Both emphases are important and confirmation of the priorities represented by each is imperative. I am convinced that incorporating more transformational development thinking into our approach to winning unreached peoples to Christ would make most Western missionaries more effective. I am also convinced that incorporating a more focused missiology into the processes employed to meet humanitarian needs would make most development workers more productive for the kingdom. We truly need each other and we are foolish to divorce these two approaches to ministry in our planning. We would be equally foolish to presume that either ministry can be accomplished without funding.

Because missions and money are inseparable concerns, we must make sure they remain married in our minds so that we do not miss the mark the Spirit of God calls us to aim for as Christian witnesses. As my professor at Gordon Conwell Theological Seminary and my mentor in Bosnia, Dr. Peter Kuzmic, is fond of saying, "Evangelicals need a missiology that is theologically grounded and a theology that is missiologically focused." That challenge is another motivation that urges me to write on this subject. If we are to take the gospel of the kingdom of God to those who are poor, our missiology must have a significant theology of stewardship (including a decidedly financial factor) woven into its fabric. Too often, I believe, modern missiology has missed the mark on exactly that point.

I hope that my effort here might help correct that shortcoming. I also hope that these reflections might influence those who follow my leadership within my own agency and others serving under larger mission umbrellas to take the risks involved in carefully reexamining troublesome issues touching on money, missions, and managing our wealth in a world still reflecting immense material need. We must be willing to reform our thinking and revise our giving strategies as we strive to be more faithful stewards of the resources God has entrusted to us. Serious attempts to serve the cause of global missions in the twenty-first century demand nothing less. An acceptable starting point might be simply to acknowledge that a consistent choice "to buy and to keep" cannot be defended as the ultimate solution for our dilemma when faced with the question of whether it is wiser "to give or not to give."

CHAPTER ONE

Doing Away with
Double Standards

The Western propensity "not to give" is a reality that we saw reflected to the shame and considerable consternation of American citizens
following the Asian tsunami disaster in December 2004. After hearing
of the initial US commitment of $15 million dollars in aid for the vic-
tims of this unprecedented disaster, Norwegian-born UN Undersecretary
General for Humanitarian Affairs, Jan Egeland, openly called unnamed
Western nations "stingy" for their miserly response to the misery left in
the wake of the tsunami. My readers will see, as they continue on, that
this critique of Western generosity is not without some foundation in
fact. Notwithstanding the eventual increase of the US pledge of tsunami
relief to more than $350 million, our overall giving track record as a
nation is not as strong as most are inclined to think. So when we decide
"not to give," the choice to hold on to our resources (to buy and to keep)

can easily be interpreted by others as an exercise in hoarding that is inde-fensible when helping more would be an equally easy decision to make.

The painful truth is that the West tends to be more responsive when crises are well publicized. Our responsiveness is directly proportional to the news coverage given to the need in question. If our inclinations to give are easy to arouse with sufficient press coverage, our attention is hard to sustain without it. Our interest and our giving tend to diminish as media reports wane, even if the pain of those who suffer does not. When the world's cameras disappear, moving on to the next crisis *de jour*, the consequences of the catastrophe left behind most often do not end—suf-fering simply moves out of sight and too often out of mind. Victims re-main in their plight with no means to relieve their pain. As C. S. Lewis so poignantly put it, suffering is like a trip to the dentist's office. "It doesn't really matter whether you grip the arms of the dentist's chair or let your hands lie in your lap, the drill drills on."[1]

Just as we need a capability for rapid deployment in response to global crises like the 2004 Christmas tsunami, we need to develop a ca-pacity for staying power as well. We need to find the kind of resolve that will insure we remain on site when others face catastrophe until stability is fully achieved. We need to be diligent to help as long as "the disaster drill drills on." That is why development plans must be joined to relief efforts and why missionaries should be intent upon a far more sustain-able strategy than just walking through the open doors that natural and manmade disasters create for the advance of the gospel.

Staying power is an issue in cross-cultural ministry even when crisis ceases to be a presenting problem. Our identification with Jesus and his kingdom mandates acts of kindness performed in his name as a matter of course (Matthew 25:31–46). We are compelled by the Great Commission (Matthew 28:18–20) to confront the many aspects of the world's cultures that need redemption and to endeavor to bring them into greater confor-mity with the will of God. So Christians are called to be more holistic gospel witnesses than we often aspire to become. Our assignment is not

---

1   C. S. Lewis, *A Grief Observed* (New York: Harper Collins Publishers, Inc., 2001), 33.

merely to make individual converts but also to disciple entire nations by introducing them to the dynamics of the kingdom of God. That is, we are to give lost people an opportunity to say yes to the person of Jesus and to the call for all cultures to embrace the values associated with a biblical worldview.

As model citizens, Christians living under the God-ordained authority of human governments are to *uphold* appropriate political and economic systems, while being willing to *condemn* them insofar as they are unrighteous, unjust, or destructive to human well-being, and to press to *reform* them into more God-honoring systems as we are able. Among this range of alternatives, conservatives stress the first (respectability), revolutionaries the second (radical and often rapid change), and reformers the third (incremental redemption of the society). Christians, living prophetically, must embrace all three of these options in biblical balance. This kind of critical participation in society is part of every believer's moral responsibility wherever he or she is born or pleased to live.

Viewed this way, the gospel tells us that all unreached people have a story in which God was involved before Christian missionaries or development workers ever came. This is another way to capture the essence of the *missio Dei,* the work God does to establish his rule among human beings—apart from the agency of human beings. God, in his sovereignty, is a part of the story of every unredeemed people, whether or not he is recognized for his role. The presence of human witnesses to the gospel does not introduce God to a culture. It simply allows people to begin seeing in an incarnated way how God was with them all along, even if he was unknown, hidden, or rejected.

The spiritual history of a community, then, is the story of God's work among a given people. The good news we bring is that God has more for them than they ever imagined—a better future and a new direction for their story. We offer an invitation to choose a new way of life, one rooted in the Bible, one made possible by Jesus' sacrifice, one compelling a new allegiance and a new alignment with the kingdom of God. The announcement of the gospel of the kingdom is an authorization to "give up, abandon and renounce other stories that have shaped their lives in false and distorting ways."[2] The gospel is thus a simultaneous call to personal rebirth and to cultural restoration.

Holding this kind of gospel perspective will keep us from two distinctly possible errors. On one hand we must not become professional proselytizers capitalizing on people's pain in the midst of crisis. On the other hand we must not approach Christian witness as a marketing process, as if evangelism is somehow about selling a salvation message to reluctant buyers. Working from a gospel perspective, we must never be satisfied with treating the message of salvation available in Jesus as a product we are trying to entice people to "purchase." We are not bartering compassion for conversions, nor are we dealing with the gospel as a commodity. We are rather caring disciples of Jesus offering incarnational testimony to his love and concern. We are believers called to facilitate an unreached people's own discovery of their true heritage as children of Abraham. A truly biblical gospel will make our sense of responsibility to Jesus and to a lost world bigger, bringing the challenge of redeeming entire nations, not just neighbors and neighborhoods into focus.

We must be prepared, therefore, to remain in a given context long-term, to sustain our presence over extended periods, to learn new languages, and to master strange cultures. Following the pattern of Jesus, we need to share the gospel by demonstration as well as proclamation of truth, and we need to be prepared to empty ourselves (and our pocketbooks) as we share the pain and relieve the strain that poverty and peril bring to so many of the world's people. Western generosity (even if it can be improved and expanded) cannot remain only a knee-jerk reaction to natural disasters or a real-time response to wars and epidemics. We need a renewed sense of global stewardship and a radical redirection of resources to meet the chronic needs of the global poor—not just chaotic needs born of crises and catastrophes. The needs associated with endemic poverty are complex and harder to resolve; they will require overwhelming commitment if they are to be overcome.

---

2   Bryant L. Myers, *Walking with the Poor: Principles and Practices of Transformational Development* (Maryknoll, NY: Orbis Books, 1999), 206.

Defining Dependency

I am writing, therefore, to propose that it is time to rec
broadly accepted missiological guidelines that tend to moderate otherwise obvious biblical mandates intended to prompt a generous Christian
response to neighbors in need. In the interest of reducing "dependency,"
Westerners have come to embrace a practice that effectively prolongs
and intensifies poverty for others. By "dependency" I mean the unhealthy
patterns of reliance on Western financial support that are presumed to
be encouraged when missionaries readily offer support for indigenous
workers, for ministry projects, or for facilities development in pioneer
settings. I am inclined to agree that whenever funds are provided at the
initiative of cultural outsiders in a manner that limits local leaders' freedom to act on their own vision, or when outside sources of financial
aid are offered in a fashion that subjugates native workers, relegating
them to a passive role or to an inherently subordinate position in relationship to their benefactors, unhealthy dependency can be the result.
Whenever funds are given without regard to the capacity of nationals to
manage, maintain, or multiply the investments made, or to make their
own contributions along the way, dependency is a distinct possibility.
No clear-thinking missiologist would intentionally promote the destructive patterns we associate with this kind of dependency. Let me state
emphatically at the outset of my argument that I do not favor—nor do
I desire to encourage others to pursue—circumstances that lead to unhealthy dependency.

I do mean, however, to challenge the widely recommended remedy
to the problem of dependency: namely, the general discouragement of
Western support for indigenous ministries. In my way of thinking, to
simply avoid giving to indigenous work is no ingenious solution to the
concerns communicated by Western leaders regarding unhealthy reliance
on outside resources. Nonetheless, avoiding the infusion of gifts that
might support or subsidize indigenous ministry has become the generally
accepted preventative measure presumed to be necessary for those serious about dealing with the dilemma of dependency. Some missiologists

merely express caution about giving to nationals, while others discourage Western funding of ministry among unreached peoples altogether.

The Dangers of Dependency

Glenn Schwartz is one proponent of a total abstinence approach to the problem. In an interview in 1997, he stated clearly his opposition to those who recommend subsidy in "a bigger and bolder way than ever before." He said, "I wish they wouldn't support church leaders with foreign funding in the parts of Africa (or anywhere, for that matter) where church leaders are doing their best to break the dependency syndrome."[3] In seminars focused on training nationals to fight dependency, Schwartz' mission agency, World Mission Associates, recommends that indigenous leaders should refuse outside support even if it is offered and that they ought to pursue the goal of being totally self-reliant. In my own denomination, Craig Ott is another leader who has expressed similar sentiments, urging mission leaders to be extremely cautious and to "think twice before you start supporting nationals in your missions giving."[4]

Ott openly declares that outside subsidies are "fraught with dangers." Among the dangers presumed to lurk in the wake of Western giving to national ministries is the creation of:

- A dependent attitude that stunts responses to God's mandate for nationals to be givers as well as receivers. Subsidies are presumed to reduce commitments to biblical stewardship among emerging churches on the mission field, encouraging nationals to become perpetual takers rather than principled tithers.

---

3   Glenn J. Schwartz, "A Champion for Self Reliance: An Interview with Glenn Schwartz," *Mission Frontiers: The Bulletin of the U.S. Center for World Mission*, Pasadena, CA (January–February 1997): 5. Available at http://www.missionfrontiers. org/1997/0102/jf979.htm.

4   Craig Ott, "Let the Buyer Beware," *Mission Frontiers: The Bulletin of the U.S. Center for World Mission*, Pasadena, CA (September–October 1994). Available at http:// www.missionfrontiers.org/1994/0910/so947.htm.

- A relational dynamic that reinforces feelings of inferiority among national workers vis-à-vis their Western partners.

- An atmosphere of jealousy, competition, and opportunism among nationals who naturally vie against one another for limited Western funds.

- A mercenary spirit that minimizes volunteerism among potential lay leaders from indigenous churches.[5]

- A sense that Christianity emerging in a pioneer setting must depend upon outside funding and is consequently a foreign faith that survives only when subsidized by the West.

- A reduction of missionary zeal and outward directed initiative by national leaders.

- An increased risk that nationals supported by outside sources will be held suspect by their own governments. How many such workers have been presumed to be agents working for the American CIA?

Missiological principles that are recognized as effective in minimizing these dangers tend to encourage us to do everything we can to insure that indigenous churches remain "self-supporting." The obvious corollary is that we should discourage outside investment as a rule. Under this line

---

5   A special note is necessary on this point. The damages associated with this supposed "mercenary danger" are dwarfed by the actual problems created by Westerners who tend to outbid one another as they seek to hire the most qualified nationals to fill staff roles within Western organizations. Though this is often deemed an acceptable use of Western funds, it is a practice that robs emerging national churches of their best potential leaders in their earliest stages of development. The result of such "bidding wars" is the removal of the most capable lay workers from their local church contexts in a process Schwartz rightly calls "shepherd stealing" (Schwartz, "A Champion for Self Reliance," 6). In effect, when national workers become mercenaries serving foreign missionary agencies, Westerners end up building the foundations of their own work in a new context at the expense of the national church. Western leaders, not indigenous workers, are therefore responsible for this dynamic, and the problem represents a weakness in us, not them. Emerging congregations among the unreached are thus often deprived of their best people at the worst possible time—when their promising leaders could help build a sure foundation for an indigenous church planting movement.

of reasoning, holding back Western financial aid is generally believed to be a more productive strategy than readily sharing wealth if we want to best advance the kingdom in unreached and impoverished cultures. One wonders whatever happened to the simple call for generous giving when God's people are faced with others who are living in significant poverty. Could it be that there is an inherent fallacy in the tried-and-true solution to the problem of dependency represented by simply holding back outside support? I am inclined to think that the root of the problem may not lie in the evils some associate with biblically legitimate generosity, but in all the strings that we Westerners have been prone to attach to our giving. I am confident that many national leaders agree.

Dangers or Duties?

Let me illustrate by sharing just a few of the insights my national colleagues in Bosnia have highlighted for my consideration. Like Craig Ott, these believers also want us to "think twice" before we give to support national ministries. But their concerns direct us to an entirely different set of reflections on the inherent problems involved. They focus less on "dangers" and more on "duties" when they address these issues. Among the thoughts they find important for us to consider before giving to indigenous ministries are the following:

- They suggest that *we have a duty to work hard at relating in humility with one another*, accepting each other on equal terms as "sons and daughters of the same Father." In the final analysis, we are not disparately blessed business partners. Neither are we in a parent-child relationship nor in a marriage model where Westerners are the undisputed "heads of the household" to whom indigenous leaders must submit. The only appropriate biblical paradigm for our relationship is one that recognizes us all as sons and daughters in the same family, eating from the Father's table. It is high time to move away from other more patronizing metaphors for our relationship. If Westerners sit at the end of the Father's table that is well-provided with food and all the bowls at the other end of the table are empty or nearly so, it is not degrading or dehumanizing or wrong for one brother to ask another to pass the bread from the abundantly supplied part of the feast set before us. Refusing to share the Father's bounty, on the other hand, is an action that is rooted in selfishness, and letting our siblings go hungry while we are well-fed is wrong. These are issues the Father has already addressed within the family. He is not pleased when we suggest that it is not in the best interests of needy brothers and sisters for those with plenty to allow their surplus to supply their siblings' want. When we refuse to share and to care for the concerns of others as readily as for our own interests, we violate the values of God's family and the most basic standards of Christian fellowship.[6]

• As we formulate strategies for our cooperative ministry in missions, *we have a duty to ensure that "good theology" rooted in biblical truth informs the principles we embrace as "good missiology."* Our basic understanding of missions must not contradict the teaching of Scripture. Bosnian believers remind us that the voice of Jesus is still speaking to his church and *we have a duty to listen attentively* (see Hebrews 12:25). Stated another way, we should not trade the truths of the kingdom of God for human theories—not even the theories of well experienced and godly people. Biblical teaching on the stewardship of material wealth should be valid in all cultures and in all eras. With this

---

6 Dietrich Bonhoeffer offers a helpful insight as we consider this alternative biblical metaphor put forward by our Bosnian brothers and sisters. Bonhoeffer discusses "table fellowship" in the family of God as a part of his treatise on the nature of true Christian relationships in one of his best-known works, *Life Together* (*Dietrich Bonhoeffer Works Volume 5: Life Together and Prayerbook of the Bible,* ed. Geffrey B. Kelly, trans. Daniel W. Bloesch and James H. Burtness [Minneapolis: Augsburg Fortress, 1996]). There he writes, "The table fellowship of Christians implies an obligation. It is *our* daily bread that we eat, not my own. We [are expected by God to] share our bread. . . . Now none dares go hungry as long as another has bread, and he who breaks this fellowship of the physical life also breaks the fellowship of the Spirit. . . . Not until a person desires to keep his own bread for himself does hunger ensue. This is a strange divine law" (73–74).

in mind, Western perspectives need to be evaluated for their relevance in settings outside our own if they are to be accepted by the entire family of God. If our ideas fit well in the West but not in the rest of the world, perhaps we are being governed by our human preferences shaped by cultural prejudices rather than by God's principles regarding the righteous use of money. Bosnian Christians see the self-supporting paradigm and the concern over dependency in this light.

• They believe *we have a duty to avoid making room for double standards in our relationships.* My Bosnian colleagues appeal to us to consider whether the expectations missionaries hold for national leaders (in terms of financial support, lifestyle choices, and practical ministry responsibilities) are the same as the expectations held for Westerners laboring in the same context. They wisely point out that we should renounce being respecters of persons, especially when the distinctions made among us are based on relative wealth—a position supported by evil motives according to James 2:4. Rather, we should endeavor to recognize and reward any and all ministers on equal terms for the kingdom work they contribute in a given setting, regardless of their cultural background. As people from both indigenous and foreign cultures are expected to do the same kinds of tasks for the same King in the same context, they deserve similar sorts of recognition, appreciation, and honor—and perhaps even comparable remuneration! God cares about justice, and *we have a duty to be equitable in our dealings with one another.*

• *We have a duty to honor the price everyone pays to be ambassadors for Christ.* Bosnians encourage us to recognize that it is inherently costly for new believers in a Muslim context to openly acknowledge their conversion from Islam to Christianity. It is difficult in Bosnia (and dangerous in many other unreached settings) for anyone to identify with Jesus and then to minister without apology in his name. It has been unpopular and not without risks to urge a gospel path for reconciliation in Bosnia's deeply divided society. Moreover, planting churches in a culture that is somewhat hostile to evangelicals is especially difficult and dangerous for indigenous believers. Westerners are wrong to assume that national church leaders in such settings are taking the easy road in pursuit of their calling as ambassadors for Christ just because they may benefit from their ministries in a financial manner. Even Paul readily acknowledged that the laborer is worthy of his hire. The truth is that Western missionaries pay a higher personal price than nationals recognize to leave their countries in order to minister cross-culturally. Likewise, it costs nationals more than Westerners realize to remain and minister as early converts in their native, unreached cultures. Financial gains and losses are not the only—and certainly not the best—measures of the costs involved in serving in pioneer mission settings.

- *We have a mutual duty to die to selfish perspectives in the interest of calling others to live as followers of Jesus.* My Bosnian friends remind us of Jesus' teaching in John 12:24–25 that death is a necessary prerequisite to fruitful ministry. To be effective as ambassadors promoting the advance of the kingdom of Christ in Bosnia (as in other unreached settings), we must all be prepared to die to ourselves, to our theological hobbyhorses, to our denominational biases, to our ministry methodologies, to our pet principles, and to our personal prejudices. Having died to self, we must then live for Christ, follow him as Lord, serve him as King, and share his message as the only Savior and Mediator between God and humankind. With that attitude, we will labor in Bosnia not as Croats, or Serbs, or Muslims, or Americans, but as citizens of heaven and as equally valuable ambassadors for Christ. Seeing ourselves as joint heirs in the kingdom of heaven and as aliens on earth will better serve to increase our unity and to enhance our sense of equality in the midst of shared ministry. Our relationships will be more effective if we all embrace the truth that no love is greater than the love that motivates us to lay down our lives for our friends (John 15:13).

The differences represented by Western concerns over "missiological dangers" and the non-Western concerns over "biblical duties" are real and they are important. They help us see why national leaders need to be included in the discussion as we seek to decide whether to "give or not to give" in support of our indigenous colleagues who share our passion for reaching unreached peoples for Christ. When we interact over these issues face-to-face, motive is one issue we have to examine honestly.

Giving with No Strings Attached

By their very nature, genuine gifts should be offered without an expectation that the recipient is obligated to the donor in some way. If the Western tendency to view giving as a means of gaining and holding influence cannot be remedied, perhaps nationals should refuse to receive the "bait" we are offering to lure them into a relationship of spiritual or practical servitude. We would do well to remember that we are all called by Scripture to give, expecting nothing in return. If we cannot give in such an unselfish spirit, Schwartz and Ott are right to suggest we should not give at all. Roland Allen makes this point plainly in his valuable book, *Missionary Methods: Saint Paul's or Ours?* when he writes, "There is all the difference in the world between gifts freely made by members of one body to another, as manifestations of the spirit of mutual charity which moves in them, and gifts or subsidies made with the intention of checking freedom of action on the part of the recipients."[7]

The kinds of boundaries that my mission, Ministry Resource Network, Inc., has established in an effort to insure that we attach no strings to our own giving are reflected in the covenant principles highlighted in chapter 12.

---

7   Roland Allen, *Missionary Methods: St. Paul's or Ours?* (Grand Rapids: Eerdmans, 1962), 57.

It is interesting to note that Jesus expounds on the principles of generosity by teaching that we ought to give with no thought of gaining in the process. He exhorts his disciples not only to give but also to lend without expecting anything in return for their liberality. Oddly enough, Jesus does not limit our obligation to respond with a generous heart to circumstances in which we are dealing with loved ones who are in need. Instead, he commands that we be responsive also to needs manifested among those who are hostile to us—treating our enemies with the same generosity we extend to friends. He urged his followers to abandon their expectations of reward when others in need ask to borrow in order to meet the basic requirements for life. Jesus thus promoted a *radical altruism* rather than a *reasoned pessimism* when he taught his disciples how to manage their finances when faced by others less blessed than they were (see, for example, Luke 6:32–38).

I am proposing a change of perspective that requires us to accept our part of the problems created when we deal with the dilemmas involved with financing missionary enterprises. As a premise, I am suggesting that dependency need not be a problem, even when outside funding predominates, if Western contributions are made without strings being attached and if national leaders are able to assert themselves by taking their rightful role in casting vision and initiating ministry. If national leaders are truly autonomous and if they remain free from control exercised by more well-provisioned partners, the negative realities we associate with dependency can be largely reduced without denying legitimately needed support for the poor.

Samuel Escobar is one mission statesman who sees this possibility. In the face of the shift of the global evangelical center of gravity from North to South, Escobar notes that the mass of mission mobilization is also shifting southward, with apostolic ministry increasingly being extended from a context of poverty. He observes that the *cooperative model* of mission activity, in which "churches from rich nations add their material resources to the spiritual resources of the churches in poor nations in order to reach to a third area" is emerging as a key to the future of global missions.[8] Youth With a Mission, Operation Mobilization, and the International Fellowship of Evangelical Students are prime examples of mission agencies expanding rapidly through the symbiotic blending of mission partners of disparate means.

Fostering Interdependency

We need not *fear dependency* as much as we need to *foster interdependency* according to God's design for the church. Healthy interdependency is a mandate for all members of the body of Christ (1 Corinthians 12:14–26). We are each called to acknowledge that we are interconnected members of one body, unable to assert either functional or financial independence from other members. We all are destined to offer contributions (material and otherwise) to other members, and we all have need of what others offer to us. If we are to fulfill our calling as Christians, we must fit into complementary, reciprocal, mutually rewarding relationships with others in God's redeemed family. Healthy interdependence presumes that we maintain the freedom to teach, reprove, offer correction, and refuse the counsel of other believers—whether or not they come from our own culture.

Daniel Rickett touches on the importance of the reciprocal dynamics that should be inherent in healthy interdependence. In his book, *Building Strategic Partnerships,* he asserts that "unhealthy dependency occurs when reciprocity and responsibility are ignored, overvalued or undervalued. . . . If resources are shared more for the benefit of one partner than for the purpose of ministering more effectively to others, the receiving partner is effectively sidelined."[9] Pressing the point, I would add that when resources are shared with the presumption that financial investments are more important than other contributions to cooperative minis-

---

8   William D. Taylor, ed., *Global Missiology for the 21st Century: The Iguassu Dialogue* (Grand Rapids: Baker, 2000), 34.

9   Daniel Rickett, *Building Strategic Relationships: A Practical Guide to Partnering with Non-Western Missions* (Pleasant Hill, CA: Partners International, 2000), 18.

try, reciprocal dynamics suffer greatly or may be sacrificed alt this sense, the problem of dependency is rooted more in *We tices that express our sense of superiority* than in *indigenous propensities for seeking subsidy as a way of life.*

William Kornfield adds, "Paternalism creates dependency. . . . There can be no genuine reciprocity between individuals or groups when one of them treats the other as a child."[10] I believe honest reflection will lead us to conclude that the problems that material disparities add to our relationships with national brothers and sisters lie at least as much with us as with them. When we make money the only measure of dependency dynamics, as if funding ratios (comparing external to internal sources of revenue) are the heart of the matter, we maximize their culpability and minimize our own contributions to neocolonial approaches that are no boon to mission advance. Until we acknowledge our own part in the stresses stemming from the misuse of money in missions, we will sustain the problems we face rather than solve them. We must remove the log from our own eye before we try to find the speck hindering our brother's vision. To pursue that objective, our first squinting glance into the mirror will require that we try to discern the source of our settled convictions about the dynamics of dependency.

One obvious place to begin weaving the material that might make for better missiology is to analyze the roots of the convictions that tend to make Western mission leaders reticent to give. The next chapter attempts to do that by describing the historical road that led to the prevailing opinion among missiologists on this subject. We need to understand where the concerns about dependency and the commitment to the self-supporting paradigm came from before we can effectively deal with their suitability for our era of mission service.

---

10 William J. Kornfield, "What Hath Our Western Money and Our Western Gospel Wrought?" *Mission Frontiers: The Bulletin of the U.S. Center for World Mission*, Pasadena, CA (January–February 1997): 1. Available at http://www.missionfrontiers. org/1997/0102/jf9710.htm.

CHAPTER TWO

The Roots of the
Three-Self Paradigm

Perhaps because of the dynamic influence of money, dependency issues have always been of prominent interest to mission leaders. Especially since the turn of the nineteenth century, this subject has remained at the forefront of mission concerns. It was an American missionary to China and Korea, John L. Nevius (1829–1893), who popularized the now venerated and almost universally valued "three-self paradigm" that presumably resolves the dilemmas associated with the felt need to make financial investments on foreign fields.

Defining the Three-Self Paradigm

Nevius' three-point formula asserts that indigenous churches and their leaders are strongest and multiply best when they are *self-governing*, *self-supporting,* and *self-propagating.* Explaining the general sense of these three factors that are presumed to insure the creation of an indigenous church, Charles Kraft writes:

> The first requisite is that a church has to be self-governing. That is, a body of believers presuming themselves to be a responsible community of Christians must administer their own affairs in terms of their own leadership patterns and personnel. Secondly, a church must be self-supporting. Funding from abroad that pays the salaries of clergy is considered to be counterproductive to the establishment of an indigenous church. Finally, any truly indigenous church must be self-propagating. The underlying assumption is that genuine indigeneity is reflected in responsible organizational, financial, and evangelistic activities. Conversely, the absence of these three characteristics indicates the presence of an undesirable foreign or Western orientation.[1]

It is generally assumed that the second of these "three-self principles" recommends against outside financial subsidy in general and that by simply refraining from infusing resources from the West we can settle the matter in the modern mission context once and for all. The seminal thoughts behind Nevius' methodology were actually the original contribution of an English Anglican leader, Henry Venn (1796–1873). Venn directed the Anglican Church Mission Society (CMS) for over thirty years, from 1841 until his death. These three priorities were also promoted broadly and nearly simultaneously by the great American mission executive, and Venn's contemporary, Rufus Anderson. Anderson led the American Board of Commissioners for Foreign Missions from 1832 to 1866.

While some dispute remains as to which of these leaders was the first to coin the three-self terminology in describing indigenous churches, many scholars agree that Venn is the original source of this phrasing. For example, Peter Beyerhaus and Henry Lefever write, "Henry Venn of

---

1   Charles H. Kraft and Tom N. Wisley, eds., *Readings in Dynamic Indigeneity* (Pasadena, CA: William Carey Library, 1979), xxvii.

the Church Missionary Society in 1854 gave currency to the three 'self's' of the indigenous church; Rufus Anderson of the American Board of the Congregational Church in 1856 emphasized that self-propagation had priority over self-government and self-support."[2]

Both Venn and Anderson deserve great credit for shaping the global mission enterprise in their era. Their lives manifested remarkable similarities: they were born in the same year; both were eldest sons; each lost his mother at age seven and his father at age seventeen; they graduated from college in the same year; and both became the corresponding secretary for his nation's largest Protestant mission agencies, where each served for over three decades.[3]

Venn was a third-generation vicar whose father was pastor to the famous abolitionist politician, William Wilberforce. Raised in a reform-intensive and socially involved household, Venn worked tirelessly, as had the generations before him, toward three primary goals: to end the African slave trade, to assert the basic rights of indigenous peoples living under English rule in her expansive colonies, and eventually to reform the British missionary practice of insisting on foreign control of national congregations.

He was among the first Western leaders to denounce the colonial aspects of mission methodology which had historically ruled the global advance of the gospel. Christian colonialism and its twin, ecclesiastical imperialism, prevailed all around the globe in his day. In what Andrew Walls has described as a spirit of "imperial religion,"[4] British Christians in that era consistently promoted a condescending and essentially paternalistic relationship with native church leaders. This perspective was a natural outgrowth of what even the most clear-thinking mission leaders

---

2   Peter Beyerhaus and Henry Lefever, *The Responsible Church and the Foreign Mission* (London: World Dominion Press, 1964), 255.

3   Pierce R. Beaver, *To Advance the Gospel: A Collection of the Writings of Rufus Anderson* (Grand Rapids: Eerdmans, 1967), 36.

4   Andrew F. Walls, *The Cross-Cultural Process in Christian History: Studies in the Transmission and Appropriation of Faith* (Maryknoll, NY: Orbis Books, 2002), 183.

of that day saw as a divine calling that linked a God-given civilizing mission to England's empire-building propensities.

I do not mean here to suggest that Britain alone was guilty of promoting a paternalistic view of native peoples. The Berlin Congress of 1850 illustrates the culpability of all developed nations of the era. In this gathering of European powers, the whole of West Africa was partitioned among the "civilized nations" that vied for a share of the region for colonial expansion. The arrogance of Western leaders is evidenced by the assumptions that guided this Age of Imperialism. As Wilbert Shenk has noted, not only was access to West African territories distributed amiably between the civilized colonial powers, the entire world was also divided neatly into two distinct groups: "the superior races and the lesser peoples." The lesser races were judged to be inherently incapable of developing to the same level as the superior races.[5] Under such blatantly racist assumptions, the civilized nations were duty bound to come to the aid of their inferior neighbors by conquering their territory, controlling their governance, and coordinating the wise use of the wealth of resources (natural, human, and financial) that had remained undeveloped until the superior peoples intervened. Missionary societies and the staff they mobilized during this period never successfully separated themselves from such condescending perspectives.

The combined forces of colonialism and conquest, directed globally in the fifteenth century from the Iberian peninsula and later from the British Isles, therefore seemed to allow "civilization to triumph over barbarism" while facilitating the guidance of "child races" toward maturity under European masters. The civilizing mandate that many presumed God had placed on British citizens was a responsibility that Rudyard Kipling called the "white man's burden"—the call to teach heathen nations the gospel of Christ and the graces of European society simultane-

---

5   Wilbert R. Shenk, *Henry Venn—Missionary Statesman* (Maryknoll, NY: Orbis Books, 1983), 107.

ously.[6] It was in this context that paternalistic passions were first accepted as appropriate motivations in mission ministry.

One byproduct of English colonial expansion was the birth of churches through mission societies whose efforts touched the four corners of the earth. The impact was ubiquitous, as the sun truly never set on the countries absorbed into the British Commonwealth. All the native churches in these remote lands were governed by the English missionaries who had planted them. Nationals were not denied leadership because they were in all cases incompetent, but because the British colonial mindset could not bear the thought of indigenous leadership ruling in the household of God. This was the very problem Venn was trying to challenge as he recognized among leaders of his era a virtually universal conviction that nationals were unable to provide their own leadership because they had not developed adequately enough in matters of faith and religion to do so.

Ecclesiastical Colonialism

Venn claimed in response that "the absence of missionary efforts to devolve responsibilities in the young church was the cause, rather than the consequence, of the low spiritual condition referred to. . . . Paternalism, racism and dependency were all part of the same problem"—namely, the domineering practices of the missionary community.[7] The lasting impact of such imperial prejudice is still felt in places like India, where the Christian faith remains all too commonly regarded by unsaved nationals as a foreign religion, a white man's imposition, forced into the Hindu culture by colonial overlords.

Wilbert Shenk reports that T. S. Johnson—who became, in 1937, the first national from Sierra Leone to reach the rank of bishop—in his book, *The Story of Mission*, vented frustration over the fact that foreign

---

6   Walls, *Cross-Cultural Process*, 179, 185.

7   Shenk, *Henry Venn—Missionary Statesman*, 34.

missionaries continued to control the national church during his tenure.[8] The pattern continued unbroken until 1953. Venn had warned as early as 1868 that precisely this was sure to be the outcome if missionaries failed to respect and trust the indigenous church. In Venn's understanding, "The Mission was the scaffolding of world evangelism and the Native Church the edifice. It was the removal of the scaffolding that proved the building was complete."[9]

Expatriate domination continued as an observable reality nonetheless, even within the ranks of the CMS under Venn's leadership. The problem lay not with the reformer but with those who followed in his institutional footsteps without honoring his deferential philosophy. Shenk asserts that, after Venn's death in 1873, his successors frequently repudiated in practice—while affirming in principle—the very ideals he promoted for transitioning supervisory responsibility to national leaders, a process aimed at what Venn called the eventual "euthanasia of the mission."[10]

Venn dared to challenge the accepted practice of colonial control over all mission institutions by introducing a plan to intentionally plant what he was the first to identify as "indigenous churches." His innovation defined as "indigenous" those congregations established for and led by national believers. His vision was to eliminate British oversight so that churches could emerge that were governed and supported by their own native members and that multiplied according to the nationals' own vision and values. This was the origin of today's three-self paradigm. Again, Venn's primary goal in promoting this formulation was to free native pastoral leaders from continued domination by colonially minded missionaries.[11] His chief concern in introducing these terms was to end missionary *dominance*, not to address national *dependence* per se. His

---

8   Ibid., 111.

9   Ibid., 46.

10 Ibid., 113.

11 Wilbert R. Shenk, "Henry Venn 1796–1873 Anglican (CMJ)," *Occasional Bulletin of Missionary Research* 1, no. 2 (April 1977): 16–19.

emphasis was on *ending outside governance*, not on *eliminating outside giving*.

Venn specifically asserted, in fact, that "missionaries could not avoid involvement in their converts' 'temporal welfare.'"[12] As he saw it, Christian love compelled action on their behalf. And though native resources were to be cultivated with the greatest possible speed and to the fullest possible extent, grants-in-aid for national leadership support through what the CMS styled the Native Church Fund were neither discouraged nor uncommon under Venn's leadership. The primary point at issue was that the emerging national leaders be paid from the National Church Fund and not through the mission directly. What Venn most desired to end was the sense among native workers that the foreign mission agency remained their paymaster and their supervisor.

This effect was achieved to Venn's satisfaction not by outlawing outside support but by segregating the National Church Fund so that support could be supplied to indigenous workers. It was also important to him that indigenous leaders be allowed to administer the National Church Fund.[13] The monies made available for support of national workers and indigenous projects still flowed from the funds of the society, but they were no longer controlled by the missionaries. Venn cited examples of instances where this approach ultimately produced self-supporting churches. An example from one of Venn's reports on Sierra Leone will suffice:

> In the second decade the experiment was made of casting upon the people the support of their elementary schools, for which the Society was paying £800 a year. This sum the Society proposed to reduce gradually by one-fifth each successive year. The people assembled in their several congregations, and determined to raise at once the whole sum necessary for the support of their schools, and to fund the Society's grants. . . . During

---

12 Quoted in Shenk, *Henry Venn—Missionary Statesman*, 26.

13 Max Warren, *To Apply the Gospel: Selections from the Writings of Henry Venn* (Grand Rapids: Eerdmans, 1971), 75.

the third decade, the support of their native pastors was thrown upon them. They willingly undertook the responsibility of nine native pastors, and immediately raised their stipends [while also contributing] more liberally than ever to the Bible Society and the Church Missionary Society over and above their native church funds. . . . Undoubtedly; the negro has a head for business and a heart for religion.[14]

Venn also specifically wrote, in a publication issued on January 8, 1866, about his openness to outside support of indigenous work, declaring that "to such a separate [Native Church] Fund the Society may contribute grants-in-aid, [which can be] gradually diminished as the native Church contributions increase, until the native Church is able to sustain the whole charge of [its financial affairs]."[15] The openness of the CMS under Venn to offer subsidies for national workers through the Native Fund mechanism is also evident from the steps taken immediately following Venn's death, in which the agency created the Henry Venn Native Church Fund as a memorial to provide grants for indigenous church development in Africa.[16]

Venn's three-tiered formula was adopted and expanded upon by John Nevius in 1890 as he contemplated reassignment from China to Korea. Nevius' adaptations added express concerns for other insensitive ministry practices still prominently followed by American and British missionaries in Asia at the dawn of the twentieth century.[17] In his *Methods of*

---

14 Ibid., 124.

15 Shenk, *Henry Venn—Missionary Statesman*, 126.

16 Ibid., 103.

17 Specifically, Nevius urged an end to: (1) Financial support practices that made nationals "paid agents" of Western powers in the early stages of mission activity; (2) Extractionist models of mobilization that served to remove native workers from their natural relational contexts in order to meet mission objectives; (3) Creating opportunistic "rice Christians" by offering financial aid indiscriminately. He saw this practice as one that created a mercenary spirit among new converts and thought it discouraged widespread volunteerism on which the rapid spread of the gospel in a newly reached culture would depend. (4) Favoritism in making commitments for financial support. Nevius thought that remuneration was awarded too often in ways that encouraged jealousy and

Mission Work, Nevius offered his own articulation of cautions against the negative effects of indiscriminant support being given to "paid agents" of the gospel, but he left open the possibility of supplying support to a variety of indigenous works:

> *I should exceedingly regret if the statement just made or any other statement in these letters should be understood or construed as intimating that the use of money in carrying on missionary work is not legitimate.* In the nature of things pecuniary aid is an absolute necessity, not only for sending out and supporting well qualified and accredited missionaries, but also for Hospital and Dispensary work, for the preparation and dissemination of a Christian literature, for establishing high institutions of learning and for furnishing, as needed, grants-in-aid for primary or preparatory Christian schools. In supplying the funds thus required, all Christians have the opportunity of sharing in the privileges and self-denials of the work of preaching the Gospel to every creature.[18]

In spite of Nevius' own qualification of his recommended reduction in pecuniary payments to national workers, the current application of the three-self paradigm, introduced originally to limit the abusive control of *outside authority*, serves instead to more generally limit the availability of *outside assistance*. The colonial domination against which Venn's paradigm was designed to be a protection has now largely passed from the scene. Venn's desired outcome has thus been achieved. But an unintended consequence also may have been produced by our modern misapplication of his three-self guideline. The original concern over *domination* has in effect been transfigured into an overriding concern about *dependence*. Not only are the issues in mind decidedly different, the outcomes produced in mission practice are also remarkably dissimilar.

---

envy among nationals while also promoting arrogance among the "chosen few" who were hired by missionaries. From John L. Nevius, *Methods of Mission Work* (New York: Foreign Mission Library, 1895), 9–17.

18 Ibid., 56 (italics added).

A Second Look at Settled Convictions

Venn's revolutionary principles and Nevius' recommended practices based upon them have become foundation stones for modern missiology. They have served effectively over the past 150 years and more to end justification for foreign control over national churches. In fact, it is now almost universally accepted that native leadership of mission churches is much to be preferred to outside governance if our goal is to see church planting movements sustained in unreached cultures. But after a century of increasingly wide reception of the three-self paradigm, some missiologists are beginning to recognize the point that I am trying to make here. It is time to take a second look at our settled convictions about dependency and the priority we presume self-support should be given. Simply stated, my concern is that today we often misapply the self-supporting principle Venn introduced into mission theory in a way that makes funding global ministry harder than it needs to be.

There are also real problems with the manner in which modern missionaries have interpreted Nevius' application of Venn's paradigm. As Jonathan Bonk reports, some mission leaders "have begun to move away from the traditional Western stresses on *independence, autonomy, and self-sufficiency* restructuring along lines more consistent with biblical teaching on the Church as the Body of Christ. . . . The emphasis is [now being placed] on the *interdependence* of Western and non-Western churches and institutions."[19]

Earlier attempts had been made to question the three-self paradigm before Bonk wrote about this issue in passing. Most prominently, Charles H. Kraft and Tom N. Wisley edited a book in 1979 entitled *Readings in Dynamic Indigeneity*. In that work they asserted that, while the three-self formula was a valid starting point in the quest for indigeneity, the approach taken by those who were following Venn's and Nevius' presumed principles was proving to be "somewhat limited."[20] Contributors to this

---

19 Jonathan J. Bonk, *Missions and Money: Affluence as a Western Missionary Problem* (Maryknoll, NY: Orbis Books, 1991), 124 (italics in the original).

20 Kraft and Wisley, *Readings in Indigeneity,* xxvii.

book added other credible missionary voices to the chorus challenging the universal validity of these accepted criteria for establishing a pioneer work as an indigenous ministry. Peter Beyerhaus noted that the three-self paradigm had never been followed consistently in any case. He observed that the last hundred years of mission history reflected that, while "some missionary societies were willing to apply the three selves formula radically, some [did so only] moderately and some hardly at all."[21]

Alan Tippett suggested that "we need a modern re-statement of the doctrine of selfhood."[22] His primary point was that indigeneity is simply too dynamic a process to be encapsulated in such a rigid scheme. This point had been made more forcefully many years earlier at a mission consultation convened by the International Missionary Council. Meeting at Willingen, Germany in 1952, delegates met to consider the revolutionary changes facing the missions community in the wake of World War II, the Korean Conflict, and the expulsion of Western missionaries from China by the new communist regime that had taken power there. (Interestingly, the communists in China used the mission community's call for indigenous churches to inaugurate its own brand of national church under government control, demanding a complete and permanent break between Chinese leaders and Christians in other parts of the world. This radical reform produced what is still today called the Three-Self Patriotic Movement in China.) In the context of the Willingen conference, D. G. Moses of India argued that the traditional three-self formula exposed a "dangerous narrowness of view" regarding self-sufficiency and autonomy and needed to be reconsidered. For him, independence was neither a biblical nor a beneficial goal to pursue.[23]

We can genuinely assert, therefore, that some key mission leaders believed decades ago that this formulation should not be considered as sacred and inviolable. But these protests in 1952 and 1979 did not turn

---

21 Quoted in Kraft and Wisley, *Readings in Indigeneity,* 18.

22 A. R. Tippett, *Verdict Theology in Missionary Theory* (Pasadena, CA: William Carey Library, 1973), 60.

23 Kraft and Wisley, *Readings in Indigeneity,* 19.

the tide of popular mission opinion. The time has come to try again to urge the mission community to reassess the validity of this assumed position.

These respected leaders combined their previous challenge to the status quo with a debate about the circumstances that might be conceived as meeting the self-supporting framework. Is it enough if a national church pays all full-time clergy from its own resources but still gets support for special projects from outside sources? Or must a church also fund all its own programs and services independently? Is the emerging national church more indigenous if it minimizes its activities and uses only volunteer workers so that outside assistance is not needed? Beyerhaus maintained that operating without paid staff was the general reality in the worldwide church through the fifth century, after which salaried clergy finally became a more common luxury of growing congregations.[24] This development was consistent with Paul's perspective on stewardship, which allowed for those who preach the gospel to make their living from the gospel (1 Corinthians 9:13–14). He and other apostolic leaders used offerings for charitable purposes as well as for interchurch assistance in times of crisis. The famine that struck the church in Jerusalem during the reign of Claudius is an apt example of one such occasion (see Acts 4:32–37; 11:27–30).

Who among us would conclude that this firstborn church in history was anything but indigenous as it manifested its full Hebrew character even after accepting the help of churches outside its cultural context? So strong were the ethnic biases in the Jerusalem church of the first century that resentment in the face of the initial conversions of non-Jews was considered the only appropriate response to the earliest missionary movements of the Holy Spirit among Gentiles. That was true even after Cornelius' conversion in Acts 10–11, an event that allowed God to gradually reorient the Hebrew Christian mindset to accept Gentile believers as fellow saints and disciples of Jesus. Not until the Jerusalem council in Acts 15 would this point of dispute be settled formally by

---

24 Ibid., 25.

the early church leaders. But the Judaizers' issue continued to plague the church, as even Peter would show his persistent Hebrew ethnocentrism in Antioch at a later date (see Galatians 2:11–14). My point is that the first-century Jerusalem church demonstrated its indigenous Hebrew character even as it received financial aid on occasion from Gentile sister churches.

If we are accurate in observing that the first-century Jerusalem church received support from faraway congregations as an expression of solidarity among Christians worldwide, why must we conclude that manifestation of the same spirit of mutuality today is somehow harmful? By the same token, who would deny that presently there are many mission-planted churches in the world that receive no outside financial support but that remain completely captivated by Western approaches to ministry? They are, therefore, self-supporting but not indigenous. William Smalley rightly concluded, "Self-support is, wherever economically possible, really the soundest method of church [finances] . . . but there certainly are situations in which it is not possible." Where insistence on self-support could make church growth nearly impossible, the presence of outside giving does not necessarily imply the absence of indigeneity.[25]

Indigenizing and Westernizing

Smalley went on to observe, "Some missions have legislated the gradual withdrawal of financial subsidy from younger churches. This is done in order to put the younger church on its 'self-supporting feet.' It is [intended to be] a step toward the day when the church will be indigenous, as the mission [defines that term], but the withdrawal of subsidy is a foreign act and not in the most remote sense indigenous."[26] He added, rather cryptically, "I very strongly suspect that the three 'selfs' are really projections of our American value systems into the idealization of the

---

25 Ibid., 33.
26 Ibid., 41.

church, that they are in their very nature Western concepts based upon Western ideas of individualism and power. By forcing them on other people we may at times have been making it impossible for truly indigenous patterns to develop. *We have [in effect] been westernizing with all our talk about indigenizing.*"[27]

As Smalley says, "It is the way the funds are administered, the way the decisions are made, and the purposes to which [outside support] is put that are diagnostic of an indigenous church."[28] Venn's paradigm was a *decisive response* that sought to curtail the *imperial passions* of his contemporaries. Could it be that the modern misapplication of his thinking has somehow become a *defensive response* that serves to support the *material passions* of those of us hailing from the West?

From the perspective of today's wealthy Western Christians, the three-self parameters are applied in a way that produces a curious result. The self-supporting aspect of the guideline, in particular, is played out in a manner that makes withholding much-needed support a principled expression of genuine concern that is somehow supposed to be interpreted as a demonstration of our *caring for others.* That is, it is predicated on the premise that poor nationals are better off when we refuse to give in response to their very real needs. The inherent paradox is obvious and not easily lost on our national colleagues in ministry. It is no wonder that they end up seeing Western appeals to this formula as simple rationalizations for those indisposed to *sharing with others.* I can easily understand that, from the perspective of those living in abject poverty, our defense against giving could be interpreted as an overt evidence of greed.

I want to propose the possibility that we Westerners sometimes open ourselves to being misunderstood because we have often misapplied Venn's principles, making them not only less practical in our day but also more punitive than he would have imagined they could ever become. Changing the application of the three-self paradigm to focus on dependency has altered our perspective in significant ways, even as

---

27 Ibid., 35 (italics added).

28 Ibid., 34.

it has shifted our concerns onto issues not intended by Venn or Nevius. Pointing this out is important because, as Os Guinness has said, "The way we *say* things shapes the way we *see* things. Say something often enough and eventually we'll come to see it that way."[29] Western clarity on the issue of dependency may be born more out of repetition of the concern than from the reality of the problem. We may be more satisfied with our sense of "missiological correctness" on this issue than we have a right to be.

The "Worst Curse" or the "Best Test" of Western Missiology

Under the logic of the presumed limits of the self-supporting paradigm, we have developed major apprehension about the downsides of using dollars to support national workers, projects, and facilities development. Paternalism is assumed to be the inescapable end of financial subsidies, and true partnership is thought to be unattainable if significant outside support is made available. The late Charles Troutman, a missionary who served with InterVarsity and Latin American Mission, put it starkly in a statement quoted by William Kornfield. Troutman dubbed financial paternalism as the "worst curse" that Western missionaries can put on the national church.[30]

I am arguing, in contrast, that an approach to sacrificial partnership that empowers and enables indigenous leaders to advance their own visions and agendas may be the "best test" of our own convictions about God's call on us to be generous in our stewardship of vast Western resources. Can we not learn to share with those less fortunate than our-

---

29 Os Guinness, *Prophetic Untimeliness: A Challenge to the Idol of Relevance* (Grand Rapids: Baker, 2003), 37.

30 William J. Kornfield, "What Hath Our Western Money and Our Western Gospel Wrought?" *Mission Frontiers: The Bulletin of the U.S. Center for World Mission*, Pasadena, CA (January–February 1997): 1. Available at http://www.missionfrontiers. org/1997/0102/jf9710.htm.

ιout also controlling their lives and ministries in the process?

uck Bennett's words again, I believe we can "help without
murting" our national colleagues in ministry.

Bonk offers a syllogism in his book as a prelude to a comprehensive list of biblical texts that ought to be explored by those seeking to understand the dynamics involved when missions and money are considered together. That syllogism is easily summarized here as a prelude to my own list of relevant passages from Scripture:

- The West is rich.

- The church in the West is rich.

- Missionaries sent by the Western Church are rich.

- Most of the peoples to whom Western missionaries are sent by their churches are poor.

- What the Bible says about the rich and the poor has a direct bearing on the Western church generally and on Western missionaries in particular.[31]

With these assertions as a backdrop, my own review of the Scriptures has led me to conclude that the biblical concepts of covenant relationships are to be preferred to business models of partnership as we look for principles to guide our relationships with national brothers and sisters. I am also persuaded that *compassion,* not *caution,* should be our ruling motivation as we respond to discernible material needs both inside and outside the family of God. It seems to me that Jesus' own teachings about what constitutes worthy ministry points us invariably in that direction.

---

31 Bonk, *Missions and Money,* 86.

CHAPTER THREE

God's Call to Generous Living

In Matthew's Gospel, the Lord makes it clear that anyone who serves those in need (feeding the hungry, offering drink to those who thirst, showing hospitality to strangers, clothing the naked, and visiting those who are sick or confined to jail) is, in essence, directly serving him (Matthew 25:34–40). Compassion for the poor and the needy is, therefore, an essential element of every Christian's calling as a child of God. I no longer believe that we can legitimately separate the gospel mandate (the Great Commission) from the social mandate (the Great Commandment). I have further concluded that compassion is generally intended by God to drive us redemptively toward the needy. Mercy is also a motivation divinely designed to create the most powerful responses in us when needs are evident, specifically among Christians. Paul makes this clear in Galatians 6:9–10: "Let us not lose heart in doing good, for in due time we will reap if we do not grow weary. So then, while we have opportunity, let us do good to all people, and especially to those who are of the household of the faith."

Biblical Reflections on Wealth and Wisdom

The simple meaning of these texts argues immediately against applying the self-supporting principle in a manner that serves to guard Christians who "have" from feeling the responsibility to respond readily to the recognizable needs of Christians and non-Christians who "have not." Both James and John add apostolic authority to "responsive giving" as a higher call than "reasoned holding back" for those who want to have a biblically defensible missiology. Consider their inspired teaching along this line:

> What use is it, my brethren, if someone says he has faith but he has no works? Can that faith save him? If a brother or sister is without clothing and in need of daily food, and one of you says to them, "Go in peace, be warmed and be filled," and yet you do not give them what is necessary for their body, what use is that? Even so faith, if it has no works, is dead, being by itself. (James 2:14–17)

> We know love by this, that He laid down His life for us; and we ought to lay down our lives for the brethren. But whoever has the world's goods, and sees his brother in need and closes his heart against him, how does the love of God abide in him? Little children, let us not love with word or with tongue, but in deed and truth. (1 John 3:16–18)

Under the weight of these passages, my former commitment to the current application of the three-self paradigm crumbled altogether. But weightier truths can and should be brought to bear for the sake of those who feel led to prop up what I see as the continued misuse of the self-supporting principle.

This context does not permit space for an exhaustive exegetical review of the biblical support for a missionary methodology that would more eagerly offer assistance to those in need when such is possible. Bonk's list of passages dealing with finances is a good reference, for it offers a more comprehensive collection that touches on money, wealth, and dealing with the poor. Interested inquirers who seek a broader treatment than the one I include below could study that list. But a simplified summary drawn from Scriptures that specifically deal with giving can serve my purposes well enough as I seek to demonstrate the clear guidance God's Word offers to govern our support of ministry to the nations. The line of biblical reasoning that I find convincing, one that demanded a measure of change in my own position regarding established mission practice in this area, follows this path:

- The earth and all that it contains is the Lord's (Psalm 24:1).

- All the silver and all the gold in the world belong to the Lord (Haggai 2:8).

- Both riches and honor come from the Lord; it is in his hand to make people great and to strengthen them (1 Chronicles 29:11–12).

- God is the one who gives us power to make wealth. Apart from him we can do nothing (Deuteronomy 8:17–18; John 15:5).

- Material blessing is not a sign of superiority nor is it a justification for arrogance between one person or nation and another. None of us has anything in the way of material goods that we did not receive from God's hand. In this respect, we are all completely dependent upon him (1 Corinthians 4:6–7).

- National origin is in God's control, not ours. So our national identity and the benefits and advantages that earthly citizenship offer us are also not to be considered a justification for arrogance toward others (Acts 17:26–27).

- Stewardship, rather than ownership, is the biblical stance from which we should view the responsibility to manage the resources God has entrusted to us (Matthew 25:14–30).

- Stewards must be faithful to accomplish the will of their masters (1 Corinthians 4:2).

- God's will in the matter of material blessing is not left unclear. *He blesses us materially because he is burdened for others spiritually.* God intends our wealth to serve his glory by making his name great and by making his ways known throughout the earth (Psalm 67).

- It is better to give than to receive, and it should be our expectation that God is moving all his people toward circumstances that will allow them to be dedicated givers rather than dependent receivers. To presume otherwise is a pejorative position born perhaps more from pride than principle (Acts 20:35; 2 Corinthians 9:6–12).[1]

- God intends all Christians to be *interdependent with*—rather than *dependent on* or *independent of*—others in the body of Christ. We are only made truly complete when we have benefited from what others add to our existence (1 Corinthians 12:14–26; Galatians 6:1–5; Ephesians 4:16). Paul specifically includes in his conception of fellowship among believers a financial aspect that is both legitimate and life-giving. He calls this dynamic the ministry of "giving and receiving" (Philippians 4:14–20).

---

1   The process by which God transforms receivers into givers may take some time. But because of his grace and his faithfulness, God's hand is moving in the lives of his children in an inexorable process that promises a greater measure of material blessing for them all. It is useful to acknowledge that this kingdom reality has been recognized practically and described in principle by church growth theorists for decades. Donald McGavran was the first to articulate the dynamics of what he termed "redemption and lift" (Donald A. McGavran, *Understanding Church Growth* [Grand Rapids: Eerdmans, 1970], 295). When God's saving grace comes to individuals in any culture (spiritual redemption), their confidence, character, and convictions about fruitful labor are impacted. They become better wives and husbands, better parents, better sons and daughters, better workers, and better citizens. They are more reliable in their work, more industrious in their patterns of life, and more focused on managing their financial affairs well. Almost invariably, their material lot in life improves dramatically over time, so that they become less needy and more able to help others (socioeconomic lift).

- As material resources ebb and flow within the family of God, the abundance of one member is intended to meet the need of another so that a measure of equality can be maintained among believers. When we recognize that we are all merely sons and daughters eating from the Father's table, the ones who gather much will not have too much and the ones who gather little will have no lack (2 Corinthians 8:13–15).

- Giving is a means to honor God and is a grace not to be entered into under duress or compulsion. God loves a cheerful giver and allows his children to express their generosity as they purpose in their own hearts. Moreover, Paul's teaching in 2 Corinthians 9 seems to release Christians from the legal requirement of tithing as set forth in the letter of the Jewish law. Instead, under the perfect law of liberty in Christ, believers in Jesus are released to give in greater measure out of a heart overflowing with love and grace. It is God's desire that all his children trust in his sovereign ability to make grace abound to us, so that always having all sufficiency, we may have an abundance for every good deed. As the New International Version renders it, God wants to make us rich in every way so we can be generous on every occasion (Proverbs 3:9; 11:24–25; 2 Corinthians 9:6–12).

- Rich and poor alike are capable of giving, though often not in equal proportions. The rich may give in greater magnitude; but in God's economy, special significance is attached to sacrifices made by the poor. It could be said that widows' mites, mustard seeds, and little jars of oil are the most prized currency in the kingdom of God (2 Corinthians 8:1–5; Mark 12:41–44; Matthew 13:31–32; 1 Kings 17:8–15).

- Only robbers and rich fools think it is wise to acquire as much as they are able and to systematically hoard the product of their efforts rather than sharing as God commands (Malachi 3:8–10; Luke 12:16–21).

- Greed, the human tendency to "buy and to keep" for ourselves more than we need, has no legitimate place in a believer's life and is to be avoided in all its forms (Luke 12:15; Ephesians 5:3).

- God has specifically promised to reward and to repay any investment his children make in offering assistance to the poor (Proverbs 19:17).

These passages offer a biblical foundation for my call to reconsider the current missiological application of the three-self paradigm. They also compel me to encourage mission leaders to reach beyond the broadly accepted presumption that giving Western financial support to indigenous ministries is illegitimate. That said, it must be reiterated that I am not promoting perpetual handouts for national workers or their churches. *I am promoting maximum investment, for the sake of the kingdom, in a manner that will not create unhealthy dependency.*

Dependency vs. Discipleship

The following chart (see Figure 1) attempts to contrast some of the distinctions I see between models of mission that create financial dependency and models of mission that result in healthy financial discipleship. Westerners should be able to model and teach biblical stewardship at the same time. If we do not practice what we are preaching along these lines, in effect showing indigenous leaders how to apply kingdom principles in financial matters, then our message will largely be lost anyway.

It should go without saying that truly committed Christians in every culture will have no desire to serve the Lord from an openly dependent posture long-term as they grow in their understanding of biblical stewardship. As noted previously, it is pejorative to assume national believers too often desire to remain dependent. Missiological principles born from such negative presumptions regarding national leaders may say more about Westerners—who doubt the efficacy of Scripture and the transforming power of the Holy Spirit—than they do about indigenous

Figure 1: To Give or Not to Give?
Charting the Appropriate Course

Dependency: A Model of Domination	Investment: A Model of Discipleship
Subjugation of nationals	Sponsorship of nationals
Selfishness and greed manifested	Sacrificial giving modeled
Competition engendered by Westerners: Patronizing their favorites	Cooperation engendered by nationals: Promoting their fellows
Complacency about multiplication induced by contentment	Capacity for multiplication enhanced by contributions
Giving minimized: Focus is on "silver and gold"	Giving maximized: Focus is on "such as I have"
Westerners set the agenda and control governance	Nationals set the agenda and control governance
Stagnates growth	Stimulates growth

Figure 1: Comparing the implications of focusing on dependency versus focusing on discipleship, this chart attempts to contrast alternative perspectives as an aid in the process of determining whether we are "to give or not to give." Note that Deuteronomy 8 indicates the danger of freely receiving is not greater hunger and increased *dependence*, but rather greater haughtiness and increased *independence*. What God desires is greater humility and *interdependence*. There is a touch of irony and paradox in the presumption that the key to overcoming selfishness among those in need is found by having those who are blessed refuse to share from their bounty. The intention of God is that those whom he has blessed might respond by giving freely, not to have them instead find reasons for "buying and keeping" their resources. In the dependency rationale, the appropriate response to need is too often greed—an unbiblical conclusion that is impossible to defend.

leaders—who deserve, as do we, to be tested in their ability to respond maturely to God's material blessing.

The Holy Spirit can and should be trusted to prevent carnal, selfish, and self-serving attitudes from being sustained in the hearts of true believers emerging from the darkness of paganism and unbelief. God's power to quickly and completely transform our perspective regarding finances is, after all, one major lesson drawn from Zaccheus' decision to repay fourfold all that he had taken from his neighbors (Luke 19:1–10) and from Paul's general instruction that former thieves steal no longer but engage instead in profitable labor so that they may have something to share with those in need (Ephesians 4:28). John's Gospel tells us that God so loved the world that he gave sacrificially when he sent Jesus to die for us. God expects us to follow his example of lavish generosity, rather than to defend our rationale for holding back resources that could be a genuine help.

The adverse outcomes that modern missiologists think may flow from Western aid being extended to needy believers around the world are, in this light, perhaps an unwarranted judgment against both our national brothers and sisters and the Holy Spirit who indwells, motivates, and blesses them as freely as he does us. That kind of thinking is motivated, it seems to me, more by our fear than by our faith; and fear should not be the driving force behind our financial decision making processes in missions. Neither should insidious greed be allowed to overrule the lavish grace God encourages all Christians to manifest as they extend themselves in giving as a humble expression of gratitude and generosity.

We Westerners would be better brothers and sisters, in my judgment, if we were willing to do whatever we could within our considerable capacity to fund the advance of the gospel—even if that means we generally give in disproportionate amounts to support indigenous ministry. Is it not logical to assume this is an obvious application of Jesus' teaching that, in the kingdom of God, "to whom much has been given much shall be required?" Because we have been blessed with disproportionate resources, we ought to bear a disproportionate financial responsibility. In the current climate that is characterized, in my opinion, by missionary defensiveness on this subject, our determination to press our case for avoiding dependency dynamics makes us less credible because we tend to define our doctrines in ways that also defend our desire to retain our wealth. We simply do not accept as readily as we ought the extraordinary obligation that comes from inordinate material blessing. We must not avoid the biblical injunctions that call us to *generous living* in order to defend our propensity to *minimize giving*.

Referring to the chart below one can easily see that our Western cautions about giving to missions have been mirrored in other evangelized areas and intensified worldwide in the church. These figures, drawn from the 2001 edition of the World Christian Encyclopedia, reveal that only about $54 million, or .02 percent, of all giving to the world's churches goes into the work of reaching the truly unreached, who are also often

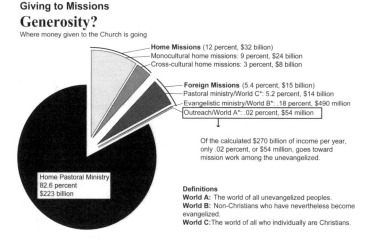

Giving to Missions

Generosity?

Where money given to the Church is going

— **Home Missions** (12 percent, $32 billion)
— Monocultural home missions: 9 percent, $24 billion
— Cross-cultural home missions: 3 percent, $8 billion

— **Foreign Missions** (5.4 percent, $15 billion)
— Pastoral ministry/World C*: 5.2 percent, $14 billion
— Evangelistic ministry/World B*: .18 percent, $490 million
— Outreach/World A*: .02 percent, $54 million

Of the calculated $270 billion of income per year, only .02 percent, or $54 million, goes toward mission work among the unevangelized.

Home Pastoral Ministry
82.6 percent
$223 billion

Definitions
World A: The world of all unevangelized peoples.
World B: Non-Christians who have nevertheless become evangelized.
World C: The world of all who individually are Christians.

Figures reflect money given by the Church worldwide in U.S. dollars.
Due to rounding, totals may not add up exactly.
Source: *World Christian Encyclopedia*, Second Edition, New York: Oxford University Press, 2001.

Figure 2: This chart was included in an article by Russell G. Shubin entitled "Where Your Treasure Is . . . A Fresh Look at Our Life and Our Resources in Light of the Kingdom," published in *Mission Frontiers: The Bulletin of the U.S. Center for World Mission,* Pasadena, CA (September 2001). Available at http://www.missionfrontiers.org/2001/03/200103.htm.

among the world's truly poor peoples. In fact, a mere .2 percent of the total of $270 billion in annual revenue of all churches goes into ministries aimed outside the church toward local evangelistic and foreign mission activities among lost people of any kind. It should be immediately apparent that something is amiss in our missiology when our cautions, concerns, and convictions about giving and dependency justify Christians keeping 99.8 percent of all church revenues for themselves. We must reexamine why the global church has fallen so far short of the generous spirit God intends his children to manifest.

If I were to select a passage that best states the general goal God has in mind in urging Christians to give liberally, 2 Corinthians 9:8–11 would be at the top of my list. The promise from Paul in that context is expressed unreservedly:

> God is able to make all grace abound to you, so that in all things at all times, having all that you need, you will abound in every good work. . . . Now he who supplies seed to the sower and bread for food will also supply and increase your store of seed and will enlarge the harvest of your righteousness. You will be made rich in every way so that you can be generous on every occasion. (NIV)

The expectation conveyed by these verses tells us that Christians are intended by God to live as generous stewards of kingdom resources. Those concerned about dependency embrace this notion in *principle* willingly enough, but I believe their arguments discourage giving liberally in *practice*. The concern over creating dependency is used to support a prevailing attitude of caution when it comes to considering maximum contributions to others in need. As I noted above, James and John both teach with apostolic authority that there is something inherently unspiritual and unloving about seeing others in need and finding a way to avoid responding (James 2:14–17; 1 John 3:16–18). Using John's language from his first epistle, I believe none of us want to end up loving materially deprived brothers and sisters in "word and tongue" but not in "deed and truth." So how should we respond in the face of incredible needs we find in places like Bosnia or the Sudan or Afghanistan? I suggest that we should try to give all that we can to see that the kingdom comes and the Father's will is done among the deprived peoples of the earth. That is what being in covenant with believers emerging among formerly unreached people groups demands of us.

I think some who argue for withholding aid point their arguments in the wrong direction, *explaining why* we well-provisioned Western Christians should give *less* rather than *exploring how* we could give *more* to impoverished mission churches. Ronald Sider predicted that this would be the case when he wrote *Rich Christians in an Age of Hunger*. He said that "it would be impossible for the rich minority to live with themselves if they did not invent plausible justifications" for ignoring the needs of the poor.[2] Nearly thirty years ago, he openly declared that "in the coming decades, rationalizations for [Western affluence] will be legion."[3] I doubt he dreamed then that many of the arguments against global generosity would come from the leaders of the mission community! His seminal work on the appropriate Christian response to the world's most needy peoples is as timely today as when it first appeared in print in 1977—and worthy of renewed attention.

Instead of quarreling with those who tend to be generous in the face of under-resourced congregations and key Christian leaders in unreached areas of the world who are willing to receive much-needed assistance, shouldn't we follow Sider's example by questioning the motives and rationales that guide Christians to guard available funds that could be of such tremendous help? In my experience, God's scales are usually slanted toward generosity as a way of life. That's the logical impact of God's lavish love expressed in Jesus! Being children of a limitlessly benevolent Father, I believe we should be extravagant givers ourselves.

Does it not make sense that a model of generosity based on obedience to biblical truths will teach a better stewardship lesson to new believers than a miserly message of frugality based on presumably legiti-

---

2   Ronald J. Sider, *Rich Christians in an Age of Hunger: A Biblical Study*, 2nd ed. (Downers Grove, IL: InterVarsity, 1984), 46.

3   Ibid., 49.

mate missiological principles? The Scriptures clearly and consistently require *responsive giving* rather than *reasoned holding back* when material needs are going unmet disproportionately. It will continue to be hard for our poorer brothers and sisters to hear our rationales for not helping them as long as they remain hungry for the most basic provisions and we remain relatively well-heeled and hoard our surpluses.

Some will suggest that giving doesn't solve the problem of the poor in any case. Daniel Grell, formerly a senior executive with my own denomination's mission, the Evangelical Free Church of America International Mission (EFCA-IM), has taken that view in defending "the logic of limited giving" that flows from a traditional view of the self-supporting paradigm. He wrote, for example, in a memo prepared for US partners sharing a commitment to Bosnia, "No matter how much effort we put into responding to the needs of the poor, we would never fully take care of them nor solve the social problem of having poor people in the world." Jesus indeed asserts in three of the Gospel accounts that the disciples should recognize the reality that "the poor will be with you always" (Matthew 26:11; Mark 14:7; John 12:8). But Grell's sense of this statement makes it sound as if the poor communities of the world are like "black holes" of financial need that place incessant demands on those who are well-to-do. That was not Jesus' point in reminding the disciples that the poor would always be present among us. Jesus was defending the lavish gift a woman was making in preparation for his burial and affirming the use of resources for that purpose when the same resources might have been given to the needy.

In no way was Jesus discouraging generosity toward the poor. He was encouraging lavish love expressed materially toward a higher priority. *Giving, when offered in a discerning way, always has God's blessing.* In later chapters I will attempt to address how we can give wisely without engendering dependency. Grell and I find considerable agreement regarding "how we can give" in ways that help without hindering indigenous ministries. It is on the "how much to give" issue that we are more significantly at odds. Having freely received an abundant supply by God's grace, the Lord has always expected Christian people of means to give freely to others in return. I don't know how we could presume God's expectation is different today for those of us living in the wealthiest and most materially comfortable society in the history of the world. Because of the magnitude of our experience of God's grace in financial terms, I believe our interests should be focused on how to maximize our giving rather than on how to minimize it.

This is, it seems to me, God's intent for those who call him Lord. Consider, for example, the clear instruction found in Deuteronomy 15:11, the Old Testament reference most closely corresponding to Jesus' reminder about the ever-present poor recorded in the Gospels. In this text, Moses commanded Israel, "For the poor will never cease to be in the land; therefore I command you, saying, 'You shall freely open your hand to your brother, to your needy and poor in your land.'" We cannot easily deny that the poor are precious to God and that they are intended to be a blessing, not a burden, to God's people. Neither can we forget that God has been specific about the priority he gives to his people developing a generous heart toward others. Isaiah 58:6–7 makes his intent obvious:

> Is this not the fast which I choose, to loosen the bonds of wickedness, to undo the bands of the yoke, and to let the oppressed go free and break every yoke? Is it not to divide your bread with the hungry and bring the homeless poor into the house; when you see the naked, to cover him; and not to hide yourself from your own flesh?

According to this text, fasting God's way doesn't even require that we stop feasting! It just directs that our consumptive ways and our tendencies "to buy and to keep" be tempered by compassion for those facing real need. God desires that we do more, not less, for the hungry, the homeless, and the naked. God wants us to give!

CHAPTER FOUR

Serving God or Mammon?

Acknowledging the Bible's inescapable affirmation of the inherent priority God gives to helping the poor, we should next look carefully at the first-century sermon found in James 2:1–13. In that text, James offers important and specific teaching about the special present and future value the poor should hold in our minds. If we are not to surrender to secular perspectives on this point, we need to grasp two particular truths that are revealed in James 2:5. These insights must be allowed to inform our Western utilitarian perspectives about less materially privileged people if we are to avoid wrong attitudes in relating to the poor around the world.

The Mammon Principle

First, James teaches that poor men and women who are chosen to be part of the family of God are to be prized because they are uniquely prepared to be "rich in faith." The point we must not minimize from this key phrase is the simple reality that impoverished believers experience a deeper trust relationship with God than do those who live in relative comfort and security. Poverty somehow creates conditions that reinforce the human compulsion and capacity to rely on God in humble ways. Prosperity, on the other hand, induces pride, self-reliance, and disregard both for God and for the poor. The corrupting influence of riches is a danger the Scriptures repeatedly warn us about—one so great that wealth alone can make it hard for rich people even to enter heaven.

We could call this the "mammon principle." Jesus taught the disciples that riches are dangerous because they have a definite demonic power at work behind them. In Matthew 6:24 he said we cannot serve God and "mammon," which is an Aramaic word defined in the New American Standard Bible's footnote as "wealth, etc., personified as an object of worship." Jesus made it clear that mammon competes with God for devotion in people's hearts and minds. Mammon has a greater hold on wealthy and comfortable souls than it does on those who are impoverished. Like a menacing lion, mammon stalks the lives of the rich far more effectively than the poor. It actively tries to corrupt the thinking of the children of God, choking the Word and keeping it from taking root and bearing fruit in our lives (Matthew 13:22).

Because we Westerners are relatively rich, we would do well to admit that we have to fight against the devilish influence of mammon. If we are not alert to the delusions of grandeur induced by our relative financial strength, we may never gain, and we may not long hold on to, a proper understanding of God's heart for the poor. We must remember that according to James 2 the poor—especially the believing poor—are to be viewed as *spiritual assets* and not as *financial liabilities*. They are with us in part because we need them to teach us about what it means to truly trust God for everything and to avoid the influences of mammon. They are in this sense richer in faith than we are.

Secondly, James 2:5 tells us that, because the redeemed poor are destined to be fellow heirs with us in the kingdom of heaven, they are to be freely accepted in the community of the King on earth. They are undeniable members of our spiritual family, and they have been granted equal standing before God even if we do not grant them equal status in our human affairs. Because the destinies of rich and poor saints are unavoidably linked in the tomorrows of eternity, fellowship between them should be wholeheartedly embraced in the world today. The poor deserve to be treated with dignity in the family of God. There is simply no room for partiality as we relate to those less materially blessed than ourselves.

Paul asserts that the reciprocal ministry of giving and receiving has a strengthening effect on fellowship in the family of God rather than weakening it. Among God's people, *genuine caring* is expressed by *generous sharing*. Paul also praises the support offered him by the Philippian church as an aspect of biblical *koinonia* (see Philippians 4:14–15). We should follow his example and affirm giving and receiving as a valuable aspect of genuine fellowship and a healthy dynamic in the body of Christ.

Turning back to James 2, we are warned that we err and overtly express evil motives when we act in partiality, favoring the rich over the poor among us. Could it be that it is precisely when we make such ill-conceived distinctions that we find suitable grounds to support decisions to keep our money at home (where we trust it will be spent well) rather than sharing with the poor in other cultures (where we fear it will be squandered)? Rich Starcher, another EFCA-IM missionary, rather callously suggests, "Money is like [battery] acid . . . it does great good in the right place."[1] The implication is that battery acid in a dry cell system creates electricity, but placed in our wallets it ruins everything. Starcher's analogy seems to be saying that material wealth is most safe and most useful when left in the right and most productive place, our own pockets. But, like battery acid, money only spoils things if it finds its way from this appropriate reservoir—Western wallets—to other parts of the world, where it is needed but presumably not managed well.

---

1   Rich Starcher, "Supporting National Church Leaders," *Africa Alive: A Publication of the EFCM Africa Office* (February–March 2000): 2.

Richard Foster speaks of mammon as the "darker side of money." Behind material riches he sees the sinister influence of a malevolent demonic power. "When Jesus uses the Aramaic term *mammon* to refer to riches, he is giving wealth a personal and spiritual character. When he declares, 'you cannot serve God and mammon,' he is personifying mammon as a rival god . . . a (demonic) power that seeks to dominate us. . . . It is the ability of money to inspire devotion that brings its dark side to the forefront."[2] Os Guinness agrees when he asserts that the spirit of mammon always presents us with a choice. We can either "serve God and use money or we can serve money and use God"—there are no other real options.[3] Therefore we need to realize that money is never a purely economic medium; it always includes a demonic element that seeks to draw our hearts away from following the Lord fully.

Foster offers several practical steps that can help us master the unholy effects of mammon in our lives.[4] His strongest advice is for us to show utter disregard for money by trampling it under foot. He encourages us to engage in the most profane desecration of all in showing our disrespect for mammon. He urges us to give our money away! He writes, "The powers that energize money cannot abide that most unnatural of acts, giving. Money [from a demonic perspective] is made for taking, for bargaining, for manipulating, but not for giving. This is exactly why giving has such an ability to defeat the powers of money."[5] Ron Sider agrees that dethroning mammon is among the most powerful first steps we can

---

2   Richard J. Foster, *Money, Sex and Power: The Challenge of the Disciplined Life* (San Francisco: Harper & Row, 1985), 25–26.

3   Os Guinness, *Doing Well and Doing Good: Money, Giving, and Caring in a Free Society* (Colorado Springs: NavPress, 2001), 79.

4   Among them are exhortations to (1) listen to the biblical witness about money; (2) consider how money impacts us personally from a psychological and sociological perspective; (3) learn to manage money so that it serves spiritual priorities; (4) identify with a group of believers who will affirm our attempts to simplify our lifestyles; (5) pray about financial decisions so that covetousness and greed are bound from our lives; (6) dethrone money by moving it down our list of priorities and defile its pretended sacred character by changing our inner attitudes and outer actions.

5   Foster, *Money, Sex and Power*, 61.

take in trying to deal with the scandal of Western greed.[6] This point must not be missed! We are more likely to serve mammon when we choose "not to give" because we assume that generosity will produce negative effects in the lives and ministries of needy brothers and sisters.

The Manna Principle

The apostle Paul says that the Holy Spirit's expectation is quite the opposite. He writes to the Corinthians about the expected response of those who are graced to receive financial aid from within the family of God: "They will glorify God for your obedience to your confession of the gospel of Christ and for the liberality of your contribution to them" (2 Corinthians 9:13).

If we presume a less redemptive response will be forthcoming should the poor living among us experience material blessing through our generosity, we may not be offering a biblical reflection of God's concern. Instead we may be betraying a pecuniary prejudice hidden deep in our own hearts. We may simply see ourselves as good stewards whom God can trust and poorer nationals as unreliable people by comparison. We must be careful to evaluate our motives for "not giving" and to guard against developing a "superior persona" just because we enjoy a financially advantaged posture *vis-à-vis* the world's poor. We dare not allow our missiological concerns for dependency issues to overrule our theological convictions about God's call to be generous financially.

We must also remember that obedience alone is not intended by God to be the only (or the primary) driving force behind our giving decisions. In fact, Paul establishes in the context of 2 Corinthians 8 the primary motivation that should prompt a generous Christian response to the need for relief aid in Jerusalem. He makes it clear that such should be *an act of compassion born of love* not *an act of obedience based on law* (v. 8). Paul's inspired teaching reveals that when it comes to generous

---

6   Ronald J. Sider, *The Scandal of the Evangelical Conscience: Why Are Christians Living Just Like the Rest of the World?* (Grand Rapids: Baker, 2005), 110–11.

responses in the face of need, he could not require it but God did desire it. He also points out that giving is a brotherly response based on the ebb and flow of material fortune that could easily be reversed in due time. Second Corinthians 8:13–15 records: "For this is not for the ease of others and for your affliction, but by way of equality—at this present time your abundance being a supply for their need, so that their abundance also may become a supply for your need, that there may be equality; as it is written, 'He who gathered much did not have too much, and he who gathered little had no lack.'"

Philip Hughes elaborates on this text in his contribution to the New International Commentary on the New Testament:

> The Apostle is careful to explain to the Corinthians the "mechanics" of this operation. He does not intend that the relief of the saints at Jerusalem should be at the cost of hardship to those in Corinth, but it is his wish that things should work in accordance, as it were, with a law of equilibrium. Under present circumstance the Corinthian Christians are enjoying a degree of material prosperity which is denied to their brethren in Jerusalem, and so the comparative abundance of the former must be extended in brotherly generosity to the want of the latter. The balance will, however, be restored should a time come when the Jerusalem church is comparatively prosperous and the Corinthian church in need; for then the extension of the abundance of the one to the want of the other will be repeated, only this time in reverse direction. And so, by this spirit of reciprocity, a principle of equality is operative in the universal Christian fraternity.[7]

We might call this the "manna principle" of material stewardship, since Paul, quoting Exodus 16:18, associates the dynamic with the experience of God's miraculous provision of a daily food supply during

---

7   Philip E. Hughes, *Commentary on the Second Epistle to the Corinthians, The New International Commentary on the New Testament,* F. F. Bruce, General Editor (Grand Rapids: Eerdmans, 1962), 305–6.

the wilderness journey following Israel's exodus from Egypt. In that specific context, in which God orchestrated events to keep living conditions standardized, food supplies equalized, and relative earning capacities neutralized, no one could generate a surplus or maintain a material advantage over his neighbor even if he wanted to do so. Paul's reference to the exodus experience seems to indicate that, in economic terms, such a level playing field may be God's preference. Certainly the inspired text points us toward unselfishness and reciprocal inclinations—at least in attitude. I am concerned that our modern application of missiological theory has undermined our commitment to the spirit of *generosity*, *reciprocity*, and *equality* that Hughes asserts is part and parcel of Christian fraternity. We have simply grown accustomed to disparate levels of wealth and power. Moreover, we Westerners have become comfortable with our being secure as we enjoy living at the more prestigious end of the spectrum of possible levels of provision.

It is perhaps helpful to note that the centerpiece of 2 Corinthians 8 is not the Corinthian church in any case. In Paul's challenge to this church that has (in context) been slow to respond to the need the apostle had made known a year earlier, he points to an example they should emulate. So it is the churches of Macedonia that are showcased in this passage. The members of these congregations were notable for their "deep poverty" and "great ordeal of affliction." These weren't rich churches helping a poorer one, but believers in want begging for the privilege of participation in the support of other needy saints. These under-resourced churches allowed their poverty to overflow in a wealth of liberality—a circumstance revealing poor Christians giving of their own accord but decidedly not according to their expected capacity. Out of the joy of sharing and relieving the burdens of others, they gave well beyond their means.

This same spirit of disproportionate generosity flowing from discernible poverty in Bosnia was easily observable to those of us who were privileged to be present during the war from 1992 through 1995. In that time frame, the West Mostar church, the first congregation to be born in the wartime setting, regularly sacrificed financially while in the midst of

To Give or Not To Give?

its own tremendous need. Under the guidance of selfless and sacrificial national pastors, this congregation offered substantial assistance from its meager resources to see other churches started in Tuzla, Jajce, Sarajevo, Bihac, and elsewhere while fighting went on across the country. They did this long before most Westerners were even thinking of being involved in Bosnia. I suspect many indigenous leaders in other settings would put us to shame in a similar way if we were to compare their example of exorbitant generosity in the midst of relative poverty with our own inclinations to hold on to our material advantages.

This pattern of sacrificial generosity expressed among nationals who work together to meet local needs is a good example, from my context in Bosnia, of the kind of generosity Glenn Schwartz has highlighted as a reasonable step away from dependency. He promotes the notion that resources should ideally flow first and fastest from the people closest to the point of crisis circumstances. Only when needs become too great or available resources are too scarce should more distant donors be called upon for help. The chart below portrays his principle of "geographical proximity" as a useful guideline for giving.

Whose Need to Meet?
Giving deference to regional structures in our aid

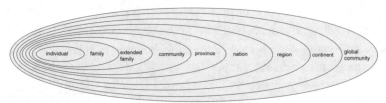

The ideal is for local needs to be met with local resources. Beyond that, special care should be given, lest the global community over-step and thus weaken the intermediate societal structures. Those people, often, yearn for the opportunity to help.

Figure 3: This chart was included in an article by Glenn Schwartz entitled "Guideposts for Giving," published in *Mission Frontiers: The Bulletin of the U.S. Center for World Mission,* Pasadena, CA (September 2001). Available at http://www.missionfrontiers. org/2001/03/200103.htm.

In the earliest days of Christian history, God used the Macedonians' example to awaken the Corinthian church to its own responsibility to be generous. I am hoping my challenge to Western mission leaders will have a similar effect. Today I believe God desires to use the under-resourced churches in places like Bosnia to awaken American congregations to our responsibility for generous giving. Where are the congregations in the West that are, like the Macedonians of old, literally begging for the privilege of giving in response to obvious needs around the world? Why are we not demonstrating a similar God-induced passion for giving an ever-greater supply to our needy brothers and sisters all around the globe?

Rather than offering resources from our considerable surplus of supplies, more generally we have been inclined to suggest that indigenous Christians should seek less costly remedies to the church growth challenges found in their unreached settings. I sometimes wonder why we don't take our own medicine in the face of similar challenges in the United States. Are we, for example, convinced that bivocational approaches to ministry that we recommend to nationals are so effective that we are willing to pursue ministry on those terms ourselves? Are we following our own advice and turning to cell church models so that we can avoid the extravagance of investing in new and larger church facilities? Recent building programs in many of the American churches that work with us in Bosnia give a clear answer to that question. Are we certain that only humanitarian grants-in-aid (the kinds that most mission leaders feel can be legitimately offered to supply basic needs for food, clothing, and shelter) are a better approach to providing for national pastors' livelihood than supporting their salaries from outside their own cultures so that they can serve as ministers of the gospel within them for a period of time? Why don't we treat these hardworking pastors as if they have earned their wages rather than responding to them as if we are offering them handouts? Do we believe spiritual laborers are only worthy of their financial hire if they are fortunate enough to work within the borders of a prosperous Western state or in the service of a well-resourced church?

Sometimes it seems to me that we are suffering in this analysis from some sort of Western missiological doublespeak. We can't teach new converts in unreached cultures to accept the concept of *generous giving* if we essentially model *selfish living* in our lifestyles and in our direct relationships with them. Neither can we expect gospel advancement without generous financial investment. I believe that the spread of the gospel depends in part on money—though others infer otherwise. One need only look at the EFCA-IM's budget to see that my own denomination has not discovered a cost-free way to do missions around the world. I believe it is time for churches in the West to stop worrying about *dependency* among indigenous believers and to start thinking about *complacency* among ourselves as affluent believers. Instead of trying to seek ways to avoid giving, we should commit ourselves to strategies that will maximize our generosity. What more could be done in world missions if we did so, rather than allowing so much needed ministry support and practical relief to go wanting because we prefer "to buy and keep" rather than to share our resources? Holding back our surplus wealth looks all too much like hoarding, and our disproportionate prosperity makes it impossible to hide our selfishness.

Second Corinthians 9:8 suggests that we are granted material sufficiency specifically so that we will have an abundance to share with others. Paul writes that God expects us to have sufficient resources for our provision and a surplus left over for "every good deed." Note that the apostle points to every *good deed*, not just every *basic need*. I believe God wants believers within resistant cultures to some day experience a measure of abundance within the family of God. I do not believe the Lord wants indigenous peoples merely to eke out an existence with only basic sustenance provided. Should it not be our legitimate role to offer a leg up on the road to greater levels of material blessing for the poorer nations of the earth? This is not a reflection of some Western prosperity doctrine; it is a recognition of God's universal promise to bless all his children in all cultures through all the ages.

If we believe God has called us to build church planting movements in unreached cultures, we must get serious about facing our financial as well as our spiritual responsibilities as we lend a helping hand. We must be willing for God to test our readiness to pay the price in dollars to see that end realized. Counting the cost and sacrificing for spiritual advances have always been kingdom dynamics. In addition to money, long-term workers and unreserved commitment to the task at hand will be necessary to see our mutual objective of global evangelism accomplished. We are only kidding ourselves if we expect extraordinary outcomes to emerge while we make excuses for not sharing more of our extravagant incomes. *We simply cannot defend responding to global need with Western greed.*

With that thought in mind, we must recognize that references to established missiological principles will not successfully mask our mishandling of clear biblical truths about stewardship and giving. I therefore cast my vote for dealing with the consequences of *giving more* to support mission work around the world rather than defending the implications of *giving less*. I would rather show nationals that we care by fighting *bankruptcy* in their lives through investing resources in those we know we can trust rather than fighting *dependency* by refusing to share from our considerable surplus.

Jesus put it plainly when he addressed the corrupting influence of mammon by declaring, "No one can serve two masters." Indigenous Christians are watching to see where we will land on these financial issues. They know (and we should readily admit to ourselves) that our choices will ultimately demonstrate which master we love more. Our conclusions may also have more influence than we would like as we model for them the process by which supposedly more mature Christians make righteous use of their material resources. Will the *mammon principle* or the *manna principle* hold sway with us? The answer to that question will be seen as we decide whether "to give or not to give" in our efforts to strengthen the cause of global mission. May God grant us grace to be more wise than worldly and more selfless than selfish as we attempt to reach a world filled with lost, poor, and desperately needy people. That kind of wisdom will not be found, in my opinion, by sticking stubbornly to the dictates of the self-supporting paradigm and the concern for dependency that is linked to it.

Some mission practitioners and many national leaders, I am confident, already agree with this conclusion. They struggle as I do with the problems caused by the tenacious application of the three-self dogma as a defense against maximizing investment among the poor. Perhaps it would be helpful to listen to the perspective of a Third World national on this issue. This we will do in the next chapter.

CHAPTER FIVE

An Alternative to the Three-Self Paradigm

Chris Marantika has spoken out about the issues I am addressing in this book for a long period of time without overcoming the inertia of established mission practice. The alternatives to the traditional three-self paradigm that he suggests have simply never captured the attention of the world's mission leaders. Nonetheless, they are worth referencing here to demonstrate that these concerns are shared by some national leaders. By God's providence, this Indonesian theologian, born on the smallest island in the largest island nation in the world, was trained at Dallas Theological Seminary and has led a seminary in his own culture for many years. His school is known for requiring its students to successfully plant a church in Indonesia as a prerequisite for graduation. For two decades Marantika, a credible indigenous leader, has advocated that the world's mission leaders move away from a strict application of the three-self paradigm.[1]

Marantika imagines the unreached peoples of the world living, as it were, in "kingdom playgrounds"—areas of the earth where the heavenly Father is watching, waiting, and working to insure that his reign and rule will one day be fully established. The Father is effectively presiding over every culture in order to accomplish his will. None are forsaken, none are beyond reach, and none escape his notice. All are waiting for others of God's children to come, to incarnate the message of the gospel, and to share in the Father's joy when new believers are born into his family. Christ's mission mandate calls those who already know Jesus to go to these kingdom playgrounds so that they may offer a culturally relevant witness to those who do not yet know the Father's great love. From Marantika's point of view, that calling is effectively an invitation to join the Father's yet-to-be-reborn children on the kingdom playgrounds our Daddy has already claimed for himself.

Viewed this way, the words of Jesus to Paul, whispered in a night vision in Corinth, echo the calming influence of the Father's heart as he watches his children at play. Like an earthly dad, the Lord God looks after his children well, knowing each one even before they come to know him. He doesn't want us to be timid about going into these kingdom playgrounds. He knows that in due time new brothers and sisters in Christ will join us there to share in his glory. This idea, though a bit fanciful, is an apt perspective to have in view when we read Jesus' words to Paul as he labored in first-century Corinth at a time when that playground seemed decidedly unsafe: "Do not be afraid any longer, but go on speaking and do not be silent; for I am with you, and no man will attack you in order to harm you, for *I have many people in this city*" (Acts 18:9–10, italics added).

Drawing confidence from the words of the Lord, Paul kept on witnessing in Corinth and established a church there. Marantika suggests

---

1   These reflections on Marantika's suggestions are recalled from notes on lectures heard in the late 1980s.

that Jesus is offering the same invitation to believers in our own day. The King of Kings wants us to occupy kingdom playgrounds and to find the "many people" God desires to save in those contexts. Marantika proposes a new paradigm to fit this playground metaphor. He suggests that we join hands as children of God, coming from all cultures, rich and poor alike, and that we willingly bring all the resources we can contribute to our joint efforts to reach the remaining mission fields of the world. He invites us to embrace a renewed call to God's kingdom playgrounds, where we can *play together, pray together, and pay together* as we serve the Father's will among the nations. Perhaps his idea is worthy of more careful consideration.

Failing to reexamine our perspective may have more ominous implications for Westerners than we might at first imagine. Indications drawn from global population trends point us toward the conclusion that the Western church's future role in global evangelism will be a diminished one. That being the case, inordinate material resources may be the best remaining and most unique blessing that we can share with other believers around the world. Already, the evangelical church is shrinking perceptibly in all Western nations. Already, the masses of missionaries mobilized from non-Western cultures dwarf the numbers sent from Europe and North America. Already, the demographic center of gravity has shifted southward, so that the majority of Christians in the world now reside below the equator in Africa, Asia, and South America. Moreover, the proportion of Christians living in the Southern Hemisphere is rising rapidly.

Andrew Walls helps clarify the implications of these unprecedented trends. He writes, "The Christianity typical of the twenty-first century will be shaped by the events and processes that take place in the southern continents, and above all by those that take place in Africa. . . . The things by which people recognize and judge what Christianity is will [for good or for ill] increasingly be determined in Africa. The characteristic decisions, the liturgy, the ethical codes, the social applications of the faith will increasingly be those prominent in Africa."[2] The self-support-ing paradigm is not likely to play well in these poorer settings, especially if it seems that Westerners are applying the principle in an effort merely to excuse hoarding their wealth. If non-Western Christian leaders ulti-mately reject our principled defenses against sharing our resources (as I believe they will), we will be left with only preferences for a practice that lays bare our more selfish propensities.

Is a Fourth Self Needed in the Traditional Paradigm?

If we are to be discerning observers of the times in which we live, we cannot afford to miss the import of Walls' observations as they relate to our stewardship of wealth. He is not alone in this vision of things to come. In fact, others see even more serious and far-reaching doctrinal issues at stake as believers from poorer southern nations arise to set the theological agenda for the twenty-first century. Paul Hiebert has said that we need to add a "fourth self" to Venn's paradigm as we observe a new trend toward "self-theologizing" among churches emerging in contexts we formerly viewed as mission fields.

C. René Padilla describes this self-theologizing phenomenon as one produced when poorer Christians begin to study the Bible for themselves. He calls this "reading the Scriptures from below" and reports that it is producing a new ecclesiology in Latin America. He says that "common people are claiming the right to think and to speak, showing that the gos-pel has a different sound when it is heard from the underside of history."[3] The biblical principles informing Christian stewardship of money will also likely have a different twist when interpreted from the perspective of the world's poorer peoples. We would be naive in the extreme to as-

---

2   Andrew F. Walls, *The Cross-Cultural Process in Christian History: Studies in the Transmission and Appropriation of Faith* (Maryknoll, NY: Orbis Books, 2002), 85.

3   C. René Padilla, *Mission Between the Times: Essays on the Kingdom* (Grand Rapids: Eerdmans, 1985), 158.

sume otherwise. Interpreted "from below," our sense of economics will likely be forced to shift as dramatically as our sense of ecclesiology.

Hiebert encourages Westerners to have confidence in this new self-theologizing dynamic, even as it holds potential to challenge the established dogmas we hold most dear. He expresses trust in the Holy Spirit to keep the truth secure as non-Western churches engage in a process that includes consideration of truths from the perspective of "saints not only within a single culture but saints in other cultures and saints down through history."[4] Hiebert sees the process of self-theologizing as one informed by a "meta-cultural" and "meta-historical" hermeneutic that promises a better understanding of God's Word than Western cultures alone have produced over several hundred years of church history. If he is correct, the theological hegemony that the West has enjoyed for centuries is waning and uniquely Western views may not prevail much longer. I believe that the self-supporting principle is one example of our prized convictions that is unlikely to hold sway in the long run.

Shifting to a missiological paradigm that makes room for Christians everywhere to *play together, pray together, and pay together* as their resources and capacities allow will also change the central concerns that hold our attention as we pursue global mission ministry. In Venn's day that concern was colonial domination. In our recent history it has been financial dependence. I believe that the future concern will be focused on practical *sustainability*—a theme that logically emerges when we add a transformational development component to our missiology.

The notion that sustainability should become the focus of our mission agenda in this modern era is, in my sense of the biblical issues involved, entirely appropriate. Turning our attention in this direction will immediately reveal that we have much to learn from others more sensitive to this issue. Sustainability has been, for example, the central focus of relief and development professionals for years. Research by missiologists into current development theory will prove to be, therefore, a

---

4 Paul G. Hiebert, *Anthropological Reflections on Missiological Issues* (Grand Rapids: Baker, 1994), 85.

worthwhile endeavor. The works by Bryant Myers, Kosuke Koyama, and Darrow Miller included in the bibliography at the end of this book offer good places to begin studying in this arena.

In any case, sustainability must become the target of prolonged missionary attention if we are to do a better job of ministering redemptively among the poor. Unquestionably, the dynamics of sustainability will vary widely from one mission field to another. It would be foolish to presume that I could prescribe general principles here that will fit every circumstance around the globe. But in chapters 11 through 14 I do attempt to offer some of the guiding considerations that can shape our efforts to be maximally generous while working toward sustainable investments on the mission field. In chapter 16, I will suggest that the time has come to redefine the concept of sustainability.

Giving attention to sustainability, missiologists will no longer be concerned about *whether* they should be investing in ministry among the poor. Rather, they will need to analyze carefully *where* and *how* their contributions to the world's unreached fields can be made in a manner that will generate lasting results, leaving an impact after the missionary's presence comes to an end. Fruit that remains, after all, has always been the focused concern of the Father in heaven (John 15:16).

If we accept the general conclusion that God's scales of financial stewardship are always weighted in favor of generosity, we can easily conclude that we must find a way to walk the path of responsiveness when we encounter people in need or opportunities for kingdom advancement anywhere in the world. But how to measure our responsiveness and the kingdom's progress is a separate issue altogether, one that bears brief reflection at this point. Andrew Walls adds light that helps us recognize transformational signs that the kingdom of God is breaking into an unreached culture—evidences that reach beyond simple conversion and church growth and impact other aspects of a given people group's experience.

Monitoring the Advance of God's Kingdom

Writing in *The Cross-Cultural Process in Christian History: Studies in the Transmission and Appropriation of Faith*, Walls offers an insightful and broadening reflection on the ways by which we might evaluate the progress of Christian witness in formerly unreached cultures. He proposes three standards: the Church Test, the Kingdom Test, and the Gospel Test.

The first, Walls' Church Test, expresses the primary benchmarks my mission organization has traditionally noted from an essentially conversion-oriented perspective. This approach sees the kingdom coming when there is a corporate witness for Jesus inherent in the culture, when we can observe the "presence of a community of people willing to bear the name of Christ, an 'Israel' that maintains his worship" as a called-out people.[5] Our paradigm has been focused primarily on developing a church planting movement in Bosnia. Our effectiveness has been measured by tracking the emergence, growth, and multiplication of congregations all across the nation. Thus, my mission's emphasis has always been on the Church Test. It is easy to measure results in this area, as the numbers we record reflect the visible *breadth* of Christian expansion.

In using the Church Test as a measure of kingdom advance in a culture newly exposed to the gospel, we err if we expect a linear and ever-progressive growth of the church in any given society. Christian expansion, depending as it does on conversion, is serial—ebbing and flowing depending upon the intensity of the faith commitments of the believers providing a witness for Christ in any period. Islam, by contrast, is a religion that has progressed largely through conquest rather than conversion. Its expansion is far more consistent and continuous in cultures where Muslims came as conquerors and maintain control over the political and military order of society. Christianity progresses where faith triumphs, not where force prevails.

---

5   Walls, *Cross-Cultural Process,* 10.

Walls puts it this way, "If the acts of cultural translation by which Christians of any community make their faith substantial within that [context] cease—if the Word ceases to be made flesh within the community—the Christian group within that community is likely to lose not just its effectiveness, but its power of resistance" against the surrounding society that holds no allegiance to Jesus.[6] For instance, Paul could boast in the first century that the gospel had been preached "round about as far as Illyricum" (Romans 15:19).[7] In the twenty-first century, however, the same area (which includes our field in present-day Bosnia) is virtually ignorant of the claims of Christ formulated in an evangelical sense. The tide of gospel witness has somehow receded over the centuries as Christians were adversely impacted by their surrounding culture and ceased to be effective evangelical witnesses for Jesus. Wherever the vibrancy of Christian witness grows cold in a culture already evangelized, congregations become increasingly nominal and the influence of the kingdom wanes. The Church Test may thus be passed in one era and failed in the next. So the breadth of the church in any given culture may be expected to advance and decline cyclically over time.

Walls, therefore, poses a second important benchmark for measuring the progress of Christian witness in a given society. The Kingdom Test involves an assessment of the extent to which standards of discipleship reveal a measure of radical and innovative faith in Jesus—faith that serves effectively to produce new movements of devotion to Christ within a given society. Evidences of reformation, renewal, and revival are the hallmarks that indicate the Kingdom Test is being met. *The kingdom rule of God is holding sway especially when the impact of Christian values and virtues moves beyond the confines of the church to touch the broader community.* Kingdom signs that meet this test are Christian witness that forcefully calls people to live under the lordship of Jesus; that

---

6   Ibid., 13.

7   John Murray writes in his commentary on Romans that "it is uncertain whether 'unto Illyricum' means that [Paul] penetrated into this country or simply reached its borders." *The New International Commentary on the New Testament* (Grand Rapids: Eerdmans, 1968), 214.

prophetically addresses injustice, immorality, and manifest evils in society; that ministers comfort to hurting human beings without prejudice or preference; and that confronts the powers of darkness. Such powerful patterns of witness represent the *depth* of Christian expansion in a given culture.[8]

The third measure of Christian expansion is Walls' Gospel Test. This is perhaps the hardest to apply and at first glance would seem to indicate the least apparent evidence of Christ's impact on a culture. *The Gospel Test seeks to assess the effect that the "good news" of the claims of Jesus is having on society as a whole.* Conceding that the principalities and powers at Satan's command are continually seeking to distort truth, destroy goodness, and detract from loving relationships among people, the evidences of "good news" taking root in a society are seen when demonic influence is exposed, confronted, overcome, and eradicated. The point is to take note of the differences being made by the resurrection of Christ not just in an eschatological sense, but also in the culture here and now.[9]

It is possible that the gospel influence in a society may produce a kingdom result—greater justice, diminished evil, and relief for the poor—without producing conversions. Paradoxically, the reality of righteousness rising in a culture still relatively void of Christians is an evidence of Christianity advancing. Eradicating slavery in America and apartheid in South Africa, outlawing the sale of young women into prostitution in Thailand, and promoting genuine reconciliation among the divided religious and ethnic factions in Bosnia are the kinds of changes that would meet the Gospel Test. (This test is not being passed greatly in Bosnia even ten years after the war there ended.) Wherever the disproportionate influence of believers responding to the good news of salvation in Christ Jesus effectively calls a culture to increasingly righteous and just living, the Gospel Test is being met.

If Walls is correct in asserting that all three measures of Christian advancement are important, I believe our aim as missionaries in Bosnia and

---

8   Walls, *Cross-Cultural Process,* 14.

9   Ibid., 19.

elsewhere should be pressed beyond simply producing converts and congregations (meeting the Church Test) to promoting a broader Christian impact on the culture (meeting the Kingdom and Gospel Tests). To do this we must seriously cultivate a sense of radical Christian commitment among the members who populate the churches we plant. Only people devoted to the genuine lordship of Christ would dare to dream of seeing the sanctification of their own lives translated into the wonder of transformation in the surrounding culture. As missionaries, our vision has often been too small, our sights have been set too low, and our expectations have been too understated to bring glory to so great a God who offers so great a salvation! We have not been adequately committed to dreaming in the Spirit about the kingdom future of unreached peoples and about our part in shaping it! Missionaries all over the world are likely falling prey to similar patterns of small-mindedness in their expectations for impacting whole cultures for Christ.

Such a loss of vision has a biblical precedent. Consider the words of Isaiah in which God urges his people Israel to think beyond the confines of their own culture to the global impact he had called them to make: "It is too small a thing for you to be my servant to restore the tribes of Jacob and bring back those of Israel I have kept. I will also make you a light for the Gentiles, that you may bring my salvation to the ends of the earth" (Isaiah 49:6 NIV).

God has called us, as he called Israel, to be a missionary people, ambassadors for Christ as it were (2 Corinthians 5:20). He commands us to go and make disciples of all ethnic groups. He inspires in us a desire to achieve the transformational development of whole cultures so that Jesus may be named as Lord among every tribe, tongue, people, and nation. But experience shows that Americans don't always readily accept the paths to responsive advance of the kingdom when they are made apparent. Perhaps examining the cultural realities that make the path to more generous living initially unattractive to us will prove helpful as a next step in our exploration of the roots of the American (and more generally Western) tendency "not to give" to the level of our potential in support of global missions.

CHAPTER SIX

Charity and the Impact of America's Culture Wars

The Roman playwright Publius Terentius Afer coined the familiar adage "charity begins at home." The premise of this chapter is that current missiological *reluctance* to express charity is likewise rooted in domestic rather than foreign soil. That is to say, the American aversion to giving to the poor of other nations may well flow from deeply ingrained perspectives that have more to do with long-term US culture wars than they do with Third World cultural weaknesses. Examining this notion will require a close look at the history of American philanthropy. Winston Churchill affirmed the value of this kind of historical reflection when he said, "The further backward you look, the further forward you can see." Examining the historical roots of American perspectives on giving will, I believe, help us better evaluate the contemporary fruit of our giving practices.

In the last decade, no one has written more cogently about charity in the United States than has Marvin Olasky. The weight of his work in this area is contained in three separate volumes that I eagerly commend to the reader. *The Tragedy of American Compassion, Renewing American Compassion*, and *Compassionate Conservatism* together offer the philosophical underpinnings associated with a contemporary attempt to readmit faith-based initiatives into the fabric of public policies addressing poverty and its abatement in the United States. Insights from this historical review may well help us understand the dilemmas we face as we decide whether "to give or not to give."

As he delves into the past to chart the road toward meaningful social reform in the future, Olasky deals with the present plight of America's poor. He concludes, in part, that our current problems with domestic poverty arise from the very welfare system that was designed in hopes of helping the less fortunate in our land. Under the influence of this system, Olasky writes, "We have seen dreams die as 'compassion fatigue' deepens. Personal involvement (with the poor) is down, cynicism is up. . . . Many Americans would like to be generous at the subway entrance or the street corner, but they know that most homeless recipients will use any available funds for drugs or alcohol. We end up walking by, avoiding eye contact . . . and a subtle hardening occurs. . . . We end up just saying no.[1]

In effect, many Americans have become welfare averse. Consequently, we are resistant to the appeals of even the truly needy who reach in our direction for a helping hand. As we choose "not to give" personally, government agencies keep stepping in to cover the lack of concerned response at a private level with programs underwritten publicly. So the welfare establishment intervenes with all the compassion of a corpse, often doing more harm than good. Over the past three decades we have fought a war on poverty that has left economic need very much alive while dealing a death blow to three of the best allies against pov-

---

1   Marvin N. Olasky, *Renewing American Compassion* (New York: Free Press, 1996), 49.

erty: shame, family, and faith in God. "When we take away shame, we take away deterrent. When we take away family, we take away the soil in which compassion best grows. When we kick out religion, we also remove the greatest incentive that motivates people to help."[2]

I am attempting here to look at history (rather than theology) to explain how the present miserly mentality toward giving became a part of the psyche of so many of America's private citizens. In the material that follows I hope to demonstrate that in understanding the rather deeply ingrained resistance toward giving in relief of the poor here at home a connection can be found to our similar struggle with giving to the poor of other nations. I will show that a predisposition against giving to our own poor neighbors (a bias born domestically as a reactionary response to a failed welfare state) makes us missiologically indisposed to giving to the poor abroad. Before we can understand our reticence to give in the twenty-first century we must trace the roots of American philanthropy all the way back to the earliest days of America's existence.

Social Calvinism

An analysis of colonial generosity makes it clear that charity was then primarily a private rather than a public virtue. Expressed by the hospitality of open homes and the availability of helping hands, generosity was a personal commitment of genuine love demonstrated by giving time and talent more often than treasure. Widows and orphaned children were commonly taken into the households of extended family members or nearby neighbors. Injured or diseased citizens were cared for by companions who were closest at hand, often at great risk and with significant sacrifice.

Personal expressions of charity were as common as they were costly in the colonial era, but consistent relief was not extended indiscriminately to all who were in need even then. Early American leaders made a

---

2   Ibid., 53–54.

distinction between the "worthy poor" and the "wayward poor" in their giving decisions. The worthy poor were victims of circumstances beyond their control: people made destitute by disaster, disease, disabling injury, physical defect, or the death of a family member. They were offered help without hesitation. But the wayward poor were viewed as vagabonds rather than victims, in the sense that they were creating their own need by their own indolence or indecency. The wayward poor were suffering not from unavoidable circumstances but from self-inflicted wounds. When personal deprivation stemmed from neglect of work or indulgences of addictive or immoral appetites, the wayward poor were not given assistance. In the colonial mindset (a perspective that endured in America until the early twentieth century), "The able-bodied could readily find jobs in a growing agricultural economy. When they chose not to, it was considered perfectly appropriate to pressure them to change their minds."[3]

Following the biblical principle expressed in 2 Thessalonians 3:10, America's early commitment to philanthropy was governed by the mantra "If a man will not work, then neither should he eat." Colonial charity reflected other faith-based biases. Among them were the convictions that:

- In God's providence, he intervenes in human affairs—proving to be a very present help in times of trouble. So men and women made in his image should also readily intervene in times of crisis in the lives of people within their spheres of influence.

- Charity is an expression of selfless love best manifest in the context of close personal relationship. Therefore, the one who gives should connect with (and not merely contribute to) the one who receives. It is interesting to note that the Latin roots for the English word *compassion—com* ("with") and *pati* ("to suffer")—literally imply that we must "suffer with" someone, sharing his or her privation as well as pain, if we are to be truly

---

3   Marvin N. Olasky, *The Tragedy of American Compassion* (Washington, DC: Regnery Gateway, 1992), 7.

compassionate. When the rich and the poor lived in close proximity, as they did in America's colonial era, this dynamic was easier to achieve than in the modern urban context where the rich and the poor live in segregated communities.

- The greatest needs faced by people in want are spiritual, not material. Therefore, learning about God and God's expectations for humankind was a matter of obligation rather than an imposition on those being assisted.

- The proper support system for a Christian society was considered to be analogous to a three-legged stool resting upon the family, the church, and the neighborhood, in that order. In America's colonial expression of what Olasky calls "Social Calvinism," the extended family was expected to be responsible to attend to its own members when tragedy struck or hard times prevailed. This priority was enforced legally in certain instances, with government officials in some areas exacting fines for violations of the normative familial commitment.

- In most cases, aid was to be provided not in cash but in kind (food, fuel, and clothing). The fallen nature of human beings was well recognized by these Social Calvinists who were rightly cautious in expressing their compassion. By focusing philanthropy on the worthy poor and by refusing relief to the wayward poor, charitably minded citizens in America's early history hoped their giving would do good and not harm in the end. They recognized that the causes of individual indigence mattered.

America's faith-based perspective on altruism prevailed into the nineteenth and early twentieth centuries. In its 1835 annual report, the Benevolent Societies of Boston reflected the typical reticence for supporting the wayward poor. The report noted that it is "disgraceful to depend upon almsgiving, as long as a capacity for self support is retained. . . . To give to one who begs . . . or in any way to supersede the necessity of industry, of forethought and of proper self-restraint and self-denial, is at once to do wrong, and to encourage [the beggar] to wrongdoing.[4]

Four guiding principles lighted the way for a Social Calvinist response to need in America's early history:

1. A distinction must be made between the wayward poor and the worthy poor as we formulate an appropriate response to material need.

2. Public statutory relief of the poor should be avoided at all costs, since such was believed to engender indiscriminant relief that actually promoted indigent lifestyles.

3. Personal involvement between givers and receivers was stressed as a means to insure that assistance extended beyond the financial to touch the spiritual aspects of life.

4. Repentance and change were seen as valid indications that personal financial aid might be appropriately continued over time. The general rule was that a person who did not go on reforming should not go on receiving.

At this stage in America's philanthropic history, the "charity consensus" guided by Social Calvinism easily allowed generous people to stand on common ground with those who were receiving assistance. The crucial understanding was as simple as it was profound: people got by best when other people took a personal interest in them and remained involved in their lives. Ministers told their congregations that it was fine to contribute money, but the larger need and the more difficult task was personal involvement with the poor. Community leaders and volunteers alike understood that the most vital kind of help involved a change in worldview, not just a temporary adjustment in worldly conditions. No one was confused about or opposed to the religious motivations that made the volunteer system effective. Neither was anyone unaware of the extraordinary demand placed on the volunteers who were central to successful private aid ministries.

---

4 Ibid., 18–19.

A report from New York City in 1854 published this explanation describing the work of volunteers in a city that was growing dramatically in numbers as well as in need: "The work is vast, complex, and difficult. To visit from time to time all the abodes of want in a population of 650,000 souls—to discriminate between honest poverty and imposture—to elevate and not debase by relief—to arrest the vagrant—reclaim the intemperate—sympathize with the suffering—counsel the erring—stimulate the indolent—give work to the idle . . . is an undertaking . . . most arduous and difficult.[5]

At great personal cost, volunteer workers, who were often motivated as much by spiritual concerns for their neighbors as by their practical needs, served as "visitors to the victims" of poverty. They kept the support system personal and redemptive, aimed as it was at reforming worldviews, reinforcing the benefits of a healthy work ethic, and encouraging poor neighbors to become more consistent followers of God's wisdom for living well in this world. Even in large cities, volunteers mobilized by the thousands to insure that recipients of relief support got help that went far beyond their material needs.

In this era, churches and charity organizations alike understood that professional social workers should be facilitators of aid, not the major or sole suppliers. Unfortunately, this largely Christian consensus was not to last. Thomas Chalmers, a Scottish vicar and leader of the Social Calvinist cause, had warned of the dangers to be associated with replacing private gifts with public grants. The involvement of government, he predicted, would change "the whole character of charity, by turning a matter of love into a matter of legislation."[6]

More than a decade later Nathaniel Ware wrote a critique of the shortcomings of American government, similarly predicting the eventual rise of a federal welfare system as one manifestation of weakness. His rationale, as Olasky observes, reflected a grasp of base human nature: "Office holders liked to appeal to poor voters who would give them

---

5   Ibid., 30.

6   Ibid., 47.

power to distribute large sums of money and [to continue] the patronage [system] that accompanied expenditure."[7]

The reality has always been that politicians know all too well the simple truth that if they are willing "to rob Peter in order to pay Paul," Paul's vote for their reelection can be counted on. The nineteenth-century French historian, Alexis de Tocqueville, recognized this internal flaw in America's elective approach to government as well. In reflecting on our great experiment in self-government he said, "The American Republic will endure until the day Congress discovers that it can bribe the public with the public's money." Government grants-in-relief were thus feared and thought by Social Calvinists to be the first steppingstones to the ruin of society. The natural bent of fallen humanity to descend into patterns of self-interest is only exacerbated when material resources are made readily available and public assistance is free for the taking.

But not all leaders of this era acknowledged the basic sin nature that Social Calvinists saw as common to all people. Nor did they fear the pitfalls that conservatives warned would follow public intervention into philanthropic endeavors. For example, Horace Greeley, who founded the New York Tribune in 1841, was a Universalist who believed that people are by nature essentially good and that every person has a *right* to both eternal salvation and temporal prosperity. Greeley believed the way to end disproportionate resourcing of individuals within a society is to redistribute wealth so that everyone receives an equal share. One step in beginning the process would be to have the government tax the prosperous citizens to fund the distribution of food and the dispersing of relief support for those who are less well-off.[8] Greeley's ideas were provocative in his day, but they produced no immediate, substantial change. They did, however, lay the foundation for the road to a new day in the twentieth century in which welfare payments would be seen as a right for all individuals.

---

7   Ibid., 48.

8   Ibid., 55.

Social Darwinism

Greeley's views were typical of a newly emerging Universalist moral premise that would eventually minimize the intensely personal approach to charity that Social Calvinism had engendered. The trend toward a more anonymous style of altruism was augmented by the relocation of people from rural settings to urban centers in America. Migration from the farm coupled with immigration from foreign lands created cityscapes filled with greatly increased populations that were also deeply divided by economic and racial segregation. In the fifty years following the Civil War, urban areas were increasingly defined by distinctly discernible pockets of rich and poor and by neighborhoods with definite ethnic and racial identities.

The growth of larger companies with thousands of workers and relatively few managers also depersonalized the employer/employee relationship. Andrew Carnegie acknowledged the breakdown of social intercourse in the workplace as a harbinger of a rigid caste system in which mutual ignorance would breed mutual distrust between rich and poor.[9] Upward mobility meant that the more affluent were less often brought into direct contact with impoverished neighbors. Since poverty no longer had a face, it became far easier for the wealthy to ignore the needy and for those in want to rely on public provision as a substitute for private philanthropy.

The indifference to human suffering that accompanied large-scale urbanization, social segregation, and vocational stratification was amplified by the intellectual justification for ambivalence and apathy that flowed from Social Darwinism. Equating the struggle of humans for economic survival with the struggle for survival in the animal kingdom, Social Darwinists argued that society should be freed from the intruding influence of people made sentimental by their religious scruples. Left to its own devices, society could be expected to follow the processes of natural order, constantly eliminating its unhealthy, vacillating, dependent members. Reductions in the ranks of the weak would consequently leave

---

9   Ibid., 66.

more room for the strong. Thus the dynamics of natural selection were perceived as a more reliable social policy than either public or private support systems.

Herbert Spencer, the British leader of Social Darwinism, wrote in this vein; but under the influence of Darwin's evolutionary theories, he supported a call not simply to let nature take its course so that survival of the fittest might fix society's problems with the poor, but promoting a more proactive plan to exterminate them on a wholesale basis. "The unfit must be eliminated as nature intended, for the principle of natural selection must not be violated by artificial preservation of those least able to take care of themselves."[10] Americans bought 368,755 copies of Spencer's books promoting this theme. His influence proved to be a great impetus for a philosophical shift in philanthropic perspective after the Civil War.

During that era, American society moved steadily away from the compassionate altruism embraced by Social Calvinists to a more ruthless alternative. Spencer's radical voice proved not to be that of a lone wolf calling for extreme innovations in dealing with the weaker and poorer elements of society. No lesser person than Supreme Court Justice Oliver Wendell Holmes lent his support to this movement by noting, "It is better for the world, if instead of waiting to execute degenerate offspring for crime, or to let them starve for their imbecility, society can prevent those who are manifestly unfit from continuing their kind. The principle that sustains compulsory vaccination is broad enough to cover cutting the Fallopian tubes."[11]

As Social Calvinists continued to preach on and to plan around the conviction that human beings are fallen but fully capable of being reformed, Social Darwinists pushed their argument to excess. Moving into the realm of eugenics, they proposed the comprehensive regulation of the reproductive habits of the weak and worthless members of society. In

---

10 Ibid., 67

11 Os Guinness, *Doing Well and Doing Good: Money, Giving, and Caring in a Free Society* (Colorado Springs: NavPress, 2001), 177, 182.

their way of thinking, no step would be too bold or too costly if it broke the power of the poor to reproduce after their own kind.

Social Universalism

Social Universalists contributed a third compelling voice to the compassion debate as the twentieth century unfolded. Informed by the underlying tenets of theological liberalism and political socialism, this chorus rapidly gained support among American's intellectual and literary elite. Finding the Darwinists too radical in their remedy for poverty and the Calvinists too conventional, Social Universalists looked for a means to effect massive alterations in the living conditions of the underclass. As the industrial revolution was proving the value of mass production and economies of scale, these secrets to modern business advancement were now being considered for application in the realm of benevolence.

Seeking the appropriate "social engine" to drive the machinery of massive relief for the poor, Social Universalists turned to government, the only Goliath thought to be big enough to face the challenge. Only government could control the breadth of distribution systems necessary to insure there was no waste, no overlapping of benefits, no favoritism, and no neglect of one community compared to another. Only government could monitor data and maintain statistics that would reflect the extent of the ongoing problems posed by poverty and unemployment and the effectiveness of relief measures. Only government could impose its will to implement change on a massive scale. And only government could punish fraud and malfeasance by those who might seek to corrupt or to capitalize on the welfare system. Government was the answer to Social Universalist aspirations for a utopian society.

Richard Ely, founder of the American Economic Association, was among the first and the most effective in promoting "the exercise of philanthropy as the duty of government." He won converts as he appealed to economists, theologians, and politicians alike to support what he called "coercive philanthropy" in the struggle to build cities of God.[12] In effect, the vision of Social Universalism promoted a shift from spiritual motivations to secular ones and from the tithe to the tax as a means to fund public support systems. Ely's book, Social Aspects of Christianity, helped lay the foundation for what has become known as the Social Gospel. The liberal theology of this movement emphasized God's love but not God's holiness and promoted the recognition of human rights without pressing the corresponding concern for personal responsibility championed by Social Calvinists. The result was a plan to meet material needs indiscriminately while paying for programs from the community chest rather than from private coffers. "Charity without challenge" was offered even to able-bodied people who simply chose not to work. This blurred the once clear line between the worthy poor and the wayward poor—between poverty and pauperism.

The Social Gospel nonetheless became a global movement shaping both public debate and public policy all over the world throughout the 1900s. William G. Freemantle, canon of Canterbury, serves as an apt representative who articulated this new perspective well. In the end, the argument fell not far short of the assertion that giving is always best expressed as a public rather than a private response to need because government is not simply good—government is God. Lest the reader react to this assertion as an overstatement, witness Freemantle's explanation of the Social Universalist reality and bear in mind that he was writing as a cleric rather than as a civil servant:

> When we think of the [Nation] as becoming, as it must more and more, the object of mental regard, of admiration, of love, even of worship (for in it preeminently God dwells) we should recognize to the fullest extent its religious character and function. . . . We find the Nation alone fully organized, sovereign, independent, universal, and capable of giving full expression to the Christian principle. We ought, therefore, to regard the Nation as the Church, its rulers as ministers of Christ, its

---

12 Richard Ely, *Social Aspects of Christianity* (New York: T. Y. Crowell, 1889), 77, 92.

whole body as a Christian brotherhood, its public assemblies as amongst the highest modes of universal Christian fellowship, its dealing with material interests as Sacraments, its progressive development, especially in raising the weak, as the fullest service rendered on earth to God, the nearest thing as yet within our reach to the Kingdom of heaven.[13]

The state was thus becoming the new ecclesiastical structure for the Social Gospel and was rightly expected by many Social Universalists to take on the church's traditional functions, among them the dispensing of charity. The twin goals of eradicating the earlier concept of humankind's sin nature and promoting the unlimited capacity of government programs to end poverty worked hand in hand to establish a new conceptual framework for government assistance as a replacement for private philanthropy. Because there was no longer a distinction to be made between the worthy poor and the wayward poor and because handouts were no longer viewed as corrupting, public welfare payments were not only possible and permissible, they were the preferable alternative to private charity. This stress on the political over the personal and the material over the spiritual became the catalyst for the government social programs of the 1930s and the community action programs of the 1960s.[14]

The key goal of government programs guided by the tenets of Social Universalism was material aid, not personal change in the individual receiving support from the new welfare system. Effectiveness could now be measured mechanically simply by monitoring the amount of material support provided. Quantitative factors therefore replaced qualitative factors in evaluating the results of public assistance programs. Rehabilitation of the chemically dependent poor, retraining of the chronically unemployed, reconciliation of families with estranged fathers, and the renewal of character in a way that indicates change in the inner person were evaluative factors dismissed altogether because they were too difficult to achieve and too elusive to measure. Getting goods into the empty hands

---

13 Olasky, *Tragedy of American Compassion,* 122.

14 Ibid., 137.

of the poor became the indisputable goal of government social service programs. Getting the lives of indigent people into a more stable state was no longer an end under consideration.

In 1909 the first state-supported programs under the new paradigm of public assistance came into being. They were designed for the relief of widows—a term broadly defined to include all abandoned women with children, not merely those whose husbands were deceased. By 1930 all but four states provided "mothers' pensions," which were sustaining over 200,000 children whose fathers were dead, disabled, or absent from the home because of divorce, desertion, or imprisonment.[15] In 1912 the US Children's Bureau was created at the federal level to augment the family support system already existing in forty-four states. The Social Security System followed in 1935 and, during the Depression era, Roosevelt's New Deal programs came close behind. A whole new age had dawned in America's attempt to assist the poor.

---

15 Ibid., 141.

CHAPTER SEVEN

Domestic Dependency Defined the "American Way"

In the transition from private to public provision of aid to the needy, an "irreconcilable difference" emerged in the welfare arena, as spiritual and secular perspectives on the problem vied for primacy. Increasingly traditional Calvinist approaches to support were rejected because they were motivated by faith-based values; social work itself was professionalized, eliminating the involvement of ordinary citizens; and many religious programs were secularized. America gave birth to "the ultimate federal bureaucracy—an anonymous public supporting anonymous machinery supporting anonymous clients."[1] In the end, secular alternatives won the day and spiritual mores were eliminated from the social safety

---

1   Marvin N. Olasky, *The Tragedy of American Compassion* (Washington, DC: Regnery Gateway, 1992), 150.

net. Universalist social philosophies provided the engine to power this sea change in philanthropic expression in America, but it would take economic reversal on a worldwide scale to put the process into high gear.

The New Deal

The crash of the stock market in 1929 and the ensuing global economic downturn that Americans experienced as the Great Depression forced poverty onto masses of people who historically had been productive. The consequent financial failures created unprecedented demands on public-sector relief programs and the new government-as-provider philosophy. Millions of able-bodied, eager-to-work citizens were put into desperate straits by a collapse of the capitalist economy that they could not hope to control or to influence. Unemployment jumped from 1.6 million people in 1929 to 12.8 million—25 percent of the labor force—in 1933. Millions more were only partially employed.[2]

With so many in need simultaneously, existing relief systems proved ineffective. Vast numbers of Americans were idle and needed to be usefully employed again. Franklin D. Roosevelt's New Deal programs attempted to blend a response to immediate pleas for aid with an ultimate plan for remobilizing the work force. Unfortunately, both sides of Roosevelt's equation were financed with tax dollars. The results tended to be a mixed bag of success and failure.

The cynicism regarding publicly funded service projects can be seen in reference to the Works Progress Administration (WPA), which was created in 1935 to put publicly supported individuals back into productive roles doing community service projects. The fruits of the WPA include mammoth positive achievements like the Hoover Dam project and countless smaller improvements in the infrastructure from coast to coast. The WPA labor force constructed 116,000 new buildings, 78,000 bridges, 658,000 miles of road, 18,000 miles of sewers and storm drains,

---

2   Ibid., 152.

and improvements to 800 airports. Still, the inefficiencies of publicly run programs were notorious. The WPA was known disparagingly among its critics as "We Piddle Around" or "We Pay for All." While the attempt to keep Americans occupied during a period of massive unemployment was laudable, inefficient workers were often maintained on the public payroll without concern for their performance or productivity. Wastefulness and disorganization reached legendary proportions.[3]

Bureaucratic oversight of building projects sometimes produced a blessing and sometimes a boondoggle. New Deal programs tried assiduously to keep the country's work ethic alive while putting a huge proportion of the population on the public dole. The long-term impact on our society was negative in some respects, especially in helping the federal government pave the way to a welfare state in the years ahead. The Depression was the seedbed for a relief system divorced from any concerns for productive work or for the worthiness of aid recipients. The New Deal initiatives became the mechanisms for major shifts in perspectives touching on public assistance. Three subtle changes in the social psyche of Americans were deeply ingrained at the end of the New Deal era. These changes included:

- *An increased emphasis on collective action*, as the government taught the public to anticipate that a federal safety net would be perpetually in place if private enterprises were to fail at a personal level in the future.

- *A decreased emphasis on personal responsibility* across the board. Individuals who were poor now had come to expect that someone else would meet their need, no matter what the cause of economic pressure. People of means who saw need and had resources sufficient to respond also presumed someone else would do so. Private citizens at all levels of society could wait and just let the government take care of problems as they arose.

---

3   Ibid., 159.

- *A newly created sense of income entitlement,* which emerged with the support of the Universalist paradigm. A presumed right to public assistance became the mainstay of our culture's conventional wisdom. The New Deal era effectively allowed the public to learn in practice what it had never been willing to embrace fully in theory. The public consensus that assumed every citizen was due a measure of basic provision was only broadly accepted when unemployment became a pervasive reality. Social Universalists won through Depression-era programs, therefore, what they had not won and could not win in public debate. They achieved widespread acceptance of a new promise of public protection against any and all personal financial failures under the guise of promoting an unprecedented mutual commitment to universal welfare. Past Calvinist convictions that limited support only to those who had legitimate needs were roundly rejected as outmoded doctrines tied too closely to religious rationales and to outdated dogmas.[4]

As Americans moved from the doldrums of the Depression to face, for a second time in the twentieth century, the trials and tribulations of global warfare, there was no longer a question among social workers and government planners about the merits of federal involvement in relief programs. But the transition to our modern entitlement system was not yet complete. Social activists were succeeding in their effort to reform America's practices regarding public assistance, but at the grassroots level the masses had not yet made up their minds entirely on the matter.

Decades later, those receiving government support were still not altogether convinced of the wisdom behind the new social support system. Olasky writes, "Recipients themselves viewed welfare as a necessary wrong, but not a right. The Protestant work ethic lived on. Dependency was thought so dishonorable that, as late as the mid-1960s, only about

---

4   Ibid., 163.

half those eligible for welfare payments were receiving them, and many of the enrolled were taking only part of the maximum allowance."[5]

Personal conscience and private shame joined the social service agent in providing an effective three-tiered system of gatekeepers monitoring the doorway to the government dole. But in the 1960s, as Lyndon Johnson declared war on poverty during his administration, the two more personal guards against dependency (an active conscience and the dynamics of shame) would abandon their posts altogether and leave the public welfare worker as the sole custodian of the community chest. In time, social workers would effectively remove the lock and throw the door wide open, offering almost unlimited access to public assistance at a subsistence level. Relatively speaking, entitlement had taken a small step forward during the Roosevelt administration. A giant leap would come during Johnson's term as president.

The Great Society

Lyndon Johnson's vision for the Great Society programs of the mid-1960s was the welfare-state fruit born from the Universalist seeds sown in the 1930s New Deal legislation. President Johnson was a master manipulator of the federal legislative process and proved amazingly adept at securing support in the House and the Senate for his War on Poverty. The result was an avalanche of new laws, the birth of several entirely new federal agencies, and the mobilization of a small army of progressive social workers. Johnson's triumphs included the Economic Opportunity Act, food stamp legislation, Medicare, Medicaid, a wide variety of public works programs, and major increases in social security benefits.

While the reality of privation in America survived the assaults of the War on Poverty, social constraints on dependency did not. The legacy of Johnson's massive legislative agenda and the unprecedented social reforms it spawned was a complete disconnect in the mind of the pub-

---

5   Ibid., 168.

lic between welfare and work and between public subsidy and personal shame. Johnson gave a final endorsement to the Universalist philosophy of social welfare. As Olasky notes, the new dictum held that "welfare payments were tokens of freedom that should be seized with a bulldog grip. . . . The goal was material goods for all without regard to the cause of destitution."[6] Congress became the midwife for income transfer legislation that gave birth to new tax initiatives conceived to effect a decisive redistribution of wealth, provisions that effectively robbed the rich in order to help the poor.[7]

The Great Society was in general an overall failure in that the dimensions of poverty in America during the 1960s increased rather than subsided. The more subtle (if less intentional) war against any vestige of personal resistance to joining the welfare rolls was, by contrast, an overt success. During the War on Poverty a far greater percentage of those eligible for federal support payments exercised their full rights to welfare with enthusiasm. Shame was no longer a factor in the charity game.

Olasky cites statistics that suggest the scope of the welfare payment explosion in this era. During the 1950s the Human Services Aid for Dependent Children (AFDC) rolls rose by 110,000 families, or 17 percent—but during the 1960s the increase was 107 percent, or 800,000 families. About three-fourths of that increase occurred from 1965 to 1968 alone, during a time of general prosperity and diminishing unemployment. Slicing the numbers a different way, Olasky observes that "the overall AFDC population increased from 4.3 million in 1965 to 10.8 million in 1974. Administrators were astounded by the sudden leap."[8]

As the decade of the 1970s began, politicians, journalists, and social workers took more careful stock of our system of personal subsidy. They concluded that the price tag for welfare provided to the unemployed placed an enormous burden on working Americans. Olasky asserts that the tragedy of the American welfare system lies in the creation of imper-

---

6   Ibid., 175.

7   Ibid., 182.

8   Ibid., 182–83.

sonal government programs that are neither compassionate nor conservative. Drifting from a colonial era commitment to the inner transformation of the underprivileged poor to the current commitment to simple (but ineffective) plans for income transfer via "tax and spend" social legislation, indiscriminate public charity has lost impact in our society. At the same time, increasingly indifferent citizens have largely lost interest in private charity. Demoralization among the chronically poor is matched by "compassion fatigue" among the those who are well provided for but who grow increasingly cynical as their taxes pay more each year for public support programs that they know don't work.[9]

Time magazine's publishers produced an issue focused on this problem on February 8, 1971. "The Welfare Maze" was their cover story. They reported succinctly that the Great Society's updated version of compassion "satisfies no one: under the system it is *unblessed* to give and to receive." That conclusion has been driven deeply into the mindset of America's general population. The deepest impact, however, has been made specifically on Christians, who largely identify with fiscally conservative and Social Calvinist convictions. Many believers are concluding that it is more to their advantage "to buy and to keep" rather than to give at all. Personal generosity is simply going out of style for a large portion of the American public.

Putting US Giving Patterns in Perspective

Let me support this conclusion statistically. In the year 2000, US taxpayers who itemized deductions for charitable contributions on their federal income tax forms made personal donations at a level equal to 1.6 percent of their total income. That means that *Americans on the whole are keeping over 98 percent of the money they earn for personal expenses or discretionary use.* One would hope that when focusing specifically on the Christian community in the United States these statistics would greatly improve. Unfortunately they do not.

---

9   Ibid., 223.

Among church members of eleven primary Protestant denominations (or their historical antecedents) in the United States and Canada, per-member giving as a percentage of income was lower in 2000 than in either 1921 or 1933. In 1921, per-member giving as a percentage of income was 2.9 percent. In 1933, at the height of the Great Depression, per-member giving grew to 3.3 percent. By 2000, after a half-century of unprecedented prosperity, giving among Christians had fallen to 2.6 percent.[10] That's only 1 percent higher than all US givers combined, a pool of taxpayers heavily weighted with secularly minded people. So even committed believers in North America appear to be keeping over 97 percent of their income. In 2002, only 6 percent of US evangelicals actually tithed.[11] This represents a 50 percent decline in the number of tithers among born-again believers in just two years, since according to George Barna's research 12 percent tithed in the year 2000.[12] This observation is consistent with the general recognition that "the richer we become, the less we give in proportion to our income."[13]

These statistics are significant because of what the lost opportunity in terms of American tithes not given represents to the world's poor. Studies by the United Nations suggest that an additional $70–80 billion per year would be enough to provide access to essential services like basic health care and education for all the world's poor. If they did no more than tithe, American Christians would have the private dollars to foot this entire bill and still have $60–70 billion left to do evangelism around the world."[14]

Interestingly, these paltry individual statistics are mirrored by churches. When we look at the allocation of the combined resources en-

---

10 John L. Ronsvalle and Sylvia Ronsvalle, *The State of Church Giving through 2000* (Champaign, IL: Empty Tomb, 2002), 40.

11 Ronald J. Sider, *The Scandal of the Evangelical Conscience: Why Are Christians Living Just Like the Rest of the World?* (Grand Rapids: Baker, 2005), 13.

12 See The Barna Group website, http://www.barna.org/FlexPage.aspx?Page= BarnaUpdate&BarnaUpdateID=91.

13 Sider, *Scandal of the Evangelical Conscience,* 20.

14 Ibid., 21–22.

trusted to churches by their members, it is estimated that 97 percent of all the money raised in the United States for Christian causes of every kind stays in our country. We must conclude that American Christians and their churches are as apt "to buy and to keep" (and therefore not to give) as are their abjectly secular neighbors. That presents a global problem, because US citizens hold 80 percent of worldwide evangelical wealth.[15]

These selfish implications for Christians turn out not to be a uniquely American problem. When we look at the global church, the statistics get worse yet. Analyzing where religious giving is allocated by all churches receiving donations reveals that the tendency "not to give" to others (the manifestation of the desire "to buy and to keep" for ourselves) is a worldwide phenomenon.

Referring again to the chart presented earlier in chapter 3 (see Figure 2 on page 53), which summarizes church revenue and spending patterns worldwide, the total amount of money received annually by all the world's churches approximates $270 billion. Of this sum, 82.6 percent, or $223 billion, is used for "home pastoral ministry"—wherever home happens to be. Another 12 percent, or $32 billion, is spent on "home missions." Only 5.4 percent, or $15 billion, is spent for ministry outside the borders of the donors' domicile. But a huge proportion of this small amount of "foreign missions" funding paid by churches goes again to pay for pastoral leadership and for ministries serving those who are already Christians. A mere .18 percent, or $490 million, goes to outreach ministries aimed at lost people living in already evangelized cultures. We may add to this pittance a much lower portion, only .02 percent, or $54 million dollars, which is spent annually trying to reach truly unreached peoples with the gospel of Christ.

We could say that Christian churches on a global scale spend .2 percent of their total revenues on cross-cultural "others" and keep 99.8 percent of their available funds for themselves and their immediate neighbors. Christians all around the world seem to be weary of giving!

---

15 Bill Bright, quoted in Ron Blue with Jodie Berndt, *Generous Living: Finding Contentment through Giving* (Grand Rapids: Zondervan, 1997), 201.

Is it any wonder that Richard Foster is so pointedly critical of Westerners when he comments on our propensity "to buy and to keep"? He writes, "Contemporary culture is plagued by the passion to possess. The unreasoned boast abounds that the good life is found in accumulation, that 'more is better.' . . . The lust for affluence in contemporary society has become psychotic: it has completely lost touch with reality."[16]

For those who might take some comfort in the thought that US government relief programs are taking up the slack as personal giving drops off, statistics show that impression also to be false. Public grants simply are not compensating for the decline in private charitable inclinations. Let me illustrate by focusing on the portion of the federal budget devoted specifically to foreign aid. I am proposing that only federal funds allocated to aid and development in other countries be counted as "US government giving to others." All domestic spending, even for relief programs that benefit American citizens and resident aliens, represents a reflection of our decision to "buy and to keep" resources for ourselves—or at least within our own borders.

As a result of a joint program conducted by the Center for the Study of Policy Attitudes, the Center for International and Security Studies at Maryland, and the School of Public Affairs at the University of Maryland, in February of 2001 Steven Kull, the principal investigator, reported that Americans have a grossly exaggerated sense of how much funding their government makes available for international assistance programs. In the program's surveys, respondents estimated that America gives 20 percent of its federal budget to assist other nations. Actually, foreign aid makes up only .14 percent of the US annual budget.[17]

Viewed in that way, we could conclude that even the US government keeps 99.86 percent of the revenues it receives—dedicating those funds to use at home! The propensity to "buy and keep" is as readily

---

16 Richard J. Foster, *Freedom of Simplicity* (New York: Harper Collins Publishers, 1981), 3.

17 Jeffery D. Sachs, *The End of Poverty: Economic Possibilities for Our Time* (New York, Penguin Books, 2005), 218.

apparent for our national government as it is for US Christians specifically or for the global church in general. On the whole, it would seem that few people anywhere are giving freely to meet others' needs. When we know the facts, it becomes harder for us to maintain a rosy estimate of ourselves. Statistics simply do not support the presumption that we Westerners are inordinately generous people in spite of our inordinate wealth.

We effectively have been conditioned over time "not to give" in both the private and the public arenas. It seems that most Americans are convinced that we have worked too hard for our money to give it away to people who are not similarly industrious, whether those people live next door or on the other side of the world. As the abolitionist preacher Henry Ward Beecher once warned his parishioners, it may be that we have reached the circumstance where our prosperity has destroyed our generosity.

I contend that welfare-state excesses have affected our perspectives on generosity in both the domestic and the international arenas. We have been so vexed by the welfare experience in our domestic context that we now export our biases on that subject and impose a wrong view of generosity when we face genuine needs among the worthy poor from other cultures. Seen in this light, concern over dependency in the mission arena is counterproductive, providing an unfortunate and unconvincing argument against giving that diminishes our material commitment to global evangelism precisely at the time when it should be maximized. A defense of my conclusion on this point is in order and will be undertaken in the next chapter.

CHAPTER EIGHT

Global Welfare or Global Warfare?

I have repeatedly stressed in the preceding chapters the general concern in mission circles about outside subsidies for national leaders or indigenous churches. The reader will recall that Western support for poor people around the world is generally viewed by some to be harmful and that many leading mission professionals see the infusion of outside resources as a step "fraught with dangers." These supposed dangers should now have the familiar ring of similar concerns expressed among conservatives in our country about the negative impact of public subsidies for the undeserving poor in America. I am of the opinion that too many missionary leaders are responding to the call for grants-in-aid to churches emerging in the world's poorer mission fields as if such support payments were just one more manifestation of America's failed federal welfare system. They are not! *It is vitally important that we come to see clearly that this connection between welfare and world missions is largely unfounded.*

Missions giving is an investment in God's international network of kingdom armies fighting for the cause of world evangelism. We must not fall prey to the kind of myopic thinking that encourages us to insist that poor Christians around the globe must be left to fend for themselves in funding kingdom advances in their unreached cultures with no outside assistance. We should also see the warning cry of "Dependency!" for what it is: a defense against extending the dole, a desire to discourage increases in "public charity," a plea to limit the transfer of wealth from the industrious to the indolent. If, as I am suggesting, the dependency concern in modern missions theory is born in part from our disappointing domestic experience with a failed welfare system, we may well be focusing on the wrong issue. I am asserting that *missions giving is not a commitment to welfare—it is a commitment to warfare*! On this point, Westerners need to revise their thinking altogether. Until we get the right perspective on the problem we will continue to draw the wrong conclusion about giving to relieve global needs.

Extending support to newborn churches and pioneer national leaders who are among the first fruits to emerge among classically unreached peoples is a way to recognize their incredible value as fellow soldiers who are willing to face overwhelming odds in order to see their countrymen set free in Christ. If Americans can see the merit of funding guerilla fighters who promote the cause of democracy around the world militarily, we should be able to see the value of financing God's warriors who serve the kingdom of God spiritually. The earliest converts from unreached cultures who are willing to join us in advancing the gospel of the kingdom in their own contexts are God's "freedom fighters," contending for spiritual revolution on the hardest battlefronts in the world. They face the most resistant religions, the most aggressive governments, the most oppressive circumstances, and the most perilous risks in order to be the "first to fight" for God's glory in their native lands. They deserve our respect and our support for their courage and their convictions! They don't deserve the denigrating treatment we often offer when we see their needs but suggest that their deprivation is not our problem and should not be our concern.

Perhaps our initial hurdle in coming to a renewed perspective on this matter arises because so many Westerners have lost the sense that witness for Christ truly involves spiritual warfare dynamics. We simply will not be able to change the lens through which we see this issue and we will not come to embrace a shift from a welfare mentality to a warfare mentality if we do not first grasp the reality that a kingdom conflict is raging in our day.

World Missions Is Global Warfare

Some explanation of this warfare must be provided, therefore, so that the reader may follow my argument on this pivotal point. In *The Handbook for Spiritual Warfare*, Dr. Ed Murphy offers this explanation of the crucial struggle we face in world missions:

A biblical worldview can be expressed in one statement: present reality exists in a state of cosmic-earthly conflict or spiritual warfare. In philosophical terms, modified dualism exists in the universe. The Kingdom of God and the kingdom of evil supernaturalism are engaged in fierce conflict one against the other. Absolute dualism affirms that ultimate reality is eternally dualistic, that evil and good have always existed, and always will exist. Biblical dualism declares a modified dualism: present reality exists in a state of dualism, but such was not so in the beginning nor will it be so in the future. "In the beginning God . . ." is the view of Scripture. There was no evil, no opposing force, only God, and God is good. Then God created moral beings, the angels, and placed them within His Kingdom. Still there was no dualism. They obeyed His will. At some point in the past, rebellion occurred within the angelic Kingdom. Dualism was born. . . . As the focus of Scripture moves through time from the "eternal" past to the "eternal" future, dualism vanishes. The

ultimate state is that of eternal monism. Only God and His perfect Kingdom will exist in the eternal future. *Dualism, however,
is a present reality. . . . Spiritual warfare rages on earth. . . .*
God and his angelic Kingdom confront Satan and his demonic
kingdom, while the children of God contend with the children
of Satan.[1]

Mission ministry, especially witnessing for Christ and seeking converts from unreached cultures, represents the frontline of spiritual warfare. Jim Petersen offers additional insight into the reality of this cosmic
struggle when he writes about the missionary task, which focuses on
taking the gospel of Jesus Christ to lost people in the world: "To be a
messenger of Christ is to participate in spiritual warfare. People are in
slavery to the world systems wherever they find themselves. The Bible
says they are under the control of Satan, ruler of this world. The problem
is not just that they don't want to understand, it's that they cannot: 'The
god of this age has blinded the minds of unbelievers, so that they cannot
see the light of the gospel of the glory of Christ.'"[2]

Christian mission involves our cooperation with God in his plan to
rescue people and nations from the grip of Satan. As Ephesians 6:12
says, "Our struggle is not against flesh and blood, but against the rulers,
against the authorities, against the powers of this dark world and against
the spiritual forces of evil in the heavenly realms" (NIV).

In missions, the reality of warfare must be an integral part of our
strategic planning. George Otis puts this need plainly: "Demonic deceptions, offensives, and strongholds are both real and sophisticated and represent a blend of unilateral initiatives against and considered responses
to divine deployments. Understanding today's spiritual battlefield means
negotiating our way through enemy zones of control or extraordinary

---

1   Ed Murphy, *The Handbook for Spiritual Warfare* (Nashville: Thomas Nelson
Publishers, 1992), 13 (italics added).

2   Jim Petersen, *Church Without Walls* (Colorado Springs: NavPress, 1992), 189.

influence (strongholds), and grappling with matters such as the strength and purposes of rival belief systems."[3]

So we must be willing to fight faithfully—pressing the battle everywhere we go and all the time. In order to face Satan's forces, God expects us to enlist in the ranks of his soldiers rather than to wait until the day we are drafted. God has, in effect, an all-volunteer army. It includes everyone who names Christ as Savior and Lord. E. M. Bounds writes about the Christian's role as a warrior for Jesus, pointing out that any description of a believer that ignores this identity misses the mark of our high calling in Christ. He declares: "The Christian must be a soldier by birth, by fortune, by trade. The most essential quality of a divine soldier is that he is not entangled 'with the affairs of this life' (2 Timothy 2:4). The elements of self-denial, courage, and endurance are vital characteristics of military training."[4]

But when we speak of spiritual warfare, we are not proposing a literal call to arms for a clash of civilizations that would pursue the course to victory over our enemies or to our mutually assured destruction. The "Crusader spirit" repeatedly has been proven to be foreign to our Christian fight of faith. Military mobilization in the name of Christ must be seen as "the barren answer of a politically minded church."[5] Conventional weapons of war are of no value in the spiritual battle raging over the hearts and minds of human beings. Furthermore, too many "conversions" already have been compelled at the point of a sword, the tip of a spear, or the barrel of a gun. Colonial conquest is a relic of the past in mission theory.

---

3   George Otis Jr., *The Last of the Giants* (Tarrytown, NY: Fleming H. Revell Company, 1991), 39. Islam, Hinduism, and materialism are three modern challenges to the Christian faith and to a biblical worldview. Otis calls these ideologies "the last of the giants" to be faced by followers of Jesus.

4   E. M. Bounds, *Winning the Invisible War* (Pittsburgh: Whitaker House, 1984), 145–46.

5   Charles H. Kraft, *Defeating Dark Angels: Breaking Demonic Oppression in the Believer's Life* (Ann Arbor, MI: Servant Publications, 1992), xi.

So our weapons, like our warfare, are spiritual rather than carnal in nature. We face our fight armed with the gospel of peace, the authority of Jesus' name, and the armor of God and with angelic hosts as our allies. The living Word of God lights our way and the preaching of the Scripture is the only sword intended to penetrate the hearts of lost individuals. The soft word spoken in response to the sinner, the listening ear of the saint, the grace gifts of the Spirit released to edify all, the prayers of the intercessor, and the love of Christ incarnated with cultural sensitivity—these are the weapons of our warfare.

But the battle demands other resources too. The struggle for people's minds will require educated leaders, published books, printed periodicals, newly translated Bibles, and creative business platforms. We will also need buildings for churches and seminaries, laborers for the harvest fields, teachers for the troops, and transportation for every needed resource. All these logistical requirements will demand the investment of large sums of money. For our war is expeditionary: it must be carried across natural barriers (oceans and mountains, rivers and deserts, jungles and glaciers) and cultural barriers (false faiths, foreign languages, exotic ways of life, and hostile governments) until it is carried to the remotest parts of the earth. It is precisely because even this kind of unconventional warfare is costly that Christians must learn to be thrifty and generous at the same time.

When we willingly part with our material resources for the sake of the global war effort that is world mission, we take up the cause being pressed by brothers and sisters all over the world. When we give to support Christians among unreached cultures, we share their suffering as they contend with the darkest cultures on earth—places where life offers far harder circumstances than does our own context. Revising Marantika's suggested substitute for the three-self formula (play together, pray together, and pay together), I think it is time we Westerners determined that we must *pay together, pray together, and stay in the fray together* with our brothers and sisters coming to Christ in unreached cultures.

In making this point, I am consciously asserting my sense that Westerners should support national workers when such is appropriate, but that we should also keep mobilizing men and women from our own nations as well to fill the world's missionary ranks. It is simply not enough to throw money at national partners. Though some mission leaders, such as K. P. Yohannan, believe it is high time to admit "that someone from somewhere else [other than the West] can do it better,"[6] I am convinced that being present and active together as coworkers for Christ is imperative.

"Warfare Allies" or "Welfare Agents"?

When wealthy Westerners do send aid to the indigenous leaders and national churches emerging among unreached peoples, it is important that we recognize clearly that we are acting as "warfare allies," not "welfare agents." This distinction is important because the motives for giving in each case are so radically different. Perhaps if we use analogies from World War II, the case I am pressing can be made more clear. After Poland was overrun by the Germans in 1939, a whole series of European nations were invaded and forced to submit to Nazi occupation. In addition to Poland, the list of countries controlled by Hitler's forces by the end of 1940 included Austria, Czechoslovakia, Norway, Belgium, the Netherlands, Denmark, and France.

When France was invaded, its Free Government leaders evacuated the country but continued to fight global fascism from French colonial territories in North Africa. At home, the right-wing Vichy Government conceded to Nazi occupation and collaborated with the Axis Powers. But not all French citizens left at home were willing to embrace German domination so readily. The Marquis, the formal name for the resistance movement in France, was formed when General Charles de Gaulle broadcast a message from London on June 18, 1940, announcing to all of France that its war had not been ended by the Nazi occupation. He urged the citizenry to hinder the occupying armies of the Third Reich

---

6   K. P. Yohannan, *Revolution in World Missions* (Carrollton, TX: Gospel for Asia, 2003), 183.

in every way possible, thus continuing France's fight against Germany. But how could so few people resist the occupying Nazi forces that had so quickly and so completely overwhelmed the nation's regular army? How could they afford to press the battle? Where would the resources for sustained resistance be found? Listen to de Gaulle's carefully chosen words in his radio address:

> The leaders who, for many years, were at the head of French armies, have formed a government. This [Vichy] government, alleging our armies to be undone, agreed with the enemy to stop fighting. Of course, we were subdued by the mechanical, ground and air forces of the enemy. Infinitely more than their number, it was the tanks, the airplanes, the tactics of the Germans which made us retreat. It was the tanks, the airplanes, the tactics of the Germans that surprised our leaders to the point to bring them there where they are today.

> But has the last word been said? Must hope disappear? Is defeat final? No!

> Believe me, I speak to you with full knowledge of the facts and tell you that nothing is lost for France. The same means that overcame us can bring us to a day of victory. *For France is not alone! She is not alone! She is not alone!* She has a vast Empire behind her. She can align with the British Empire that holds the sea and continues the fight. She can, like England, use without limit the immense industry of [the] United States.[7]

In effect, de Gaulle was promising an ongoing supply of resources to make ongoing resistance possible. He was clear that the necessary material and arms would come from the Allies, especially from Britain and America. He was broadcasting from London, where he was gathering the Free French Forces to join the Allies on the battlefields of Europe and North Africa. He was counting on support from the other nations who were fighting against the same foe. The Allies' common enemy guaran-

---

7   Quote available at http://en.wikipedia.org/wiki/Appeal_of_June_18 (italics added).

teed their camaraderie in a common cause. In England and in America, these Frenchmen looking for material assistance were not seen as a *band of beggars seeking alms*. They were viewed as a *band of brothers seeking arms*.

Note the words de Gaulle used with reference to the availability of arms and ammunition. "France is not alone! She is not alone! . . . She can, like England, use without limit the immense industry of [the] United States." How could de Gaulle promise access "without limit" to America's industrial might? He could do so because the Roosevelt administration had made a virtually unbounded commitment to supply a maximum store of military aid to those nations fighting for democracy against the global fascist tyranny that threatened the whole world.

The Lend-Lease Act

In a proposal that would later be codified in the Lend-Lease Act (passed by Congress March 11, 1941), Roosevelt had positioned America, still technically a neutral nation in the growing global conflict, to serve as the "great arsenal of democracy." The notion behind this policy was that America alone was uniquely situated to provide arms and logistical support to England and eventually all the other countries that would become part of the Allied Powers. America alone possessed the wealth, the industrial capacity, the technical expertise, and the means of distribution to arm and outfit for war all the nations that would come to be identified as our allies. In the original legislation, $1.3 billion in aid was approved without regard to the technicalities of repayment. By the end of the war, more than $50 billion dollars in military aid had been distributed globally.

Lend-Lease was actually the third major program the United States had inaugurated in its efforts to help England and China successfully face the Axis Powers. Initially, under the dictates of the Neutrality Act of 1935, America supplied military and logistical aid only on a "cash and carry" basis. As Britain ran low on cash reserves, the United States

traded older naval destroyers for long-term lease agreements that provided new military bases for America in various parts of the world. When it
became apparent that England could not possibly continue paying for all
the military aid it needed to sustain a war effort that had reached the four
corners of the earth, Roosevelt turned his administration to the Lend-
Lease alternative. At its peak, the United States was supplying arms,
food, and logistical support to more than forty nations.

It is interesting to note that this provision of immense quantities
of military resources was made without charge, yet these supplies were
never considered as offerings of charity or as expressions of American
benevolence. In fact, Roosevelt described the Lend-Lease program essentially as a selfish policy from the US perspective. In a press conference on December 17, 1940, the president offered an off-the-cuff explanation for this new policy:

> In the present world situation of course there is absolutely no
> doubt in the mind of a very overwhelming number of Americans
> that the best immediate defense of the United States is the suc-
> cess of Great Britain in defending itself; and that, therefore,
> quite aside from our historic and current interest in the survival
> of democracy, in the world as a whole, it is equally important
> *from a selfish point of view* of American defense, that we should
> do everything to help the British Empire to defend itself. . . .

> Orders from Great Britain are therefore a tremendous asset to
> American national defense; because they automatically create
> additional facilities. *I am talking selfishly, from the American
> point of view*—nothing else. Therefore, *from the selfish point of
> view,* that production must be encouraged by us. . . .

> The best defense of Great Britain is the best defense of the
> Untied States, and therefore . . . these materials would be more
> useful to the defense of the United States if they were used in
> Great Britain, than if they were kept in storage here.

> Now, what I am trying to do is to eliminate the dollar sign.
> That is something brand new in the thoughts of practically ev-

erybody in this room; I think—get rid of the silly, foolish old dollar sign.[8]

Britain was not bankrupt, but she was badly outnumbered and in the fight of her life. She didn't need financing alone; she needed friends and allies to share the burden of war. Taking the dollar sign out of the equation and eagerly sharing resources was Roosevelt's way of cementing American collaboration with the United Kingdom in times past. I am suggesting that a willingness to share resources with our spiritual allies is an equally prudent way to cement our commitment to and our collaboration with fellow citizens of the kingdom of God today.

A War Chest for World Missions

The philosophy behind the Lend-Lease program was essentially based on the notion that grants of military aid under the act were not a system of debits and credits. They involved neither gifts, nor loans, nor transfers of cash. They were, instead, a system of mutual war supply designed to make possible the maximally effective combined operations by which the Allies were fighting and winning the war. On the basis of "equality of sacrifice," concerns were focused on each ally contributing to the war effort in whatever terms that investment could be made and measured. Norway and the Soviet Union could not be expected to field armies of equal size, and America and Australia could not reasonably offer the same amounts of war material. Contributions were evaluated on a relative and proportional basis, not dollar for dollar.

Disproportionate devastation of national infrastructure and disparities in losses measured in soldiers killed, wounded, or missing in action were also recognized. How could the Soviet Union's nine million military dead and eighteen million wounded be compared with the United States' loss of three hundred thousand troops in each category? How was the dramatically unequal loss of life magnified when one considers

---

8   Quote available at http://www.fdrlibrary.marist.edu/odllpc2.html (italics added).

that the United States suffered virtually no civilian casualties while the Soviet Union saw the war take the lives of an additional nineteen million noncombatants during fighting on its soil? Financial comparisons failed completely and ceased to be meaningful in the face of such staggering losses measured in war dead rather than war dollars.

Beyond the net effect of body counts and budgets, it seemed only right that some attempt should be made to measure the relative postwar stability of the various governments and the war's effect on national economies. In the process, American attempts to account for balances due under the Lend-Lease transactions in financial terms alone became hopelessly untenable. In the final analysis, the United States had invested more money and material than any other allied nation. At the same time, America had not been bombed, its homes and factories had not been damaged, and its soil had not been devastated by enemy invasion. Strictly economic accounting seemed to fall short, far short, in any approach to settling accounts. So most Lend-Lease bills were considered "paid in full" after the armistice. In effect, all the allied nations were given credit for making their own maximum investment in the war effort on their own terms. It is this mutually magnanimous spirit that I believe should guide missions giving today!

The World War II Lend-Lease plan had nothing to do with international welfare and everything to do with international warfare. So should current mission support strategies. Every effort should be made by believers allied in spiritual warfare to see that kingdom forces on every front are equipped to fight, that they are sustained in battle, and that they are supported as completely as possible. Current concerns over dependency and the self-supporting paradigm have little relevance when we allow this sort of wartime perspective to guide our decision making processes.

America's visionary leaders during the World War II era succeeded in making our nation the "great arsenal of democracy." They did this because the United States alone in the world of nations could afford to foot the bill. Why should we not now become the *war chest for world missions* for the same reason? The relative circumstances found in today's global spiritual warfare approximately mirror those of World War II. Our relative wealth, our material and industrial capacity, our technology, and our ingenuity make us far more able than any other nation in history to support the expansion of the kingdom all over the world. Jesus once made clear the kingdom principle that "To whom much has been given, much will be required."

As we debate whether "to give or not to give," we demonstrate the reality that we have lost sight of the biblical perspectives that should undergird our commitment to financing global missions. We also betray the fact that we have forgotten (and worse, no longer feel moved by) our disproportionate obligation to God and to people. Being inordinately blessed in material terms, we should be inordinately committed to sharing with others in kind. The goal is to allow America's contribution to the global war effort to become great again. But first we must look beyond our "giving patterns" and consider the problems created by our "keeping propensities" as we attempt to be thorough in grasping the issues associated with dollars, dependency, and doing the right thing in twenty-first century missions.

CHAPTER NINE

Missionary Lifestyle Choices

Earlier in this book I referenced Dr. Jonathan J. Bonk's book, *Missions and Money: Affluence as a Western Missionary Problem.* I also shared the impact his writing has had on my own thinking regarding the interplay of wealth, wisdom, and world mission theory. His insights have special import when we consider missionary lifestyle choices and their relationship to the natural tendency Westerners have "to buy and to keep" rather than to share their resources with the poor.

Doing Good in Order to Do Well

In a sentence, Bonk asserts that, from the perspective of the poor whom missionaries ostensibly desire to serve sacrificially, it seems obvious that many missionaries endeavor to "do good in order to do well."[1] That is to say, in spite of the sacrifices apparent at home to those who watch well-intentioned friends and family members "forsake all" in order to serve the gospel in foreign and faraway parts of the world, missionaries to the poor often arrive on unreached fields only to find that they are fabulously wealthy in relative terms. Surrounded by poverty in the new mission setting, the Western missionaries' attempts to abandon worldly wealth often serve only to magnify their material abundance.

In the social context of most unreached peoples, newly arriving Western ministers simply enjoy incredible economic and practical advantages over their neighbors. The disparity is reflected in comfortable, well-appointed quarters; clean and/or hot water; the quality and quantity of apparel; the variety of nutritious food; available medicine, medical care, and medical insurance plans; and access to automobiles, airplanes, technology, education, and information. Missionaries generally even have greater access to people in positions of political power in the country they are serving than do their national neighbors. The security of retirement funds, the relief of regular vacations, and the reassurance represented by connection with a broad, even if unseen, network of relationships set the missionary apart from those born into the poverty of the mission context. Such an extended network of supporting relationships (whether within the missionary's agency, denomination, or sending church) provides an invisible but nonetheless real and significant safety net that nationals in the same setting could never hope to have. The availability of emergency resource assistance adds icing to the already sumptuous cake that puts the missionary in a decidedly advantaged posture when viewed from the less-fortunate perspective of the poor. On the whole, the indigenous neighbors cannot miss the reality that *missionaries seem to do very well as a result of their desire to do good for the kingdom.*

Less apparent to the national onlooker would be the availability of a wide variety of "support services" enjoyed on the field that would not

---

1   Jonathan J. Bonk, *Missions and Money: Affluence as a Western Missionary Problem* (Maryknoll, NY: Orbis Books, 1991), 55.

be within reach of a missionary's budget had they remained at home. Housekeepers, cooks, child-care workers, private language tutors, gardeners, and other "menials" (to use Bonk's painful term) can be afforded in the context of poverty when they would not be financially feasible at home. Pointing to these kinds of privileges broadly enjoyed by Western workers serving Christ as witnesses to the poor debunks the notion that missionary mobilization is always an act of self-denial.

How is it that patterns viewed by missionaries as evidence of self-sacrifice could be viewed by nationals as overtly selfish? Searching for an answer, Bonk cites the comments he heard from the Ethiopians he recalls from his childhood experience as a missionary kid. Though grateful for employment offered by the missionary community, the Ethiopians could not easily understand "why, with so much wealth, the missionary seemed unwilling to share with those who were poverty stricken."[2] Bonk thus begins to build a case that, more than we may like to readily acknowledge, Western missionaries are not only less sacrificial than we presume but also more selfish than we would care to admit, when judged from the perspective of those being served.

For readers who may already be beginning to feel the pain that awoke in me when I first read *Missions and Money*, I warn that deeper hurts are yet to come. Bonk offers facts and figures to show that the typical modus operandi of Western missionaries only reflects the increasing prosperity of their homelands in a world where the gap between the rich and poor is ever widening. Using the UN's International Comparison Project figures as one example, industrial economies are growing at a rate nearly three times that of low-income economies. But the disparity reflected in this statistic is even more significant than this comparison would at first seem to show. That is because the base used to calculate expansion rates in industrial economies was sixty times greater than that found in low-income economies of the same period (comparing 1984 per capita GNP levels of $11,430 and $190 respectively).[3] In other words,

---

2   Ibid., xiv.

3   Ibid., 5.

the problem of what Bonk calls "insular prosperity" is not new, and it is not receding. Rather, the disparity of relative poverty is getting steadily worse as the twenty-first century begins.[4]

Citing more recent UN statistics, Douglas Johnston confirms this point that the economic gap between the "haves" and the "have nots" is growing steadily worse. With the global population now officially set in excess of six billion, it was estimated in 1999 that the wealthiest 20 percent of humanity consumes 86 percent of all goods and services while the poorest 20 percent of the world's inhabitants consume only 1.3 percent.[5]

But this problem has been with us for centuries. Quoting David Picton Jones, a nineteenth-century missionary serving in East Africa with the London Missionary Society, Bonk shows that affluence was apparent as a central problem for missionaries as early as 1884. Serving in a context of profound poverty, Jones wrote to his mission secretary, sharing his concern about his national neighbors: "Our life is far above them and we are surrounded by things entirely beyond their reach. The consequence is that they . . . *cannot* follow us."[6] Bonk's thesis is that insular prosperity, though advantageous to Western missionaries, "has an inherent tendency to isolate [would-be witnesses] from the cutting edge of missionary endeavor, rendering much of their effort either unproductive or counterproductive, or sometimes both."[7]

The roots of the missionary propensity for insular prosperity are nurtured in the rich soil of Western cultural conditioning. Material plenty, a common (though not universal) condition of American life, has had a pervasive influence upon the American people. Missionaries from the

---

4   Ibid., xix.

5   Douglas M. Johnston Jr., "Religion and Foreign Policy," chapter 6 in *Forgiveness and Reconciliation: Religion, Public Policy and Conflict Transformation,* Raymond G. Helmick, SJ, and Rodney L. Peterson, eds. (Philadelphia: Templeton Foundation Press, 2001), 118.

6   Bonk, *Missions and Money,* 10.

7   Ibid., xix.

United States have not escaped the congenital forces of the culture in which they were conceived. Rather, the affluent religious womb in which American missionary passions are developed also shapes a pattern of privilege that survives conversion to Christ and is nearly impossible to reform. As Bonk notes, "Born and bred in the economic abundance of the West, the character, outlook, values, preoccupations, and strategies of missionaries have naturally been deeply affected."[8] It is hard to refute the conclusion that we Westerners carry in our psyche a mentality of entitlement that inherently weakens our evangelistic potential.

Thus, Americans especially tend to manifest a presumptuous claim to providential privilege. We expect to play a dominant role as saviors of the civilized world. With this perception, as Bonk observes, we carry a variety of "gospels" around the globe. We promote the gospel of "science, technology, modern weapons, democracy, and of course, of religion." But even if we manage to focus primarily on a truly evangelical Christian witness, our message is too often only a "comfortably incarnated gospel."[9]

Jesus made the calling to true discipleship costly. He demanded a general renunciation of material affluence as a goal for Christians when he said, "If anyone wishes to come after Me, he must deny himself, and take up his cross daily and follow Me" (Luke 9:23). Pursuing the Great Commission with what we might call the Great Renunciation in mind, first-century believers in Jerusalem chose not to consider any of their material possessions as their exclusive property. Instead, they sold what they needed to sell in order to lay stores at the apostles' feet in an effort to insure that no needy person would be found among them. Perhaps we should be more challenged by that early church economic example! I am not proposing a communist-style common purse or that everyone needs to sell everything in every case in order to follow Jesus, though the Lord himself made just that demand on occasion (Luke 18:22). Rather, I am promoting a covenant-oriented concern for others that has its roots

---

8   Ibid., 17.
9   Ibid., 26, 17.

in both Jesus' teaching and the apostolic tradition (Luke 12:33; Acts 4:32–35; Philippians 2:3–4).

It seems obvious that Jesus intended us to limit our lifestyles to some degree so that we might share the resources entrusted to us with those less fortunate. John Piper makes this same point: "Jesus presses us toward a wartime lifestyle that does not value simplicity for simplicity's sake, but values wartime austerity for what it can produce for the cause of world evangelization. . . . The point is: a $70,000 salary does not have to be accompanied by a $70,000 lifestyle. . . . *No matter how grateful we are, [wealth] will not make the world think that our God is good; it will make people think that our God is gold.*"[10]

In spite of admonitions from Scripture, we maintain a variety of rationales to defend our tendency to hold on to affluence—to buy and to keep—as we put our hands to the missionary plow.

Defenses for Missionary Materialism

In *Missions and Money*, Bonk summarizes the following four streams of thinking often used to support the relatively high standards of living enjoyed by Western missionaries to the poor. They offer practical and sound considerations—explanations that deserve to be taken seriously—even as they often lead us to unfortunate economic choices on the world's mission fields.

- *An Economic Rationale.* Especially in the early developmental stages of pioneer missions among tribal people and among cultures teeming with the threat of disease and the danger of death from wild animals and wicked men alike, mere survival on a foreign field has historically been no forgone conclusion. In anticipation of the predictable reality that some of their number would not survive the experience of penetrating lost cultures with Jesus' message of salvation, many early pioneers carried

---

10 John Piper, *Let the Nations Be Glad* (Grand Rapids: Baker, 1993), 106 (italics added).

their supplies to inhospitable lands in coffins rather than crates. Conventional wisdom quickly came to hold that "the cheapest and the most effective missionary was, beyond doubt, the live one; the live missionary was [also] the healthy one; the healthy one was [also] the comfortable one; the comfortable one was [also] the one whose way of life when abroad most closely approximated that to which the missionary was accustomed back home."[11] Thus, *missionary wealth* and *missionary health*, from the earliest missionary experiences, were assumed to go together.

For the typical missionary to become fruitful in a cross-cultural assignment requires several years of preparation, including Bible school or seminary courses, language training, and specialized orientation. Prior to arriving on the field, equipping, deputation, and transportation add yet greater investments of money and time into the effective missionary's development. Therefore, early departure from the field as a result of disease, death, disunity, or even discomfort imposes a staggering loss to the sending agency. Current concerns among mission leaders over the too prevalent reality of "first term failure" demonstrate that this issue is as relevant an issue today as ever—one measured as much in dollars and cents as in the diminished ranks of missionary workers. In this modern era, discomfort and disunity are probably more common causes of early departures from the field than either death or disease. But economic realities still dictate that the most cost-effective mission is the one that can keep missionaries on the field and get out of them the best service they are capable of offering.[12] Taking good, practical care of missionaries is an obvious and logical decision. So goes the economic rationale for maintaining missionaries in relatively lavish means on the fields in which they serve.

---

11 Bonk, *Missions and Money,* 33.

12 Ibid., 31–33.

- *A Domestic Rationale.* The second argument for comparatively affluent missionary lifestyles has been evident in my own
  agency's experience in Bosnia. In 1992 we began to send missionaries (mostly short-term team members) to serve in refugee camps during the war in Bosnia. In these early efforts we
  mobilized mainly single missionaries, some of whom made the
  first long-term commitments to our field. First one marriage
  and then another between our single American missionaries
  and national citizens later occurred. Then children came along
  in each household. Though our staff lived initially in refugee
  camps and then in housing accommodations similar to that of
  our target population, wives and children created a noticeably
  greater focus on creature comforts for the missionary home.

  Then, in 1999, we sent two American couples, along with their
  children, to Sarajevo. They took to the field a cargo container
  filled with household effects, furniture, automobiles, and even
  a piano for each family. Why the increase in amenities in these
  instances? Because we reasoned that helping the wives and
  children make a successful transition to the new culture was
  essential to the long-term service of each couple. If the wives or
  children in these households were not able to cope with cross-
  cultural adjustment, the survival of the family on the field was
  questionable. Such domestic concerns are the most emotional
  of all married missionary issues. The simple reality is that families are more complex and more costly to deploy and maintain
  in mission service than are singles. We will never send another
  cargo container to the field. But attending to the comfort, care,
  and educational needs of children is still a powerful and in-
  stinctively legitimate rationale for a measure of missionary
  affluence.[13]

- *A Social Rationale.* Even with the best of intentions, Western
  missionaries who attempt to "go native" in identifying closely

---

13 Ibid., 35, 37.

with the poor do so with great difficulty and with only marginal success. This is because the people among whom we serve invariably define our identity—usually doing so by reflecting their sense of our usefulness to them. Part of that usefulness is measured by our ability to access material resources. Denying that Western missionaries have greater wealth is a dishonest foundation for relationship. Such denial may even reinforce an impression that we are greedy and prone to hoarding our possessions. Thus, pretending to be poor is a detrimental deception on the mission field. The end of such approaches usually engenders distrust, skepticism, or mockery among national neighbors.

Escrowing funds at home and limiting our lifestyle choices on the field is only a slightly better pretense. It is not helpful to assume that anyone should aspire to be poor or that Westerners should mask the reality of their relative riches. A better general perspective is that contextual *parity* rather than contrived *poverty* should be our aim. That goal still demands hard choices as missionaries attempt to moderate their lifestyles. Self-imposed moderation is a wise and worthy reflection of our commitment to work toward a genuine contextualization of our presence in cross-cultural settings.

Ultimately missionaries face the unavoidable challenge of learning to live as stewards of great relative wealth in a sea of great relative poverty. Bonk concludes that the essential economic challenge for Westerners is to allow their national neighbors to help forge a concept of what it means to be *righteous rich people* living among the poor.[14] It is not enough for missionaries to decide what the Scriptures require of them in this respect. Nationals need to be invited into a dialogue on the subject.

---

14 From a lecture Bonk gave at Gordon Conwell Theological Seminary, South Hamilton, MA.

Their insights will be informative as well as discomforting but we need to see their perspective clearly.

In my own experience, many missionaries are made immediately uncomfortable with the prospect that indigenous Christians should be included in a dialogue on this subject. For obvious reasons, they don't want the national voice to be heard. In suggesting that we include Bosnian believers in discussions about money management and lifestyle choices, missionary responses have ranged from open anger to dismissive contempt. The tenor of these responses is captured cryptically by one American missionary who offhandedly defended his own consumptive choices with the judgment that, on this point especially, "Bonk's belief is bunk!"

- *A Strategic Rationale.* Western mission strategies tend to be money intensive.[15] They depend increasingly on expensive technology, personal mobility, rapid systems of international travel, and the ability to hire laborers at low rates of pay to attend to mundane duties so that missionaries can focus on higher, more strategic ministry priorities. In the process of seeking efficiency at a price, Westerners invariably serve not only as religious teachers but also as employers. For some mission strategists, it seems only right that providing financial resources should also permit and perpetuate Western control of staffing, vision, and direction as indigenous churches emerge. For more colonially minded leaders still serving in the mission community, dominance flowing from financial superiority might be the most important strategic rationale for sustaining a measure of affluence.

As the saying goes, "The world's version of the Golden Rule is that the ones who have the gold get to make the rules." For some Westerners, *missionary affluence* is the recognized price of maintaining *missionary influence*—an important strategic

---

15 Bonk, *Missions and Money,* 40.

advantage. The simple but sad reality is that dollars still buy dominance over poorer national neighbors in many settings.

These apparently logical explanations are the common points raised in defense of the lifestyle advantages missionaries often enjoy when serving among impoverished peoples. But these benefits come with other hidden costs that we also need to bear in mind.

CHAPTER TEN

The High Cost of Missionary Affluence

The advantages flowing from sustained health, relative comfort, personal security, and ministry efficiency are—on the surface—logical, and expenses incurred to maintain them seem justifiable. But Westerners ministering the gospel among the poor sacrifice a measure of apostolic effectiveness and spiritual credibility when they defend the financial advantages they are accustomed to enjoying. Bonk warns that our "failure to counter wealth's insidious effects upon missionary endeavors will ensure the continual ebb of the Western churches as a Kingdom force."[1]

---

1   Bonk, *Missions and Money*, 44.

The Downside of Mobilizing Upscale Missionaries

Like the Laodicean church in Revelation 3:17, we Westerners may say we are rich and have become wealthy and are in need of nothing, without being aware that, in God's economy, we are wretched and miserable and poor and blind and naked. Following in the footsteps of this self-satisfied church in Asia Minor, we might do well to consider whether we have arrived at a place where our lifestyles indict us as people who need *too much materially and too little spiritually* in our service of the kingdom. Secure in our relative wealth, we too often think and act as if we are certain the world's poor people need us, but we fail to see that we also need them. Bonk cites five major consequences that flow from the presence of rich missionaries witnessing in a world of hunger.[2]

- *Insulation from the Culture.* Disparate wealth simply has the power to cushion the mission community from the harsher realities of life faced by the poor and needy neighbors who surround them. Affluence and the goods and services wealth can provide constitute what Bonk calls the "non-conducting material" that protects the missionary from the sights, sounds, heat, cold, and smells of the world experienced by impoverished people. We too often live as missionaries segregated in compounds, complexes, bases, or enclaves, not realizing that we are effectively insulated from those we seek to serve.

- *Isolation from Our Neighbors.* The propensity for protecting ourselves from the ravages of poverty also serves simultaneously to isolate us from our neighbors. Modern sociologists call this "cocooning" in the context of suburban settings where well-to-do Westerners normally live. Gated communities, electronic garage door openers, Internet shopping services, and delivery systems for products and services including fast food, groceries, dry cleaning, and parcel post are just a few examples of the modern amenities that allow us to live in relative isolation behind closed doors. While not all these Western advantages are

---

2   See Bonk, *Missions and Money,* chapter 4, pp. 45–58.

available on the world's mission fields, many are; and functional equivalents of these privileges abound in foreign settings.

Even if circumstances in our mission contexts (such as refugee quarters or wartime accommodations) force us into cramped environments, we still prefer when possible to at least arrange for a private room. So it is that we seek separate facilities when we are admitted to hospitals, select a table in a public restaurant, look for a hotel room with its own toilet, or even when we use public transportation. Fewer people, more personal space, and increased privacy are all Western values that play poorly in ghetto conditions, refugee tents, or the cardboard hovels that are houses for the disenfranchised in the world's poorest communities.

If our passion for privacy does not adequately isolate us from the poor, then the pace of our lives often does. The sheer speed with which we conduct ourselves works against the processes required to form deep relationships. If we can conclude that segregation hinders the development of relationships, we need to acknowledge that speed also kills our capacity to build affinity with others. We would be less prone to isolation if we would simply slow our pace. In Bosnia, for example, lingering long over Turkish coffee with one's friends is a singularly important national pastime. Americans, by contrast, are more accustomed to getting their coffee "to go" with the expectation of drinking it in solitude as they drive hurriedly to their next appointment. Immediate benefits come when we choose to slow down. We need to make a conscious choice in our fields of service to take a bus rather than a car or to walk rather than ride. Kasuke Koyama captures the isolating dynamic inherent in our pace of life when he reminds us that we all serve a "three mile an hour

God" who designed people to walk and talk with friends, not to ride or fly in private compartments at high speed.[3]

- *Illusions of Superiority.* Financial disparity is also a barrier to developing true friendship between families when the households attempting relationship do not share similar means. As long as there is an economic chasm between missionaries and their converts, social relationships will be hampered. In essence, the rich are inherently prone to lord their authority over the poor. As Bryant Myers states, disparate resources typically make relationships oppressive and disempowering, "a result of the non-poor playing God in the lives of the poor."[4] Having inordinate wealth in relation to one's neighbors naturally engenders a sense of superiority. Too often nationals draw the wrong conclusion as we perpetuate the illusion that relative Western wealth is a consequence of relative Western righteousness. We must more carefully acknowledge, as did 160 mission practitioners in the Iguassu Affirmation, that "material blessings come from God, but prosperity should not be equated with godliness."[5]

Undeserved deference heightens the sense of superiority that is presumed by the wealthy and conceded by the poor who relate to the rich from a position of decided economic disadvantage. This is a natural dynamic, but it misses the kingdom expectation anticipated by James 1:9–10: "The brother of humble circumstances is to glory in his high position; and the rich man is to glory in his humiliation, because like flowering grass he will pass away."

---

3   Kosuke Koyama, *Three Mile an Hour God: Biblical Reflections* (Maryknoll, NY: Orbis Books, 1980).

4   Bryant L. Myers, *Walking with the Poor: Principles and Practices of Transformational Development* (Maryknoll, NY: Orbis Books, 1999), 13.

5   William D. Taylor, ed., *Global Missiology for the 21st Century: The Iguassu Dialogue* (Grand Rapids: Baker, 2000), 18.

- *Intensification of Advantage.* Bonk writes, "While missionaries have naturally stressed the self-giving altruism of their service, outsiders have often regarded the relative affluence, security, and social status enjoyed by missionaries to be a sign of darker, essentially self-serving motives."[6] Many missionaries simply are far better off financially on the field than they ever were at home. On the mission station they may have access to more living space, more leisure time, more servants, more buying power, more privileges, and more prestige. Their advantages are effectively intensified by the context of their service for the Lord. All too often under such circumstances, affluent apostolic witness, "while creating little hunger and thirst for righteousness, has whetted native appetites for the material benefits enjoyed by [missionaries]."[7]

  Historically, material wealth has caused lost neighbors among indigenous people to manifest utter indifference to what a missionary *says* while attracting rapt attention to what he or she *has*. When a native neighbor exhibits an unabashed desire to share in the spoils the missionary so richly and openly enjoys (in effect, seeking only to mirror the example set by the teacher), both motive and character are called into question in the would-be follower. Imperious spiritual leaders deem such ambitious disciples selfish and worldly. The result is a vicious cycle of mistrust, suspicion, and faultfinding on all sides.

- *Instigation of Envy and Hostility.* Poverty is a relative reality, just as affluence tends to be. In fact, it may be important to note that the experience of poverty can be even more profound when the people who are poor today were relatively comfortable at a time in their recent past. Such is the case in our Bosnian context, where a prolonged war ruined what had been the most

---

6 Bonk, *Missions and Money,* 52.

7 Ibid., 53.

prosperous economy in Central Europe. Responses of envy and anger can be even more dramatic under such conditions.

Standards of compensation among emerging churches and national leaders are seldom set to insure parity among workers. The level of available personal financial support; the monies set aside for funding social security, retirement, and other employee benefits; technologically advanced ministry tools (computers, copiers, projection equipment, sound systems, etc.); and even privately owned automobiles and personal housing standards are not enjoyed in a uniform manner. Nationals who learn how to "work the West" often enjoy far greater prosperity than the rest of their colleagues. Envy is, therefore, not merely a cross-cultural issue; it exists within intra-cultural relationships too.

As Bonk observes, "Envy almost certainly operates most efficiently in regards to near neighbors. It is not directed toward the distant rich but toward the well-to-do with whom we share life and ministry most closely."[8] Generally speaking, we might expect that the closer the social ties among people of uneven means the greater will be the likelihood of envy to creep in and choke the hearts of even the most committed believers.

In the face of obvious advantages, missionaries are sometimes ridiculed behind their backs, subjected to malicious destruction or defacement of their property, or victimized by becoming the repetitive targets of opportunistic thieves. Missionaries with inordinate means occasionally may also be threatened with bodily harm. Such hostile treatment is hard for many Westerners to understand, and it occurs only to some that these evidences of envy, anger, and resentment are directly tied to our roles as Western purveyors of a gospel of abundance. When we lament our losses, in many ways we are merely grieving over the pain of self-inflicted wounds.

---

8   Ibid., 56.

We should not be surprised, as we attempt to share the gospel of Jesus from a position of privilege, if Western missionary lifestyle choices that flaunt financial advantage inspire contempt rather than conversions.

The Interplay between Affluence and Deference

The goal of the evangelical missionary, no matter the means employed, must be the telling, proclaiming, preaching, and sharing of the good news of Jesus with a view to convincing, converting, baptizing, and discipling men and women from every tribe, tongue, people, and nation. That goal is directly dependent upon our capacity to have our model of faith heard, understood, and followed by lost people from other cultures—even poor ones. That is why a missionary model of the Christian life that is imitable is so important. That is why it is so important that the Christian life modeled by the missionary be imitable. Affluence among Western witnesses is a great hindrance to the process of sharing the gospel, because the lifestyle in which we incarnate our message as Christians is too often inaccessible to our audience.

But not all missionaries are rich or Western. In most unreached areas of the world, Christian ministers from within the target cultures or from nearby societies have also pioneered the way. We have deigned to call these indigenous workers "national evangelists," "paid agents," or "native workers," while assiduously reserving the term "missionary" for those wealthy enough to do missions in the money-intensive Western way.[9] In effect, we generally hold that unless a person has enough money

---

9 I have maintained that practice in the context of this discussion for simplicity's sake. It is difficult to arrive at language to distinguish missionary expatriates from those native to the cultural contexts we are trying to reach with the gospel. Using words like *indigenous, native, national,* or *non-Western* to describe target populations is much preferred to previous popularized terms like *savage, barbarian, undeveloped* or *heathen peoples.* I trust that my desire to avoid offense in making a distinction between one individual's place of origin and domicile and another's can be received without attributing insensitivity to my intent. Being consistently politically correct is especially difficult when we are referring to people from multiple cultures and a variety of geopolitical nations.

to buy a return ticket for an international flight from the field and sufficient funding to live overseas as he or she is accustomed to living at home, that person is not a missionary.[10]

We often speak of mission mobilization from the Third World as if it were a recent phenomenon. We presume that missions naturally proceeds from the politically, militarily, and economically powerful centers of the world to those margins of global society that are either dominated or impoverished or both.[11] Our perspective degrades and denies the powerful, pervasive, and persistent witness of "national evangelists" who have manned the front lines of kingdom advance from the first century to the twenty-first century. Beginning with those scattered from Jerusalem to Antioch following the persecution of the church after Stephen's martyrdom to our own day, lay workers, indigenous Christians, native witnesses, and national evangelists have often carried the primary load of mission responsibility. It is time to put away the artificial distinctions made by degrading terminology and demeaning categorizations that serve to deny credit where credit is due. When we fully embrace the value of national workers, perhaps we will more fairly fund them as well.

Dr. Davorin Peterlin, a faculty member of Regents Park College in the University of Oxford, director of the Keston Research Institute, and former director of graduate studies at the Evangelical Theological Seminary in Osijek, Croatia, has argued for a change in terminology to reduce the degrading distinctions made when we reserve the title "missionary" for Westerners. He speaks with a strong and unapologetically cynical tone as he writes on this subject in an article entitled "The Wrong Kind of Missionary: A Semi-Autobiographical Outcry":

> In the West the ministry of *church organizers* is usually a full-time salaried job. In the non-Western world they also usually minister full-time, but without remuneration. The reason for this state of affairs is that national denominations have no funds for financing such positions. As a result, many able indigenous

---

10 Bonk, *Missions and Money,* 72.

11 Ibid.

Christians with gifts of administration or teaching . . . look for secular jobs to sustain their families. Furthermore, the efforts of indigenous *church organizers* are often regarded with disinterest or with a mildly patronizing attitude by foreign *gospel spreader* missionaries as they ride off into the sunset of more spiritually evangelistic efforts. And so it is forgotten that the *church organizers'* ministry of *making disciples* is as important as the *gospel spreaders'* ministry of *proclaiming the Good News.* . . . I propose that for purposes of financing, [indigenous] *church organizers* should be placed alongside [foreign] *gospel spreaders* in one large category of *Missionaries.*[12]

Peterlin's passionate outcry against the inherent injustice of usual mission community practice is offered in hopes that his perspective as a national leader will convince Western agencies that they "should recognize that there is a great need for, and good logic in, more active financial support of indigenous missionaries."[13] Peterlin actually goes so far as to say that Western support of qualified nationals (where such are available) should be given priority over funding expatriate missionaries. He asserts that such a shift will require the rethinking of our philosophical perspectives and long-term goals in managing mission finances—the very aim of the material I am offering here.

Nowhere in the world's marketplaces has the goal of "equal pay for equal work" found adequate expression. The workplaces populated by professional missionary "gospel spreaders" and national "church organizers" are unfortunately following the world's pattern in this regard. The benefit of full compensation that missionaries often enjoy but seldom earn by making a disproportionate contribution to shared ministry is out of reach for most indigenous workers. It need not be so. We cannot justly avoid consideration of this reality as we face the issues arising from the interplay of missions and money. The pretentious presumption

---

12 Davorin Peterlin, "The Wrong Kind of Missionary: A Semi-Autobiographic Outcry," *Mission Studies* 12, no. 2 (1995): 173.

13 Ibid., 174.

of a privileged role for Westerners is a part of the bad fruit born from the financial advantage enjoyed by many foreign missionaries. On closer examination, the injustices created by disparate compensation in the world of missions only make the issue loom larger.

The simple truth is that, all over the world, non-Western leaders often are proving more effective in producing both quantitative and qualitative church growth than many of their Western counterparts. Much of the West is increasingly becoming a mission field in its own right, and the flow of deference due to effective ministry should rightly be reversed in many situations. Honor should be extended to those from among the poor who have demonstrated their passion for God in the midst of impoverished conditions. They should be affirmed for their survival skills, which were developed long before supposedly more spiritually mature missionaries entered the scene. They knew how to live in harsh conditions before we ever came along! They possess contextual and cultural expertise that far exceeds our own. And they have their own "kingdom vision" for their own people. It should be our role to serve rather than to supplant that vision.

CHAPTER ELEVEN

The ABCs of
Compassionate Conservatism

In chapter 8 we explored the impact of Roosevelt's Lend-Lease program. The magnitude of America's investment in wartime provision for our World War II allies may have been offered in part for selfish reasons, as Roosevelt readily admitted. But the sheer scope of our investment was exceedingly generous nonetheless. The Lend-Lease Act no doubt helped to secure the eventual Allied victory over the Axis Powers. But US largess was not limited to wartime investment overseas. Our altruism was manifest after the war as well. When hostilities ceased, the Marshall Plan became the centerpiece of America's postwar diplomacy in Europe and the guide for global recovery.

Through this initiative, the spirit of generosity manifested in a time of war was matched when peace finally came. For our purposes, the postwar Marshall Plan offers a valuable model for modern mission involvement. I am proposing that Western Christians should adopt the general format of this historical philanthropic milestone as a guide for giving today. Our dilemmas over granting support in the interest of global evangelism would be greatly reduced if we were to create a "Missionary Marshall Plan" for the twenty-first century. To explore this possibility we must look at the parameters of the original agreement that rebuilt Europe after World War II.

George C. Marshall had been the Army Chief of Staff during the entirety of the war, commanding over eight million men and women in uniform and supervising all US military personnel, including senior theater commanders Dwight D. Eisenhower and Douglas MacArthur. When the war ended Marshall became a special envoy to China, appointed by President Harry S. Truman in hopes of negotiating an end to the civil war raging between communist forces and citizens loyal to Chiang Kai-shek. In 1947 Marshall returned to America and accepted a seat in Truman's cabinet, serving as Secretary of State until 1949. While in that role Marshall prepared a peacetime plan for global economic recovery, showing the same logistical and administrative brilliance that had characterized his military service.

In a speech offered at Harvard University's commencement ceremony on June 5, 1947, he first put forward the outline of the plan for rebuilding Europe and reviving the global postwar economy. Faced with massive starvation, a continent-wide recession, many of Europe's currencies virtually worthless, disruption of commerce at all levels, and severely reduced European industrial capacity—with manufacturing systems largely devastated and still awaiting rehabilitation—the world was paralyzed and longing for a viable plan for a return to normalcy. Marshall offered the template that was so desperately needed. Speaking with no podium and without referring to notes, the Secretary of State offered in a surprisingly brief and informal speech the outline of a game plan aimed at making individual nations in Europe prosperous again and self-sufficient in a recovered and robust world economic community.

Here's a portion of his speech:

The truth of the matter is that Europe's requirements for the next three or four years of foreign food and other essential products—principally from America—are so much greater than her present ability to pay that she must have substantial additional help or face economic, social, and political deterioration of a very grave character. . . .

It is logical that the United States should do whatever it is able to do to assist in the return of normal economic health in the world, without which there can be no political stability and no assured peace. Our policy is directed not against any country or doctrine but against hunger, poverty, desperation, and chaos. Its purpose should be the revival of a working economy in the world so as to permit the emergence of political and social conditions in which free institutions can exist. Such assistance, I am convinced, must not be on a piecemeal basis as various crises develop. Any assistance that this Government may render in the future should provide a cure rather than a mere palliative. Any government that is willing to assist in the task of recovery will find full cooperation, I am sure, on the part of the United States Government. Any government which maneuvers to block the recovery of other countries cannot expect help from us. Furthermore, governments, political parties or groups which seek to perpetuate human misery in order to profit therefrom politically or otherwise will encounter the opposition of the United States.

It is already evident that, before the United States Government can proceed much further in its efforts to alleviate the situation and help start the European world on its way to recovery, there must be some agreement among the countries of Europe as to the requirements of the situation and the part those countries themselves will take in order to give proper effect to whatever action might be undertaken by this Government. It would be neither fitting nor efficacious for this Government to undertake to draw up unilaterally a program designed to place Europe on its feet economically. This is the business of the Europeans. The initiative, I think, must come from Europe. The role of this country should consist of friendly aid in the drafting of a European program and of later support of such a program so far as it may be practical for us to do so. The program should be a joint one, agreed to by a number, if not all, European nations.[1]

Congress passed this plan in the form of the Foreign Assistance Act, and President Truman signed it into law on April 3, 1948—just ten months after Marshall's speech at Harvard. Over the next three years more than $13 billion dollars were invested in Europe. Even this tremendous sum was too small to remedy all of the continent's economic woes. But the Marshall Plan did encourage an unprecedented level of international cooperation among nations, some of which had been long-term wartime enemies. It also facilitated the free exchange of interstate commerce in Europe and helped to prevent the lingering hyperinflation that had followed the end of World War I.

A Revitalized Philosophy of Philanthropy

On June 5, 1997, Madeleine Albright, then serving as America's first female Secretary of State, represented Bill Clinton's administration when she too spoke at a Harvard graduation ceremony. On this occasion, the commencement celebration also marked the fiftieth anniversary of the introduction of the Marshall Plan parameters. In her remarks Albright reminded those present of the remarkably redemptive resolve America had displayed in 1947, and she called us to the same high standard in our day. She said, "Because the situation we face today is different from that confronted by Marshall's generation, we cannot always use the same means. But we can summon the same spirit."[2]

---

1   Speech available at http://www.georgecmarshall.org/lt/speeches/marshall_plan.cfm/.

2   Speech available at http://gos.sbc.edu/a/albright3.html.

I am suggesting the Western church should recapture, for the sake of world missions, the extraordinary spirit of American generosity that motivated the Lend-Lease program and that moved America to fund the Marshall Plan. It is time to revitalize America's philosophy of philanthropy so that our enormous national wealth (public and private) can serve kingdom purposes at home and abroad. If secular interests in the World War II era could inspire magnanimous investments in support of antifascist allies, why shouldn't spiritual interests move the church to make similarly generous investments globally today? The primary defense raised as an argument against Western infusions of funds in needy areas has been the self-supporting paradigm and the related desire to avoid creating dependency.

It is ironic that in a period when the West in general and America in particular are more interested in the spread of Christianity than any other people in history, and at a time when our nation is more financially able than any nation ever hoped to be to fully fund the cause of global evangelism, we would choose to limit our expression of generosity because of the ostensible danger of hurting the cause of Christ by helping others materially to the best of our ability. I am asserting that the reasons for our unreasonable restraint in missions giving are absurd, that they should be seen as abhorrent to selfless and servant-minded Christians, and that they should be abandoned. The unprecedented opportunities we face for the advance of the kingdom should be met with unprecedented openness to giving.

I am not, however, so naive as to simply call for the rejection of the three-self formula that has guided mission practice for so long. In the place of these outdated boundaries to our charitable intentions, new parameters should be developed to help define the scope of wise giving practices. But our goal should be the reawakening and release of a truly Christian spirit of grace and benevolence. We should seek to renew the philanthropic inclinations of our forbearers and to fortify them. We should find a way to give more rather than less, to go farther without fear, and to grace unreached cultures with the gospel of Jesus Christ in a measure far beyond all previous experience and far in excess of our present expectations. A Missionary Marshall Plan for the twenty-first century could point us in that direction.

Patterned after the simplicity of the original program that rebuilt Europe, I propose the following philosophical perspectives and practical principles for the Christian community's consideration. Like a three-legged stool, the approach to global giving I am recommending is supported by the following vital elements:

- a return to compassionate conservatism as a guideline for Christian charity;

- an understanding of the dynamics of covenant relationships;

- a commitment to Christlike generosity.

The first leg of this stool will be the focus of the remainder of this chapter.

Seven Marks of Compassionate Conservatism

In order to avoid creating an international welfare state as we consider infusing wealth from the West to the rest of the world, we must intentionally avoid giving indiscriminately to the "wayward poor" of other nations. We can learn to give wisely on a global scale if we follow Olasky's domestic advice and return to the principles of "compassionate conservatism" that ruled America's giving patterns when Social Calvinism held broader sway in our own culture. He suggests seven marks that characterized legitimate expressions of compassion in the eighteenth and nineteenth centuries. These qualities are presented in an alphabetically ordered acrostic that literally establishes the ABCs of wise giving patterns.[3] I offer his main ideas in a modified form that accommodates them to the mission application I have in mind.

---

3   Marvin N. Olasky, *The Tragedy of American Compassion* (Washington, DC: Regnery Gateway, 1992), 101–15.

- *Affiliation.* Interpersonal networks that offer support to indigent people provide the first wise ingredient of prudent philanthropy. The priority concern is to help destitute people rebuild human relationships before bringing them humanitarian relief. Getting to know those in need sufficiently well to recognize where their family and friendship circles have broken down is the place to begin lifting them up. Efforts to restore connectedness allow the fabric of family and friendship ties to be rewoven over time so that it may serve as a safety net that money alone could never buy. Nobel Prize-winning economist Joseph E. Stiglitz asserts that these relational connections are irreplaceable. "In the process of development, [we must] do what we can to preserve these bonds."[4]

Volunteer workers were the key to encouraging affiliation when private organizations were the primary caretakers in America's past domestic setting. In world missions, this role will likely be played not by volunteers but by vocational missionaries and development workers resident within unreached cultures. As Christ's ambassadors, they should focus on creating communities that can support people with chronic needs. The goal is to be in close enough contact with recipients of aid to be able to support their efforts to rebuild fractured families, to assist them in reconnecting with nearby neighbors, to help orphaned or abandoned children find care and comfort in the security of a home rather than an institution, and to offer the church as a kingdom refuge—a community characterized by love, acceptance, and forgiveness. Compassionate giving requires that we help desperate people reestablish affiliation with meaningful support systems before we lend material assistance.

As a member of the board of directors of Food for the Hungry, I can testify that this organization's "Vision of Community"

---

4   Joseph E. Stiglitz, *Globalization and Its Discontents* (New York: W. W. Norton, 2002), 84.

(VOC) is an example of a ministry methodology that marches under this priority. Food for the Hungry staff members world-wide are steeped in a corporate ethos governed by their VOC core values. These values assume that effective ministry must involve a strategy that simultaneously links leaders, families, and churches in any attempt to rehabilitate or revive a needy community. The VOC perspective shapes all of Food for the Hungry's development and relief efforts by making sure those efforts are consistent with a philosophy that connects these elements of community in every expression of compassion. VOC is a practical manifestation of the recognized priority for making affiliation central to relief and development projects.

- *Bonding*. As missionaries and relief personnel encouraging reconciliation and reconnection with the poor, it must be assumed that material support will be accompanied by our ongoing personal commitment. Remember that true compassion suggests our willingness to "suffer with" those in need. That distinction explains why *charity* was a suitable synonym for the word *love* in the English vernacular of bygone eras. "Bonding" presumes that personal involvement will be a hallmark of our benevolent philosophy, even in cross-cultural settings. A revitalized philosophy of philanthropy will require the mobilization of workers who are committed to incarnational ministry and to lifestyle choices that make close-up and personal contact with the poor easy to maintain.

Our goal is to share Christ's love. We cannot be satisfied with dispensing aid at a distance. We must develop a deep affection for and a personal connection with the people we serve. After all, Jesus made it clear that love would be the telltale sign of his disciples' true devotion to him as Lord. So the poor among the nations should be reconnected not only to the communities they inhabit—they should be linked to the world through our commitment of love. By bonding personally we become better able to help redemptively.

- *Categorization.* This aspect of compassion focuses on the very real necessity of continuing to distinguish clearly between the worthy poor and the wayward poor. Those who cannot work because of their age, health, or mental state should be comforted and treated kindly. The wayward, by contrast, should be helped only to find or to create job opportunities. They should not be readily offered relief in material terms. The process of categorization can be kept simple or made more sophisticated depending on the context of the work. Establishing appropriate circumstances to test the willingness to work, teaching social and employment skills, and evaluating reliability and accountability are three distinct parts of the categorization process. Personal referrals and background checks may also be included. The key to effective categorization is to be intelligent when acting on good intentions to help the poor, maintaining a distinction between the indigent and the indolent and offering the gift of industry as eagerly as the gift of mercy.

  Sometimes we may not be well enough informed to evaluate the legitimacy of a need. Our national brothers and sisters will likely be better acquainted with the circumstances and the people than we can be. Westerners must be ready to listen and learn from their more experienced indigenous colleagues in a way that reflects our respect for their native wisdom and their intuitive sense of the situation. Part of manifesting humility in the midst of our service to the poor involves our willingness to admit that "we do not know what we do not know." When our personal knowledge and experience in a given culture is limited, our need to listen well increases.

- *Discernment.* As Christians, we dare not engage in spiritual warfare without keeping spiritual weapons and spiritual armor close at hand. Gifts of the Spirit, including discernment, are part of the "divinely powerful" endowments God grants us for battling Satan's minions (2 Corinthians 10:3–5). We must seek spiritual insight in our work and avoid relying merely on human instinct and worldly wisdom. This priority assumes that we lend assistance without forfeiting our biblical bearings. We must not lose sight of the "lostness" of human beings. Our fallen nature is such that fraud comes easily when material resources are made available free of charge. In offering financial support, humanitarian aid, or church subsidies, we must act on Jesus' counsel to be wise as serpents and as innocent as doves (Matthew 10:16).

Spiritual discernment is aided by the practical steps taken to deepen relational awareness in pursuing affiliation and bonding as outlined above. We can also be forewarned by the mistakes of others, and we should avoid repeating them. As Olasky observes, one lesson from the welfare legacy in America is that "well-meant interference, unaccompanied by personal knowledge of all the circumstances, often does more harm than good."[5] Human judgment is limited to outside observance, but God sees into the heart. Keeping a spiritual component at the center of our compassionate response will make the care we provide more effective and more efficient.

Biblical discernment will also help us restrict material relief to those contexts where giving is truly an act of love that blesses the weak and not a boondoggle benefiting the wayward. Some practical guidelines borrowed from a nineteenth-century relief agency, the St. Louis Provident Association, can help us gauge the appropriate measure of response to the poor that we encounter in a variety of settings. Adapting the lessons learned locally in Missouri to fit our mission application, it is prudent to bear in mind that we should:

- Give relief only after personal investigation of each case.

- Give necessary articles and only what is immediately needed.

- Give what is least susceptible to abuse.

---

5   Ibid., 107.

- Give material aid always in lesser amounts than might be procured by labor (unless the need is the result of disaster, disease, or disability).

- Give assistance "at the right time" and only "for the right time." We should suspend support as soon as circumstance allows.

- Give only if the recipient agrees to abstain from drugs, alcohol, and immoral conduct while obtaining assistance.

- Give no longer when it becomes apparent that the recipient's work ethic or work interest is in serious question.[6]

• *Employment.* In the interest of long-term sustainability, the useful employment of all able-bodied heads of households must remain a higher goal than offering aid. In effect, relief workers should desire that their constituents should quickly work them out of their role as support providers by assuming responsible and rewarding jobs. Olasky notes in very certain terms that "labor is the life of society, and the beggar who will not work is a social cannibal feeding on that life."[7] Even when grants supply funding for temporary relief, aid recipients can be required to work in service to the immediate community in return for the help they get, whether that community is a neighborhood, barrio, or refugee camp. This is possible even when the local economy provides no easily available job opportunities.

One African leader told his neighbors, "You have no money and no jobs. I also have no money, but I can give you jobs. I want to start a school and I need your help." The community followed his vision and started offering classes for children

---

6   This list of guidelines is adapted from pages 22–23 of the third annual report of the St. Louis Provident Association, published in 1893. The original list is quoted by Robert and Jeanette Laver in an article entitled, "Will a Private War on Poverty Succeed? The Case of the St. Louis Provident Association," *Journal of Sociology and Social Warfare* (March 1983): 16.

7   Olasky, *Tragedy of American Compassion,* 109.

that otherwise would have had no educational opportunities. In short, they chose industry over idleness. We too should encourage workfare over welfare whenever possible. Aspirations to productive labor should make even a poor-paying job preferable to poverty or prolonged personal support. The dynamics of "redemption and lift" should also make those being won to Christ and discipled in faith increasingly employable over time (see the first endnote for chapter 3, on page 48). When all else fails, Paul's principle for the unemployed should be employed with the able-bodied poor: if a man will not work, then neither should he eat.

- *Freedom.* This element of compassionate conservatism does not suggest everyone should be allowed to do as he or she pleases. Freedom in an economic sense is an observable component of the environment for working people, not the liberty to do our own thing at all times. Free enterprise presumes the opportunity to make a career of what one chooses, to labor in a location of one's own preference, to negotiate a fair day's pay for a fair day's work, and to aspire to transition out of the labor force to serve as an employer—if one so desires. Freedom in this sense also includes the opportunity to work and to worship without government restriction or criminal coercion.

Ron Sider recognizes this element of economic justice as well. In *Just Generosity,* he writes, "Justice in economic relationships requires that people be permitted to exchange and use what they own—including their own time and energy and intellect as well as material objects—freely so long as in so doing they do not violate others' rights."[8] Freedom in the workplace grants everyone access to the lowest rungs in the employment ladder and rewards those who desire to climb for their hard work, education, vocational training, and marketplace experience. Freedom

---

8 Ronald J. Sider, *Just Generosity: A New Vision for Overcoming Poverty in America* (Grand Rapids: Baker, 1999), 55.

allows the investment of long hours and the virtues of good character to move almost anyone out of poverty over time.

Our commitment to freedom in the marketplace means that we promote justice and equity and that we stand up for the poor against oppression, nepotism, favoritism, and inequities that keep them in poverty.

- *God's grace.* God is the ultimate motivation for all redemptive expressions of mercy. A burden for others that moves us to sacrifice is a benevolent reality born of the Spirit. God grants the power to make wealth (Deuteronomy 8:18) and prompts our desire to share what we have earned. God's grace is the last element mentioned in this list, but it is certainly not the least meaningful component of true compassion. Because God is personal, knowable, and all-powerful, he can put the seal on social relationships by teaching people what it means to live in a covenant family serving the King of Kings and Lord of Lords. With God's help, our passion for right living is empowered, our character is reformed and strengthened, and our responsibility to others is embraced. Redemption brings lasting change to individual lives and to whole communities. God's power to transform extends even to the most depraved and deprived human beings. God's promise of *shalom* and our vision of sharing his peace combine to give all persons hope when they also embrace faith and love. God's compassion is the foundation of our covenant with him.

God's compassion demands redemptive change. Through the indwelling Holy Spirit, God motivates, supports, and sustains changes in our inner being. Emulating him, our compassion must also promote personal revival and renewal. Our goal is that by lending a helping hand we might restore those who are fallen and helpless to self-respect and self-support. Remember, our calling to transformational development is pursued in hopes that God will use us to help unreached and impoverished people find true identity, true unity, and true destiny in and through the Creator who empowers us all.

Moving beyond the ABCs of compassion, we must proceed to the 123s of covenant keeping if cross-cultural giving is to be fully released and fully redemptive at the same time. Walking in covenant, despite disparities in wealth, is the second leg of the revitalized philanthropy stool.

CHAPTER TWELVE

The 123s of
Covenant Relationships

From the experiences of sixteen years of ministry in Bosnia, the following are the most helpful insights I can offer for those desiring to relate to nationals from a biblical covenant perspective rather than from a business partnership paradigm. Operating in a covenant dynamic was made possible for us because of our intuitive attempts to pay attention to the ABCs of compassion ministry early in our exposure to Bosnians. Because we had worked at affiliation, bonding, categorization, discernment, and freedom, and because God was at the center of our relational commitment to our national neighbors, trust levels between indigenous leaders and our missionaries have generally been high.

Notice that *employment* was left out of the list of efforts we have made to this point in working in the spirit of compassionate conservatism. That is because Bosnia's economy has not yet recovered from the ravages of war. Relief and development agencies have, for the most part, lost interest in this desperately troubled and still deeply divided country. They have moved their staff and relief resources to other global trouble spots, such as Kosovo, Afghanistan, Iraq, Indonesia, and the Sudan. The humanitarian NGOs are gone, but human need is still very much present.

Sixty-five percent of the Bosnian work force remains unemployed, which is more than twice the number out of work at the height of America's Great Depression. Jobs are scarce and money is in critically short supply for many. To make our challenges even greater, the earliest converts we won to Christ were from the less educated and less skilled segments of society. We are still experimenting with micro-enterprise projects and job-creation alternatives. Economic recovery will come in time, and employment of nationals will one day be a larger part of our experience in Bosnia. While we look for future job-creation strategies that will work in this broken economy, we are committed to making sure that we do not miss the present opportunities God is providing for spiritual impact beyond employment.

The Unique Aspects of Our Covenant with Bosnians

Beyond our commitment to giving according to the dictates of compassionate conservatism, we work alongside Bosnians as brothers and sisters in covenant rather than as partners in a contractual relationship. As the nationals have reinforced repeatedly, we are first and foremost sons and daughters of the same Father. So we labor alongside each other more as members of God's family than as colleagues sharing a business venture. Some of the important elements of our covenant commitment with Bosnians include the following:

1. Our sense of covenant begins with *a joint agreement on pursuing a common goal: advancing the kingdom worldwide in fulfillment of the Great Commission.* Our missionaries and the

national ministry leaders are fully committed to the creation of an indigenous church planting movement in Bosnia as one aspect of that common global goal. All of us know that establishing this country's new churches and equipping its emerging leaders makes Bosnia the beginning, not the end, of our joint efforts. Nevertheless, establishing the church in Bosnia is the first mission priority for us all.

2. Our covenant commitment to move beyond Bosnia with a global vision *defines in principle an exit strategy for our mission to Bosnia.* Because the whole world is on God's heart, the whole world must be on our hearts too. We have agreed that we will eventually extend our mutual efforts beyond Bosnia's borders, taking the gospel to other unreached peoples. When that time comes, we will not end our relationship; we will pursue mission together in a new context! From the beginning of our work during the war, we have consistently clarified for all parties that as Westerners we are a temporary help to the national church and should not be viewed as a permanent resource. It is our intention, at the earliest possible opportunity, to leave Bosnia in a new mission mobilization aimed at another unreached people group in cooperation with Bosnian missionaries. In Venn's terminology, this recognized goal is an expression of our covenant commitment to the "euthanasia" of our mission in Bosnia. Though the timing of our exit from this field to the next is left uncertain, the terms of our departure are known to all.

3. In our covenant relationship, *paternalism has no place.* We walk as brothers and sisters, coequal children of one heavenly Father, serving a mutually agreed-upon agenda. No special deference is due Westerners because of our relative wealth. Bosnians are generally viewed as wiser than us in understanding their own culture and in strategizing how to reach it. We are governed in our relationship with nationals by the transformational development perspectives discussed earlier in this book. As Westerners,

we serve as learners under the blessing, approval, instruction, and counsel of the national leadership.

All our efforts are bent toward building the national church and serving the national agenda, not our own ministries. Therefore we do not hire national workers to serve as our employees. We endeavor to build up national workers and support them financially as we are able and as the national presbyters ask us to do so. The initiative remains with the national leaders when it comes to identifying and funding new vocational workers, who in turn serve the developing indigenous churches and not our agency. We don't give money to individuals. Rather, we support national churches, which then hire their own staff directly. Westerners are generally discouraged from assuming any ministry roles that can or should be performed by national leaders. If a Westerner is put into a functional role in support of a national church, every effort is made to train a national replacement in the shortest possible time frame.

4. In our covenant relationship, *we are committed to extravagant generosity.* That is, all parties to the covenant have a responsibility to give all possible resources to serve the mutually agreed-upon agenda. This foundational commitment to maximum giving means that we are holding back nothing within reasonable capacity that could help the church planting movement in Bosnia advance. Anything in the way of possessions or personal expertise that might help us achieve our mutual objectives is made available for the mission we share. All contributions have value, no matter what their magnitude and no matter what their nature. *Money is neither the only nor the primary measure of worth to this team effort.* Contributions of funds do not buy influence or control for the donor churches, agencies, or individuals from either culture.

Because our church and mission are relatively small, we actively recruit other US churches to join in bringing missionaries and material aid to Bosnia. The resource potential of our "small bucket" is therefore reinforced by our efforts to bring "more and larger buckets" to the field. We have recruited more than twenty other American churches that now share a focused commitment to Bosnia. While my mission was created by a church of just over two hundred members, I led this coalition of larger churches called the Bosnian Church Planting Fellowship (BCPF) for a number of years. One of the BCPF churches has twelve thousand members; yet during my tenure their mission leadership readily accepted my service as director of our consortium. This kind of mutual submission without regard to resources and size is an inherent aspect of our covenant relationship. The BCPF churches are in regular fellowship together (meeting twice a year in the United States), and we encourage each other to honor the covenant dynamics we have promoted in Bosnia.

5. In our covenant relationship, *the most contextually relevant parties take the lead.* They do this in ways that affirm and utilize everyone's gifts, experience, calling, vision, passion, and credibility to their maximum potential. Leadership influence is not dependent upon the relative size of anyone's resource pool. In recognition of this reality, we have generally allowed national leaders in Bosnia to set the agenda and take the initiative in advancing our mutual service in support of a church planting movement designed to reach the entire country. The national leaders have prioritized a list of more than forty Bosnian cities that have no Christian witness as targets for church development. We have tried to raise money for the projects they desire to pursue, including the acquisition of church facilities. When adequate funds are available, they have identified the properties they think are worthy of consideration. They have also negotiated the purchase terms and they hold title (as a denomination) to the properties purchased.

This arrangement only makes sense given that their insight pertaining to real estate matters in Bosnia is more contextually relevant. When it comes to theology, they appreciate the unique contribution Westerners can offer because of the seminary training many missionaries have enjoyed. In this area, we have been their teachers. On the other hand, Bosnians have a better understanding of how best to interface with government officials, so they help us often in that arena. We have more experience with issues touching on church governance, so they seek counsel accordingly on occasion. In effect, we try to submit to each other's strengths and to protect each other's weaknesses as we walk in covenant. This kind of give-and-take is a valuable part of our approach to shared ministry.

6. In our covenant relationship, *all parties are agreed that all churches (whether Western or indigenous) should be accountable—even if they are self-supporting, self-propagating, and self-governing.* From our perspective, being *indigenous* does not equate to being *independent.* We are committed, along with our national partners, to remain accountable at some level for our stewardship of all human, material, and monetary resources entrusted to our care. Accountability is, therefore, a part of all covenant relationships and not an evidence of hierarchical positioning.

Stewardship is a serious responsibility in our covenant, and it is made more effective when supported by accountable relationships that extend beyond reporting on financial matters. Therefore, in appropriate settings and at regular intervals, all leaders (nationals as well as expatriates) willingly share how they are doing in their ministry progress, their family systems, and their personal walk with the Lord. Almost all my interactions with national leaders begin with their expressions of genuine interest in my personal life. That interest is usually shared in questions they raise about my spiritual health and my family—not about our joint ministry. Because we are partners in covenant we are committed to one another at a personal level. We care, we share, and we offer prayer in support of one another. I have learned from Bosnians that time spent over meals and enjoying their beloved Turkish coffee is best reserved for building intimacy, not for the business of ministry. They are teaching me what personal commitment in covenant should look like.

7. In our covenant relationship, *initiative for developing new vocational workers, planning and implementing new projects, and launching programs for new facilities development originates with national leaders rather than with expatriate missionaries.* Westerners are free to offer their ideas, experience, and creative thinking, but the national leaders have the final say in strategic planning for most new initiatives. We are there to serve the indigenous leaders' agenda, not to establish a competitive plan of our own.

Let's take our approach to financial accountability in providing funds for national workers as an example. In the interest of promoting healthy financial management, a national presbytery approves all ministry assignments for national workers in Bosnia. As I mentioned in the third point above, vocational workers are identified and mobilized by national leaders rather than Westerners. The four-member national presbytery also sets support levels for indigenous staff, even if their workers are funded from outside sources. Those workers are employed by the national church and answer to national leaders in their assigned responsibilities. To the best of our abilities, no monies are permitted to be passed to individuals or to churches in Bosnia without prior approval from the presbytery.

The US churches participating in the BCPF are accountable to this priority. In honor of our sense of accountability, all Western partners are asked to give a monthly financial report to the national presbytery revealing all funds flowing from their ministries to any project, person, or church in Bosnia. The contribution of Western cash does not increase missionary clout. Competency, character, consistency, and commitment are the qualities that increase influence in our covenant relationship.

8. In our covenant relationship, we have agreed that, *in the interest of sustainability, Western investments in programs and facilities will be approved only after careful evaluation of the national church's capacity to maintain, manage, and operate the ministries created by the proposed investment of funds.* This is a vital step in trying to insure that the project being funded can be kept going after an initial investment is made. A project is not sustainable if its viability rests on the need for ongoing outside support. To illustrate, consider the issue of facilities development in Bosnia. Our mission has helped the national church acquire five different buildings over the past decade. We have generally, however, not given additional funds for operational support or maintenance after the initial purchases were made. In all cases, national leaders have managed not only to maintain but also to substantially improve the facilities we helped finance. They are sustaining the properties we helped them acquire.

9. In our covenant relationship, *biblical principles of stewardship and financial management are taught to all members associated with national churches.* It is expected that a commitment to generous living and liberal giving in support of the Lord's work will be embraced as a high personal priority for every follower of Jesus. Western missionaries endeavor to model this priority in their own lifestyle choices and in the personal example they offer to others. Nationals reflect the same priority in their own stewardship decisions.

Covenant Keeping and Kingdom Economics

It may be helpful to share how our investment experience over sixteen years is working to bless our church in the United States as much as the churches we support in Bosnia. When we adopted Bosnia in 1989, the missions giving for our church totaled approximately $89,000 per year. This sum was provided through faith-promise giving by a congregation of just over two hundred members. Over the course of the last decade we have created a 501(c)(3) nonprofit corporation, alongside our local church, that helps to facilitate mobilizing long-term missionaries under our own auspices. We now combine our faith-promise giving with other donations to our mission organization from inside and outside our church to estimate our total giving to Bosnia. Members of our church may not *give all* these resources directly, but our church does *get all* the funds that we then send on to the field.

Our giving had risen to $380,000 per year in 1997, when I wrote my first book recounting our journey to Bosnia.[1] Since that time we have raised as much as $1.2 million in a single year for the mission in Bosnia—still representing the flow of funds through a small congregation hovering around two hundred people. Our missions giving has regularly approached $1 million a year. We do the possible in raising funds for Bosnia and God keeps doing the impossible by multiplying our resources, even providing "manna from heaven" at times![2] The funds raised have been spent for the support of US missionaries, for compensating national workers, for special projects, and for the acquisition of facilities for four churches, a drug and alcohol rehab center, and a Bible school in Mostar. The covenant commitment our church made to missions has benefited Bosnians, but it has also catapulted us to a level of giving most American church watchers would find impossible for an assembly our size.

I believe our experience demonstrates that God's kingdom economy works on an entirely different basis than the world's financial system. Supernatural provision only comes and kingdom dynamics only "kick in" if we operate on the biblical principles of grace and lavish generosity. We need not fear that pouring out resources will eventually cause our supplies to be drained, because God promises that giving will generate blessing so great that our store will overflow! Remember Jesus' promise, "Give, and it will be given to you. They will pour into your lap a good

---

1   John Rowell, *Magnify Your Vision for the Small Church* (Atlanta: Northside Community Church, 1999), 224. Available at Amazon.com.

2   See chapter 5, "Manna from Heaven," of *Magnify Your Vision for the Small Church.*

measure—pressed down, shaken together, and running over. For by your standard of measure it will be measured to you in return" (Luke 6:38). The promise from Scripture is that our cup will run over rather than run dry as we keep giving sums of money away. In Luke 12, Jesus tells the story of the "rich fool" who hoarded his possessions rather than sharing. The point of the parable is that we should focus not on laying up treasures for ourselves but on being rich toward God (v. 21; see also vv. 33–34). The dynamic of blessing seems to be predicated on our willingness to tap into God's supernatural supply by intentionally moving to meet others' needs.

This is an Old Testament as well as a New Testament concept. In Proverbs 11:24–25 Solomon explains, "There is one who scatters, and yet increases all the more, and there is one who withholds what is justly due, and yet it results only in want. The generous man will be prosperous, and he who waters will himself be watered." Similarly, in Malachi 3 God exhorts Israel to be generous and to stop withholding their tithes, a practice God characterizes as robbing him. Malachi declares the Lord's invitation for Israel to consider the viability of the kingdom supply system through which giving results in greater blessing. God speaks through the prophet's pen, saying, "Test Me now in this [and see] if I will not open for you the windows of heaven and pour out for you a blessing until it overflows" (v. 10). *God disdains rich fools and robbers and delights in robust givers. The kingdom economy is activated when we move in generosity!*

Our experience verifies this aspect of kingdom living. I believe our capacity to give has been increased because we keep seeking ways to be more generous. I am convinced that the influx of God's supply usually awaits the outflow of our generosity. As churches and individuals participating in kingdom dynamics, we are designed to be rivers—not reservoirs—when it comes to managing God's resources. Western means are often limited because we set miserly limits for our giving. The reality is that most large and small churches alike have room to magnify their vision for their capacity to give!

Let me share a couple of examples from our journey in Bosnia to show how infectious a generous spirit can be in a missionary context. Included in the church facilities we have financed in Bosnia is a building for a congregation in the Evangelical Church denomination in Sarajevo and another for a second-generation church plant in the nearby town of Breza. Both properties were acquired in 2003, for $150,000 and $70,000, respectively. Interestingly, our ministry initially had raised $220,000 to secure the Sarajevo church's building, but after nearly twenty months a suitable site in that price range had not been located.

In the interim the Breza church found an ideal building for its ministry at an extraordinarily favorable price. But the new church plant had no funds for the purchase. So the parent congregation in Sarajevo asked permission to share the gift we had raised for their building with the church it had planted. Asking our blessing on this act of benevolence was a courtesy, not a matter of control. In their integrity, the national leaders were sensitive to our intent as donors when we gave them money for their building, and they felt accountable to us for the possible use of these funds in a different application. With our hearty agreement, they gave nearly a third of their resources to bless a daughter church with a building before they had secured one for themselves.

That act of extreme generosity was clearly going to make the Sarajevo church's search for property more difficult, but deciding "to give" under these circumstances was in the best interest of the national church planting movement. So the Sarajevo leaders put the interests of others before their own. That's what people in covenant always are inclined to do! Within a short period of time, the Sarajevo church leaders discovered a perfectly located new property listing as it first came on the market; and they were able to negotiate a purchase price within the limits of the funds they had left after buying the building in Breza. Now both churches were blessed with new facilities to highlight their presence in the respective communities they serve!

Following these acquisitions, late in the summer of 2004 the Sarajevo church communicated the need for installing a central heating system for its three-story building. They had saved $4,700 of a total project cost of

$8,200 from their own offerings over the preceding year. An appeal for help in funding the needed heating system came in August, not because the nationals in this church were unwilling to wait and to save the balance required, but because winter was fast approaching and alternative methods of providing heat temporarily would drain funds already set aside for a permanent solution to the problem.

Our American partners, individuals and churches alike, responded quickly to meet this modest request for special project funds. In fact, so many small gifts were offered to complete the heating system that soon more money was coming in than was needed. Pastor Slavko Hadzic immediately asked our mission to stop forwarding funds to his church. Instead, he and his leaders suggested that we consider redirecting these resources. Could he have used more money for other refurbishing needs his building required? Certainly. But just a few miles down the road, the Breza church was faced with the same winter weather dilemma. The small-town congregation required $6,000 to install a similar central heating system in order to be prepared for the cold temperatures that were soon to come. Remember that Sarajevo and its surrounding communities hosted the 1984 Winter Olympics. These people understand what winter weather means! The believers in Breza had saved $3,500 toward their need. They asked for nothing from the West. But Pastor Hadzic was aware of their challenge, and in his usual selfless manner he made an appeal for help on their behalf. Could gifts provided for his church be redirected to this nearby congregation's need? Our immediate answer was yes!

Brothers and sisters committed to walking in covenant care for each other's interests as much as for their own—even before their own (Philippians 2:3–4). They steward material resources sacrificially. They don't "buy and keep"; they give as often as they can and as liberally as they can. This is not a reflection of dependency—it's a covenant dynamic! Mladen Tomicic, the pastor in Breza, was grateful when we indicated that he could expect our ministry to fund the $2,500 needed to finish his heating project. But when the church in Pennsylvania that collected the funds for this grant sent the money, they gave $3,000 rather than $2,500.

The mission director who sent the check explained the extra gift this way, "My reason for suggesting $500 more than requested is that there are always added, unexpected expenses in projects like this. (Don't we know?!) I want to be sure there are enough funds for Mladen to complete the job."

Do you see how the grace of giving became contagious in this instance, infecting Western donors, national pastors, and Bosnian churches alike? Positive experiences like this are the reason why I get so frustrated with the constant cautions others offer regarding the "dangers of dependency." Giving done wisely need not be a disaster—it should advance the kingdom and multiply blessing on all sides!

The grace that flows from giving is a kingdom reality we are supposed to see in operation regularly. But we experience such examples all too rarely in modern missions. I believe we often miss out on the blessings God intends (for givers and receivers alike) because we have missed the truth that generosity is the starting point of the kingdom economy. Sacrificial giving has always been the impetus for extending the gospel. It was so even with God's part in initiating the plan of redemption: "For God so loved the world that he gave!" So should we! As we do so, we are wise to offer support with discernment and in the context of covenant relationships. It is not helpful simply to throw money at people we know only casually in an effort to solve a problem we understand only minimally. The ABCs of Social Calvinism and the 123s of covenant relationships can guide us toward better ways to give generously over longer periods of time. Following these guidelines, perhaps more Westerners can learn to help without hurting our indigenous brothers and sisters.

The Missionary Marshall Plan, the third leg of our revitalized philanthropy stool, offers still more insight into how we can make generous giving a blessing rather than a curse.

CHAPTER THIRTEEN

A Missionary Marshall Plan for the Twenty-First Century: Part I

Four Principles for Those Who Send

The proposal I am making here is not intended to provide a detailed strategy that will satisfy the needs of every possible mission context in the world. Rather, I am offering principles for maximizing Western investment in world mission warfare while minimizing the downside we associate with the misuse of welfare at home and abroad. As I have asserted before, my goal is to promote sustainability and minimize our concerns about dependency at the same time. Sustainability will be addressed more directly in chapter 16.

To Give or Not To Give?

As we proceed, the reader should bear in mind the foundations laid in all the forgoing material, but especially the content of the last two chapters. The tenets of compassionate conservatism and the dynamics of covenant relationships are the backdrop against which I wish now to unveil the design of a Missionary Marshall Plan for the twenty-first century.[1] I am using the key concerns that George C. Marshall had in mind in 1947 as a structure for the outline below. Review with me the key components that guided Marshall's articulation of the American response to Europe's pressing needs following World War II:

- He observed that it was "logical" for the United States to assist other nations.

- He was responding to a world that was characterized by "hunger, poverty, desperation, and chaos."

- He was searching for "a cure" for the problems Europe faced, so he therefore called for a comprehensive solution to the world's needs, rejecting piecemeal steps.

- He advised massive investment in a time of turmoil, when investment involved greater risk than in less troublesome times. Marshall desired to help restore confidence in the viability of future peace and prosperity in postwar Europe.

- He was willing to cooperate with any government available to partner in a shared vision for the recovery process.

---

1   In choosing to use the Missionary Marshall Plan as a template for actions appropriate in making wise use of money in modern missions, I am trusting my readers will not be put off by the choice of a model provided by this great leader from the World War II era. Though George C. Marshall was indeed a great wartime general, I am especially intrigued by the change in direction he managed as a peacetime leader in his postwar career, retiring from the army to pursue diplomatic service as the US Secretary of State. In our day it is not politically correct to favor examples from war leaders or to militarize our language. Here I am affirming Marshall for his leadership as a man of peace, and I am drawing on one of the most magnanimous examples of American generosity extended toward the world in all our history as a nation. I trust this choice will add weight to my call for a more generous spirit in our own era, rather than detract from it.

- He aimed at relief that would help imperiled people help themselves toward recovery.

- He wanted the initiative for the plan to flow from Europeans rather than Americans.

- He presumed America should help because we were uniquely able to do so and because the needs of most European nations far exceeded their own ability to pay for aid.

- He sought to establish a joint effort that would bring governments, political parties, and civic groups together in common cause. Acting in a spirit of reconciliation, he saw no room for politics or personal prejudice to play a part.

Interestingly, for all the goodwill Marshall intended, not all nations were excited to join in his recovery proposal. The Soviet Union and its new satellites in Eastern and Central Europe wanted no part of a capitalist plan. Under heavy-handed Soviet influence, the Iron Curtain countries refused to participate. The Free World's concern over communist expansion, and the general sense that Stalin's government fit Marshall's description of an administration intent on perpetuating "human misery in order to profit therefrom," created a circumstance that disqualified the Soviet Union and its satellite nations from participation in any case. As a consequence, the inevitable chill in the air over Europe gave way quickly to the Cold War realties that would endure more than four decades. The tension between East and West was so pronounced that the formation of the NATO alliance for Western European security purposes ensued in 1948. So only the democratic leaders of Europe responded to Marshall's call for action by convening a meeting in Paris to frame a response to the Harvard speech. They did so urgently, gathering not five weeks after Marshall made his initial proposal public.

History is a good teacher! Just as the rift between the communist and capitalist states started in earnest when the Marshall Plan was proposed, it would be naive to think that a spiritual version of that original vision for magnanimous giving would be any better received today. Embracing a shift in established ideology or philosophy of ministry is simply hard for many people—even when a change is truly in order. Peter's paradigm shift (from Hebrew ethnocentrism) in Acts 10 and the Jerusalem church's negative response (in Acts 11) to his newfound and God-ordained openness to fellowship with Gentile Christians is a good biblical example of this kind of reluctance to change. I therefore expect this proposal for change to meet with mixed reviews.

As Solomon so wisely puts it, "There is an appointed time for everything. And there is a time for every event under heaven" (Ecclesiastes 3:1). More specifically, he says there is "a time to keep and a time to throw away" (Ecclesiastes 3:6). I believe we have come to such a time for change, and I hope to describe the means for a redemptive shift in perspective and practice in supporting world missions. For any Christian individuals, churches, mission agencies, or nongovernment organizations willing to join me in calling for a more aggressive policy of assisting indigenous leaders in winning unreached peoples to Christ and for those eager to offer their maximum material contributions in alleviating human suffering, I offer the following nine principles (in two parts) as an outline for a Missionary Marshall Plan for the twenty-first century. Let me begin with four principles that apply uniquely to those who send missionaries to unreached and impoverished peoples living in the harshest conditions prevailing on our planet.

The Principle of Primary Responsibility

Nothing close to massive mobilization of resources for world missions will ever occur until local churches realize that it is not only "logical" for them to assist in reaching unreached peoples but that this is a God-given mandate they have somehow overlooked. It is time for churches to reclaim the primary responsibility for completing Jesus' plan for world evangelization.

When the church I founded embarked on the road to Sarajevo, we were attempting to play a small part in reaching the unreached Muslims of Bosnia. We did not intentionally set out to do this work on our own initiative following a synergistic, church-based mission paradigm. As we were sovereignly led into this methodology, however, we have become increasingly committed to the principle that *mission ministry is the primary responsibility of the local church and only secondarily the purview of professionals serving in mission agencies.* The nature of "parachurch" ministries should dictate that agencies come alongside the local church in fulfilling this responsibility rather than to co-opt or compete with it.

The assignment of primary responsibility for global evangelism is not left unclear by Scripture. In Acts 1:8, for example, Jesus repeats the mandate of the Great Commission by reminding the apostles leading the Jerusalem church, "You will receive power when the Holy Spirit has come upon you; and you shall be my witnesses both in Jerusalem, and in all Judea and Samaria, and even to the remotest part of the earth." This reiteration of God's call to take the gospel to all nations and to advance the church throughout the world was issued to a handful of leaders presiding over a local assembly of only 120 people.

Jesus' audience on this occasion was not comprised of hale and hardy workers eager for the challenge of global outreach. The eleven men charged to lead were ordinary, uneducated people who were in no way confident of their competence for the task. They were frightened by the events of the immediate past, uncertain about the security of their present circumstances, and timid about taking the future by storm. Their response to Jesus' words was not to hurl themselves headlong into a hostile world. Instead, they hid themselves in a secret upper room with just over a hundred other frightened Christians. Even after the Spirit's power came at Pentecost, they ministered only in Jerusalem—apparently apprehensive about mobilizing to take the gospel to the four corners of the earth.

Their reluctance is understandable. What local church, especially a small one, would be bold enough to presume that a worldwide scope of ministry lay within its reach? Like these early disciples, most of us who lead small churches in the twenty-first century feel ill-equipped, unprepared, under-resourced, and overmatched when we are urged to consider taking a full share of responsibility for the remaining task in world mission. Contemporary leaders of small churches are easily able to identify with the reticence of these first apostles and their followers.

But we should also be urged to identify with the eventual success enjoyed by that first small church in Jerusalem. In spite of their meager numbers and the enormity of the task to be done, God's Spirit empowered them to serve his purposes and Jesus proved faithful to his promise to build his church through them. I firmly believe the Lord Jesus wants to do the same through us today, whether we are part of a large church or a small one.

Until churches accept the primary responsibility for world mission and the corollary duty of mobilizing a maximum supply of human and financial resources for that purpose, global evangelism will remain a secondary priority and we will choose more often "not to give" rather than "to give" to this cause. Under the present realities, where agencies are generally left to lead the way, even most "mission-generous" churches in reality give minimally to global outreach. We can become "mission-minded" again, however, if we begin to think, act, strategize, mobilize, and give as if the whole of world mission success depended only on our own congregations. That was the mentality that ruled in the first century, guiding the church in Jerusalem and then in Antioch to get serious about their role in this impossible task! Churches willing to move in that direction again could change everything.

Our local church is an example of the fruit that such a shift in perspective can produce. Because we considered Bosnia "our unique responsibility," our local body of two hundred members gave multiplied millions of dollars to missions in just over a decade. Our mission commitment has generated almost three times as many vocational workers on the field in Bosnia as we have in Atlanta; and our annual budget for global ministry is 200–300 percent of our local budget, depending on the demands of a given year. Few churches of any size are coming close to that kind of commitment. Far fewer churches are beginning to touch their potential in funding missions. They are not even trying to explore greater possibilities because they do not see missions as one of the central contributions God intends them to make to the kingdom. If the Missionary Marshall

Plan is to work, local churches will need to reclaim this role, acting (and giving) as if global outreach is their primary responsibility.

The Principle of Providential Provocation

The second foundational principle for this plan tells us that it is important to seek a focused objective for each local church desiring to minister among unreached people. Relatively few Western churches have "adopted" a specific people group to labor among. In 1947, Marshall could easily point to Europe because the whole continent had been ravaged by war. Everyone in America was aware of the loss of life sustained by the combined armies of the Allied and Axis Powers—over sixteen million dead! Adding the destruction of cities, factories, mines, and railroads all over Europe, knowing where to aim our efforts in relief was simple then. That is not always the case in global mission today.

Most churches have no clue where to point their plans for cross-cultural involvement, even when they determine to make them. Without a particular people in view, it is impossible to make a maximum contribution to the world mission war effort. Too many churches aim nowhere and end up doing nothing exceptional in global outreach. Others try to act but their efforts are indiscriminate. They aim everywhere and consequently do little of substance anywhere. So how should we decide where to focus our efforts? I suggest that we often can find the greatest need and the greatest opportunities if we look for areas that are experiencing the greatest trauma. We should, in effect, look for what I call "providential provocation."

The Jerusalem church did not immediately move toward the mission fields of Judea, Samaria, and the remotest parts of the earth just because Jesus conveyed that responsibility in Acts 1:8. Instead, the apostles, and those who followed them, timidly remained in the familiar confines of Mt. Zion until persecution literally pushed them out of their city. In Acts 8:1, following the martyrdom of Stephen, we are told that all the members of the Jerusalem church (except the apostles) were scattered throughout Judea and Samaria. Saul, and probably other Jewish zealots who opposed the early church, used intimidation, incarceration, and brute force in an attempt to extinguish the light of the gospel before it could penetrate the world's darkness.

God used governmental and religious persecution to get the Jerusalem church actively involved in the mission mandate. He made first-century believers into refugees in an effort to mobilize them to the uttermost parts of the earth. They initially moved involuntarily and under duress as God provoked them to obedience to the Great Commission. I have come to believe that such instances of "providential provocation" should be viewed as *divine direction toward doors that have been sovereignly opened for new ministry efforts.* This principle points the way toward people and places where potential for fruitful ministry is enhanced by God.

In Bosnia, circumstances that the natural eye could only see as disastrous proved to be the divine means by which God intended to advance his church. Our eyes of faith should be able to discern this kind of providential provocation in a variety of situations that can make unbelievers uncharacteristically open to the truths of the Scripture. Political upheaval, military conflicts, economic reversals, relational stress, famine, and natural disasters are some of the events that magnify human suffering and heartache around the world. Such hardships often work to open the hearts of those who most need the love of God and who have been most closed historically to the message of salvation available in Jesus' name.

Let me be clear as we talk about the impact of providential provocation. I am not recommending an opportunistic strategy that would make missionaries into professional proselytizers who capitalize on other people's pain. Rather, I am urging mission-minded church and agency leaders to be spiritually discerning about the circumstances God is using to create a special openness to his Spirit's offer of healing, hope, and eternal life. In the hardest of circumstances, Christians should commit themselves for the long haul, incarnating the gospel and introducing unreached masses to the power and purity of the Master's message of saving grace.

Patrick Johnstone, perhaps the world's foremost prayer researcher, has for decades mobilized specific intercession for all the nations through his regularly updated *Operation World* prayer guide. In another book, *The World Church Is Bigger than You Think,* he has offered a helpful analysis about the relationship between crisis and opportunity in evangelistic ministry that reinforces the point I am making here. Referencing Jesus' teaching in Matthew's Gospel, Johnstone focuses on the Lord's prophecy concerning end time troubles yet to come upon the earth: wars and rumors of war, nation rising against nation, famines, and earthquakes. All these signs Jesus characterized as *birth pangs,* not *death knolls.* They are part of God's grand plan for redeeming the world, a plan in which negative circumstances are an essential component.

Johnstone states, "Somehow [God's] redemptive purposes are worked out in love, but also in the context of tragedies that open hard hearts and break down barriers to the gospel. One fact has become clear to me in my gathering of information from around the world; the sound bites and the news flashes on our television screens do not tell the full story. God is doing an unprecedented work in our day. [That work is] not occurring in spite of disasters but because of them."[2]

We must be poised and responsive without delay when God's hand moves to open a door for the gospel through providential provocation. If we follow the leading of the Holy Spirit, chaos will create "*kairos* moments." *Kairos* is the Greek word for times of special opportunity, pregnant periods in human history when God's people can capitalize on events orchestrated by the sovereignty of God for the sake of the advance of the kingdom. When hard times are shaped by God's hand to make people more receptive to the gospel, we should be prepared to share—materially as well as spiritually—with those who suffer. We should also expect that many will accept the truth of the claims of Christ as they experience his love through us. As we offer, and they accept, practical support from our presence and our provision in dealing with

---

2 Patrick Johnstone, *The Church Is Bigger Than You Think* (Great Britain: Christian Focus Publications/WEC, 1998), 10–11.

their desperate difficulties, we all will discovery that God still ordains divine appointments for kingdom purposes.

The Principle of Preeminent Grace

A third principle underlying this Missionary Marshall Plan touches on the issue of resource allocation in the face of extraordinary need. In 1947, Marshall suggested that piecemeal solutions were inadequate. They are in our day as well. We must mobilize sufficient resources to effect a cure rather than merely to trifle with a society's symptomatic needs. With the combined material stores of an entire nation available at his discretion, Marshall's call for a huge response made sense from an earthly perspective. But for most churches and mission agencies, access to money and humanitarian aid supplies seems to be far more restricted. Few individuals, churches, or agencies can routinely draw on giant treasuries as they respond to missions opportunities around the world. We do have, however, the unfathomable depths of God's grace from which to garner resources.

I had never viewed the phrase from Romans 5:20—"where sin increased, grace abounded all the more"—as a statement with missiological implications until we began our work in the midst of Bosnia's war. But involvement in the context of this conflict soon changed my mind. From the very beginning, we encountered military force, ethnic cleansing, mass rapes, concentration camps, torture, genocide, war crimes, ethnic hatred, and religious animosity. All these horrors came our way before we even began to imagine how we might move our people into this war-torn mission field. The overwhelming evil amassed in this bedeviled place made the obstacles in our path unimaginably difficult. Even the secular media discerned the uniquely desperate context Bosnia had become. One ABC television news special dubbed Bosnia "the land of demons."

But demons should never deter the determination of our mission priorities! We entered Bosnia in the name of Jesus, the Lord of Hosts. We went forward with his authority and power. We were serving the purposes of the one who purposes to offer deliverance from every stronghold hell can devise. I am embarrassed to admit how feeble my faith was as we took our first steps on the road to Sarajevo. We advanced with timid caution, always feeling concerned that the Spirit of God was speeding the pace of our journey beyond our capacity to keep up. By his might, however, every crooked way was made straight and every obstructing mountain and hill was made low. By his grace we made steady progress.

Reflecting often on the unmerited favor God has demonstrated on our behalf, we have come to recognize that Romans 5:20 does indeed have definite missiological implications. "The Law came in so that the transgression would increase; but where sin increased, grace abounded all the more" The English rendering of the Greek words Paul chose to use does not do full justice to the contrast the apostle is trying to communicate. Paul uses two different words for "increase" or "abound" in the second part of this verse. Where sin "increases" (*pleonazo*), grace is caused by God to "abound," or "increase," "all the more" (*huperperisseuo*). More literally, the text might read, "Where sin increases incrementally, grace is lavished overwhelmingly." Grace multiplies exponentially wherever sin is added to the environment. Greek scholar, Kenneth S. Wuest, catches this nuance as he offers an alternative rendering of this phrase in his helpful word study book. He translates this part of the verse, "Where sin increased (*pleonazo*), grace super-abounded, *and then some on top of that*" (italics added).[3]

Think for a moment about the point Paul is making here. This verse promises that wherever demented human beings or the demons of hell sow evil on the earth, and in whatever measure, we can expect God to produce a far greater supply of grace. That is to say, the harvest of wheat sown from heaven will always outstrip the yield of tares sown from hell—if the church will simply till Satan's ground in the power of the Spirit. This principle from Romans 5:20 teaches us that *wherever sin is poured out, grace can be released in preeminent proportions.* But

---

3 Kenneth S. Wuest, *Wuest's Word Studies from the Greek New Testament, Volume One* (Grand Rapids: Eerdmans, 1984; first published 1973), 88.

God's guarantee of preeminent grace is often contingent upon the mediating presence of his people. Sin can't win in situations where Christians sustain their witness for the kingdom of God. If we are willing to take our message of saving faith in Jesus to the hellholes of the earth and remain there, grace will overcome evil every time. That's the missiological promise inherent in Romans 5:20—the persistent hope of those who believe in God's ability to provide preeminent grace.

If we want to be effective in missions today, if we prefer to do mission service where the Spirit of God is most anxious to break down barriers to faith in Jesus Christ, we should remember the principle of preeminent grace. It teaches us that we should not be looking for easy assignments, but for opportunities in the places where evil is being visited upon the helpless with unprecedented viciousness. Where satanic forces and sinister people are most malevolent, the grace of God's Spirit promises to be the most magnificent. It is in the heart of darkness that God's light will shine the brightest. The demonstration of God's ability to overcome evil with good is one of the special fruits of his special favor. The principle of preeminent grace should give missionaries boldness to choose the most difficult places to serve. It is in the haunts of hell that heaven will most clearly prove its power. In such places the grace of God will grant us victory—if we will abide persistently, suffer patiently, and stubbornly refuse to lose heart.

One of the evidences of God's preeminent grace in our journey toward Sarajevo was his repeated willingness to provide "manna from heaven" when we had no resources to draw on. God's supernatural supply of a $3 million facility for our church in Atlanta—an outright gift, funds for vans for the team on the field, and resources for acquiring buildings in Bosnia are examples of how the Lord made it possible to sustain extravagant giving along the way. His grace truly did super-abound to us over these years![4]

---

4   Again, see chapter 5, "Manna from Heaven," of my book *Magnify Your Vision for the Small Church.*

The Principle of Prophetic Investment

When Marshall called for a massive infusion of resources into Europe, the whole continent was essentially bankrupt. Traditional economic theory and the terrible postwar circumstances made this whole region a decidedly unattractive investment locale. But the Secretary of State knew that only great commitment from America could generate great confidence in Europe's future. The recovery he envisioned would require considerable risk. The subsequent outpouring of $13 billion ($100 billion in today's terms) jump-started Europe's economic engine and drove a continent-wide recovery that is now legendary. Giant leaps of faith of similar magnitude are often required in mission settings. The future risks we must run in order to reach the unreached world will sometimes be completely irrational. But they need not be irresponsible or unfruitful.

Consider our experience in Bosnia when we made our first really large investment, just after the Dayton Peace Accords established an uneasy truce ending four years of fighting in the fall of 1995. Even though Implementation Force (IFOR) troops seemed suddenly omnipresent in Bosnia by early 1996, lasting peace was not yet assured and Sarajevo was not yet safe. It was in that uncertain moment that a new ministry opportunity was presented for our consideration. We had been in touch with the leaders of the Evangelical Church denomination in Sarajevo for over a year by this time. This small but stalwart assembly of a handful of believers had survived the war together and had managed to continue meeting for Bible study and encouragement all through the years of siege. Under the threat of constant shelling, they had taken refuge in the shadow of the cross and had even led others to faith while fighting raged on day after day.

Now that the war was over, this growing assembly needed a place to meet. More importantly, the church needed a visible location to be identified with its Agape humanitarian aid ministry. We were asked at that time to raise $125,000 to purchase property for the Sarajevo Evangelical Church. Before the smoke had completely cleared from recent shelling, this church's vision had come sharply into focus.

To Give or Not To Give?

I remember visiting Sarajevo in January 1996 to inspect the proposed church site near the center of the city. The three-story building
filled only one quarter of the plot of land it occupied, leaving ample room
for expansion. The structure was one of very few in Sarajevo showing no
appreciable damage from the four years of daily bombardment that had
scarred so much of the city. Sheltered by surrounding high-rise apart-
ments, the small community of believers were convinced this was the
perfect place for them to establish a tangible presence for their tenacious
congregation.

I wondered about the wisdom of making a real estate commitment
in the most beleaguered city in the world. As we wound our way to and
from the proposed church property, the roads were still lined with empty
cargo containers, burned-out buses, and disabled tramcars stacked like
cordwood three and four high. These makeshift walls throughout the city
made use of the useless wreckage of war to provide important protection
from indiscriminate enemy fire. The building was just a block away from
"sniper's alley." It was hard to believe that this was really a reasonable
proposal to consider. Soon I was to see that God's ideas don't have to be
reasonable in order to be wise and responsible.

As I thought and prayed about the request being made of us, I was
led to review an unusual passage in Jeremiah 32. The story this text re-
counts occurred in the final days before the fall of Jerusalem and the resulting Babylonian captivity. Jeremiah had long since been prophesying
the imminent overthrow of the Holy City and the coming deportation to
Babylon. The prophet's faithfulness to his message of doom and gloom
had evoked the personal wrath of King Zedekiah. Jeremiah was therefore
being held under house arrest in the king's court while Zedekiah tried
desperately to avoid the fulfillment of Jeremiah's vision of impending
disaster.

The circumstances Jeremiah faced were very similar to those in
Sarajevo in 1996. Both cities had been under siege for an extended period of time. Both were surrounded by hostile armies whose intentions
were anything but good. Neither city was a safe place to be making long-

term plans—especially not long-term plans for real estate investment. But that is exactly what God had in mind for Jeremiah.

The prophet had heard the Lord commanding him to buy a parcel of ground in Anathoth just as the doom of Jerusalem was approaching. Under these circumstances, one would think that Jeremiah was uncertain that he was really tuned in to the voice of the Lord. But God confirmed the command by sending Jeremiah's cousin with a specific invitation for the great prophet to redeem his uncle's property precisely at this perilous time. Jeremiah then confidently grasped the idea that God had in mind a prophetic investment in Israel's territory.

It seems obvious to me that Jeremiah never assumed he would enjoy a vacation home in Anathoth when he bought this lot. *His interest was in posterity, not in prosperity.* The passage makes this clear. Jeremiah purposely made the closing on this real estate transaction a very public and profound event. Gathering witnesses and long-lasting clay jars, the prophet had the deed signed, sealed, and stored away as a testimony to God's promise for the future. The city would indeed fall. Its inhabitants would indeed become a complete desolation. But houses and fields and vineyards would be bought there again, and the city would later be re-settled. God was confirming his promise to that end by causing Jeremiah to act in a manner that confounded his countrymen.

Jeremiah's "prophetic investment" was a divinely designated illustration, a token of the promise that God's plan for Israel's eventual return would surely come to pass. The nation would be punished, but by God's power his people would also be preserved. The Lord was sending them into captivity, but he would also call them back again in due time. Was such a sequence of events possible? Jeremiah 32:17 gives an unflinching answer for anyone lacking faith in this prophet or in the word of the Lord: "Ah Lord God! Behold, You have made the heavens and the earth by Your great power! . . . Nothing is too difficult for You." This text from Jeremiah opened my eyes to the principle of prophetic investment. *Somehow, in God's economy, it is prudent to acquire property in perilous places.* As God wills, such purchases can have prophetic impact.

The Missionary Marshall Plan will require visionary investors who will respond when they are asked to give generously for kingdom purposes—being prompted by faith in what the Spirit says rather than prevented by fear due to what their eyes can see. In God's economy, prophetic acts take priority over prudent assessments at times. Just ask Jeremiah! Prophetic investment will be required to build God's kingdom among unreached people in the twenty-first century, just as it was on the brink of the Babylonian captivity and in the aftermath of World War II.

CHAPTER FOURTEEN

A Missionary Marshall Plan for the
Twenty-First Century: Part II

Five Principles for
Those Who Go

Turning attention from those who send to those who serve as missionaries among the unreached poor, I offer five additional principles that I believe will help Western stewards of immense means to better enable their indigenous brothers and sisters to advance their own kingdom agendas within their own cultures. Like Marshall's plan for rebuilding Europe after World War II, our twenty-first century plans for effective mission must be aimed at helping the unreached poor help themselves. The poor and the unreached need our friendship as much as our finances, and for that reason alone we begin this chapter focusing again on the priority of establishing covenant relationships.

The Principle of Personal Covenant

The 123s of covenant keeping in our mission context were covered in chapter 12, so they need not be reiterated here. Suffice it to say only this much more: Pioneer ministry among unreached peoples is a marathon commitment, not a sprint. When we mobilize in response to *kairos* moments, we must enter new fields with a long-term presence in mind. Success will be achieved through the relational connections produced by long-term incarnational approaches to sharing the gospel. *Ministry under the vision of a Missionary Marshall Plan must, therefore, be covenantal and not merely commercial or contractual.* In twenty-first century missions, we are not establishing *business connections in foreign cultures;* we are establishing *brotherly connections in the kingdom of God.* The difference is qualitative.

Let me illustrate how easily contractual arrangements can frustrate covenantal aspects of relationship in modern missions. I met a missionary couple recently who were in a situation where a poor single parent was blessed to be employed as their full-time nanny. The nanny was a believer and had soon become a valued sister in Christ and trusted friend as well as a household servant. Her care for the children she was hired to attend in the missionary family rivaled her care for her own two children. Reassignment then took the missionaries to a new field. Employment was hard to come by in the nanny's impoverished context; so, in deference to the nanny's need for a stable a source of income, she was invited to move with the missionaries to their new ministry assignment. The nanny felt blessed to maintain her job and the missionaries were glad to be a blessing (as employers), even as they benefited from the continued domestic support the nanny provided.

The fact that the nanny was leaving her own two children behind, in the care of other family members, in order to remain a servant to her missionary employers seemed to go unnoticed and unaddressed by all. From the posture of the poor nanny, this arrangement made sense economically. It also made sense from the perspective of the relatively well-to-do missionaries who were enjoying a service in both field assignments that they could not have afforded were they assigned to minister in the United States.

Were the missionaries in this instance acting in the spirit of biblical covenant relationships? Might there have been a way to employ the nanny and allow her children to remain with her as she serves her role as a part of the missionaries' larger *oikos*—their extended family circle? Was this arrangement driven by kingdom values or by the dynamics that the domestic servant culture found virtuous in this context?

I believe that focusing on covenant practices instead of business principles will lead us to better decisions for missionaries *and* the impoverished people they serve. The primary point is that in covenant relationships money is not the thing that matters the most and compassion is not the concern that counts the least. The commands of the kingdom call us to higher ground and to healthier relationships, in which loving concern for the well-being of others transcends concerns for self. In the kingdom, women and children have great value and are not to be made the victims of plans formed after human wisdom—as seemed to be the case with this nanny.

The Lord makes it clear, in fact, that love is to be the hallmark of our ministry motivations (John 13:34–35). As a result of love, indigenous leaders come to know that we are committed because we care and that we are dedicated to doing all we can to eradicate the oppressions and injustices that keep people locked in cycles of deprivation. We are of no value to the poor if we serve as bystanders who simply feel their pain and pity them. We must commit to being present and personally connected so that we can suffer with them until the kingdom has come and their culture has been revolutionized by Jesus. This kind of personal, covenantal, and incarnational approach to reaching the unreached is an integral part of the Missionary Marshall Plan.

The Principle of Purposeful Promotion

For far too long Westerners have presumed to fill the senior seats of authority in guiding the global mission agenda. That role is passing and oversight by indigenous leaders is becoming a practical reality in global outreach. Nationals will increasingly lead the way in world missions as this century progresses, and well they should. *Granting indigenous leaders their rightful role in governance in their own cultures is imperative, and purposeful promotion of nationals is the right goal to pursue.*

Too often we do analysis with professional proficiency and then presume to speak for those we assume have no voice. As Bryant Myers states, "This implies that the poor are unable to diagnose their own situation and that they, in truth, have no advocates of their own. This does not have to be the case and, in ensuring that it is not the case, a transformational frontier may be crossed. The poor will be less poor when they learn to do their own analysis" and to speak for themselves.[1]

All one has to do to grasp the significance of voices that speak from within a culture is to recall the impact that leaders like Mahatma Gandhi, Martin Luther King, and Nelson Mandela have had as spokesmen for their own oppressed peoples. Their contextual relevance and their critical eloquence were more revolutionary than any outside influence ever could have hoped to be. The impact of their lives came in large part because they spoke for their people from an insider's vantage point. We are wise to help people see their potential to follow in the footsteps of such great reformers.

Indigenous people need to be taught to see with spiritual eyes and to speak for themselves and for God's kingdom from within their native cultures. It is important in this process that we not impose our understanding of Scripture on our national neighbors. Part of empowering indigenous people is releasing them to develop their own theological perspectives—to add a "fourth self" to the three-self paradigm, mak-

---

1   Bryant L. Myers, *Walking with the Poor: Principles and Practices of Transformational Development* (Maryknoll, NY: Orbis Books, 1999), 124.

ing room for their role in "self-theologizing." This kind of respect for indigenous people is a reflection of good discipleship, in my opinion, and therefore a valuable aspect of good missiology. A deferential attitude that promotes the potential of native leaders to guide ministry reflects the reality that in the kingdom of God the natural order of things is usually reversed. Those whom the world sees as powerless populate the kingdom: the poor (Luke 6:20), the meek (Matthew 5:5), and the persecuted (Matthew 5:10).

Care should be taken that we reinforce the strengths latent in a native culture and that we not inadvertently add to an already present sense of hopelessness, helplessness, and disempowerment among the poor. Our goal should be to help those whom we serve to see their history in the new light of the gospel. We must allow them to discern the ways that God has always been at work among them: seeking them, blessing them, and preparing them for a better future aligned with the kingdom. By promoting the capacity that nationals possess to perform their own self-analysis and to develop their own contextually relevant understanding of Scripture, a positive mindset can be developed that lays foundation stones for long-term transformation of the indigenous culture.

From Myers' World Vision experience, he offers a few key questions that may help us remain positively focused as we pursue our missionary calling in various cultures around the world.[2] Summarizing his suggestions for "appreciative inquiry," one might ask:

- What life-giving, life-embracing forces do you have in your community? What gives you the energy and the power to change and to cope with adversity?

- Thinking of the last one hundred years of the community's history, what has happened that you are proud of, that makes you feel you have been successful?

- What are your best religious and cultural practices? What traditions have helped you when times were tough?

---

2   Ibid., 177–78.

- What do you value that makes you feel good about yourself?

- What skills or resources have enabled you to do things your children will remember you for having done?

These sorts of questions fuel the dynamic of redemptive self-analysis and help shape an affirming assessment of our task in missions. An attitude of "purposeful promotion"—a mindset that appreciates national believers' competencies, valuing their sensitivity to the guidance of the Holy Spirit and their desire to pursue their own sense of destiny in the Lord—is more effective than our best efforts as outsiders to lean on our own understanding in guiding their spiritual development. Our recognition of national leaders' ability to problem-solve in their own settings will be part of the successful completion of world evangelism. This conclusion has historical precedents worth noting.

America could well have assumed a superior stance as Marshall led our national response to unprecedented international need for reconstruction and rehabilitation. But he was wise enough to *defer* rather than to *dominate* in the process that addressed the crisis in Europe following World War II. In his Harvard speech he said, "It would be neither fitting nor efficacious for this Government to undertake to draw up unilaterally a program designed to place Europe on its feet economically. This is the business of the Europeans. The initiative, I think, must come from Europe." And it did! Marshall purposefully promoted established European leaders and in the process he communicated his confidence in their capacity to perform. Leaders from Europe stepped up almost immediately to begin drafting a response to America's invitation to take the initiative in strategic planning. They led the way to their own recovery and found success sooner because the process depended mostly upon their own visionary vitality.

In conceiving a Missionary Marshall Plan for the twenty-first century, I am suggesting that we need to assume the same deferential posture today that America took when Marshall called forth the creative capacities of European politicians in 1947. If we are courageous enough to purposefully promote non-Western leaders, we will likely see national pastors demonstrate the same extraordinary qualities of leadership their political predecessors mustered in postwar Europe. Credible Christian voices from the non-Western world—no longer content simply to plead for the privilege to lead—have begun to insist that the time has come for native leaders' rightful influence to be recognized and released. This trend can be seen in the writings of K. P. Yohannon, René Padilla, Vinoth Ramachandra, Vinay Samuel, Kwame Bediako, David Tai-Woong Lee, Orlando Costas, and Samuel Escobar, among many others. They are harbingers of the increasing influence of non-Western leaders on a twenty-first century understanding of missions that is only now coming forcefully to the forefront of debate.

David Tai-Woong Lee, a mission agency director from Seoul, Korea, states overtly that missiology done from the West alone is no longer adequate. He shares his sense of a consensus among several Third World Christian leaders attending the Iguassu Consultation on Missiological Issues (hosted by World Evangelical Fellowship in October 1999), predicting that the influence of Third World leaders will soon be so significant that "most of the missiological text books written from a Western perspective will become obsolete."[3]

The drastic shift in the locus of the global evangelical church to the Southern Hemisphere and the rapid growth of the Two-Thirds World mission force demand a change in perspective. Peruvian leader, Samuel Escobar, observes the emergence of a "post-imperial missiology," a new approach to the practice of global outreach in which Western domination is gone and the contribution of nationals is fully engaged. In the new reality, "Third-world churches are seen as agents and originators of missionary effort [offering] a missiological reflection that is valid in its own right."[4]

---

3   David Tai-Woong Lee, "A Two-Thirds World Evaluation of Contemporary Evangelical Missiology," chapter 9 in *Global Missiology for the 21st Century: The Iguassu Dialogue,* William D. Taylor, ed. (Grand Rapids: Baker, 2000), 135.

4   Samuel Escobar, *The New Global Mission: The Gospel from Everywhere to Everyone* (Downers Grove, IL: InterVarsity, 2003), 108.

In the Missionary Marshall Plan, it is therefore "neither fitting nor efficacious" for Westerners to continue imposing their will in missions. Initiative in non-Western cultures rightly belongs to the indigenous leaders native to them. Their prerogatives and primacy should be supported, not supplanted, by Westerners. I readily acknowledge that giving nationals the opportunity to guide their own path into the future does not guarantee a powerful outcome. But biblical history would seem to stand in favor of optimistic expectations. After all, turning to a twenty-first century missiology that promotes spiritual proclamation by the poor represents, in essence, a return to first-century methodologies for missions.

In that early era of Christian history, a marginalized church with no political support and no economic power base advanced the gospel from a position of abject weakness. In the end, first-century believers turned the known world upside down. The same result may well be reached today if we recognize, release, and honor the leadership capacities of Christians from non-Western cultures.

The Principle of *Paraklesis*

As we honor the initiative and insights of national leaders, what role are Westerners to play in the Missionary Marshall Plan? Our rightful place is to stand at the side of national leaders, not above them nor under their feet. Whether they are poor or rich, our role is to support their leadership inclinations as best we can. We are most valuable to them when we are most available to aid in their success in ways they find meaningful. We should serve them just as the Holy Spirit serves us. We should be the chief advocates of their personal potentials and the best champions of the possibilities latent in the plans they propose. We should help empower them for greater service than they could achieve acting alone.

From a biblical perspective, it is interesting to note that Jesus used the Greek word *parakletos* in describing the role that both he and the Holy Spirit would play in the life of all believers. And in 1 John 2:1 the word is used to comfort the readers of the apostle John's first epistle: "My little children, I am writing these things to you so that you may not sin. And if anyone sins, we have an Advocate (*parakletos*) with the Father, Jesus Christ the righteous." The Greek word in this context is used in its classical connotation, conveying the sense of a defense attorney allied to our side in a legal dispute. In his *Word Studies in the New Testament*, Marvin R. Vincent notes that the advocate is "one who strengthens the cause and the courage of his client at bar."[5] An advocate encourages, defends, presents truth to support our case, and promotes our cause in a manner biased toward insuring our success.

The same Greek word is used in John's Gospel repeatedly in reference to the Holy Spirit. In most English translations, a broader connotation is considered and the word is rendered as "Comforter," "Helper," or "Counselor" rather than "Advocate." These alternative renderings imply a less classical and more literal sense of the word. *Parakletos* is derived from the Greek roots *para*, "alongside," and *kaleo*, "to be called." Thus, the Holy Spirit as Comforter or Helper or Counselor is called alongside believers to aid in their service for Christ and his kingdom. This connotation lends itself to the picture of someone who "suggests true relationship to our minds, and true courses of action for our lives, who convicts . . . the world of wrong, and pleads our cause before God our Father."[6]

A *parakletos* is essentially a committed ally. When Jesus speaks of the Holy Spirit as the *parakletos*, he explains how the Spirit will fulfill the promise of God's presence with us for fellowship and for personal support. The Comforter is an aid in our weaknesses (Romans 8:26) and, being God, is "a very present help in trouble" (Psalm 46:1).

Another member of this Greek word group is *paraklesis*, which can be rendered "comfort," "encouragement," or "consolation." In the Missionary Marshall Plan, it is a *paraklesis* role that Westerners should play—though admittedly from the posture of an equal as opposed to one vested with the power and sovereignty of the Holy Spirit! We should

---

5   Marvin R. Vincent, *Word Studies in the New Testament* (Mclean, VA: MacDonald Publishing Company, n.d.), 244.

6   Ibid.

simply come alongside to serve as allies in battle and support, enable, encourage, counsel, and advise as friends and family members. As Escobar suggests, we should aid nationals "by applying biblical principles of reciprocity, solidarity and mutuality [so that] poor Christians will be empowered to become agents of their own liberation, not passive recipients of handouts. . . . Today missions should consist of service—service both of the spiritual in proclaiming the Word and of the physical in meeting human needs. . . . In this new era of globalization this means new patterns of cooperation and new forms of partnership."[7]

Let us identify and practice "the principle of *paraklesis*" in ways that will help our indigenous brothers and sisters penetrate their own cultures for Christ's sake. Our acts of support will vary from one context to another, but in every circumstance they will allow Westerners on the mission fields of the world to emulate Jesus' passion to serve rather than being served. In this approach to ministry, the Missionary Marshall Plan will be instrumental in putting an end to the "imperial missions" practices of the past.

The Principle of Proportional Sacrifice

The foundations for this principle have been introduced in the forgoing material sufficiently to require little additional clarification. The concept is too important, nonetheless, to be left out of the necessary elements that are integral to the Missionary Marshall Plan. Gaining a sense of parity in ministry is predicated on all parties cooperating in joint outreach efforts with resolve to make a maximum contribution to the common objective. Money, manpower, language acumen, managerial expertise, contextual credibility, and native knowledge of the culture are all valuable aspects of pioneer ministry and of holistic response to the unreached poor. In the same way that America honored the Allies' contribution to the joint military effort during World War II, Western mis-

---

7   Escobar, *New Global Mission,* 148, 154.

sionaries must honor the meaningful contribution of national Christians to world missions today.

This will not be accomplished until we succeed in renewing our minds so that we raise our estimate of the relative value of nonmaterial contributions to the cause of missions. In a warfare mentality, the principle of proportional sacrifice suggests a commitment to maintain a measure of disciplined austerity at home, to exhibit extraordinary generosity abroad (in support of troops in the field), and to value a devotion to unity that mandates high regard for all allied support of the common effort. Just as God's Word declares the extraordinary value of widow's mites, mustard seeds, and little jars of oil, we must become convinced that proportionate worth in the kingdom of God is not a function of personal wealth.

Proportionality in giving is determined, therefore, not by what we have invested financially in a kingdom venture, but more by what we have kept for ourselves. This calculation will help us see how insidious our propensity for buying and keeping really is. In God's economy, treasure is accumulated not by saving for a rainy day but by sacrificing for kingdom initiatives. Material security is found not in maintaining our financial reserves but in meaningfully sharing our personal resources.

The widow's mite was considered lavish because the desperately needy woman kept nothing for herself. If we would like to get a better glimpse of the proportionality of our giving, I have a suggested formula: We should *divide what we saved by what we gave* every time we make a donation. The resulting quotient will show whether we are selfish or sacrificial. The higher the quotient, the lower our proportionate commitment to the work of missions.

Evaluated on this basis, Americans do not fare very well in an analysis of relative generosity. Consider the statistics presented earlier that indicate US believers keep more than 97 percent of their wealth. We tend to assume Americans are unusually generous givers, but it appears that proportionately our contributions represent little real sacrifice. In terms of total dollars, American giving may be comparatively prodigious.

When viewed in light of the wealth we *retain*, however, our giving reflects a relatively paltry sum.

Following this proportionality formula, Westerners will see better the true limits of their generosity. This approach to analyzing altruism may also help us acknowledge and affirm that the contributions nationals make to our mutual objectives in mission are far more sacrificial than we have recognized. In the revealing light of proportionate reflection, Westerners will likely conclude that nationals are by far the more dedicated donors. In this aspect the Missionary Marshall Plan is designed to clarify the true measure of Western generosity, dignify the disproportionate giving of the poor, and honor the nonmonetary wealth and inherent worth that indigenous people bring to the mission enterprise.

The Principle of Peacemaking Prayer

In presenting this last element of the Missionary Marshall Plan, I want to return to the warfare perspectives discussed in chapter 8. We are not merely soldiers in the cosmic conflict raging over people's hearts and minds. As Paul tells us in 2 Corinthians 5:18–20, we are also ambassadors, with a special role to play as we confront unreached cultures with the claims of Christ. In that role we have been given both "the word of reconciliation" and "the ministry of reconciliation." We are called, effectively, to show a world that is inclined toward war how to live in peace. Jesus, the Prince of Peace, compels those who follow him to love strangers and enemies as readily as they love neighbors and themselves. The transforming power of Christ and the Holy Spirit call us to tear down all walls of partition and to put enmity (not our enemies) to death (Ephesians 2:14–15).

Using Miroslav Volf's simple but profound language to describe what it means to live with a "reconciliation perspective," we may say that we are to embrace the "other" rather than live in ways that exclude those alien or hostile to us. This reconciliation mandate applies as readily to historical enemies as it does to present friends. In an act of embrace inspired by the Spirit of God, "the open arms of the 'father' receiving the 'prodigal' son and the healing embrace of the Jew by the Good Samaritan" are the images that must shape our mission.[8] The act of embracing acknowledges the reality that God has no enemies whom he does not love. Following our Lord's lead, neither may we. We are under God's divine calling to live with a genuine commitment to a reconciliation perspective. We are called to embrace rather than to exclude the others around us.

But this sort of "embrace" is not simply a sentimental process. "God's love for us and our neighbor can be a tough, truth-telling, there are consequences, your soul is in danger kind of love. But there is never hate; the enemy is never demonized or declared hopeless. The offer of grace is always there."[9] Reconciliation, not retribution, is ever God's redemptive goal. So we, his ambassadors, must lean in this loving direction. That is the strategic priority at the center of our divinely ordained diplomatic mission. Reconciliation must, therefore, be at the heart of the Missionary Marshall Plan. In the spirit of reconciliation, not only the message of our ministry but its various means should be bent toward encouraging peace.

Cultivating a reconciliation perspective will also force us to focus greater energy on "strategic intercession." This is the term John D. Robb and James A. Hill use for specialized prayer calling for the supernatural suspension of hostility, hatred, and warfare between individuals and between nations. In their book, *The Peacemaking Power of Prayer*, they write about the importance of intercession in our pursuit of peace and reconciliation.

In war, there is such a thing as a preemptive first strike which seeks to destroy the enemy's capacity before he is able to unleash his own assault. Sun Tzu's *The Art of War*, the ancient

---

8   Miroslav Volf, *Exclusion and Embrace: A Theological Exploration of Identity, Otherness and Reconciliation* (Nashville: Abingdon, 1996), 29.

9   Bryant L. Myers, *Walking with the Poor: Principles and Practices of Transformational Development* (Maryknoll, NY: Orbis Books, 1999), 51.

Chinese classic on military strategy still read by war planners today, says: "What is of supreme importance in war is to attack the enemy's strategy. . . . Attack plans at their inception." We believe that in spiritual warfare, the same principle pertains. It is much better to be proactive rather than reactive. Knowing full well that the number of complex humanitarian emergencies is on the rise, God's people need to have a preemptive prayer strategy to deal with them. . . .

All human progress has occurred through the adoption of new paradigms or ways of thinking about reality which have enabled human beings to be more effective in dealing with the challenges we face.[10]

In introducing this Missionary Marshall Plan for the twenty-first century, I am aligning myself with Robb and Hill in their assertion that progress in global evangelism, as with all aspects of human history, requires new ways of thinking about reality. It also depends on the priority we give to prayer. That is why this last principle links intercession and initiatives aimed at reconciliation under the power of peacemaking prayer.

In seeking new ways of thinking about world mission, it is high time for us to move beyond the box defined by the simplistic analysis of the three-self paradigm. It is also time to stop using dependency concerns as an excuse for denying Western capacity and Western responsibility to greet the world's desperate material needs with generosity. I am praying for a general renewal of covenant commitment within the international body of Christ. I am asking God for a revival of real unity that will be expressed in shared resources as well as shared relationships. I am also trusting that this book will help others decide to move in this very direction.

---

10 John D. Robb and James A. Hill, *The Peacemaking Power of Prayer* (Nashville: Broadman & Holman Publishers, 2000), 3–4, 199–201.

CHAPTER FIFTEEN

A World of Strategies for Overcoming Poverty

In the forgoing material I have offered principles for restoring Western generosity in a world awash in need, but I have not attempted to present a detailed program for ending poverty per se. More specific plans for relieving global deprivation have already been advanced by others in both Christian and secular arenas. This chapter is intended to familiarize readers with some of those detailed plans in hopes of providing information on existing strategies that could offer a track to run on for those who desire to move toward increasing their personal efforts to aid the poor. Some may, after all, find an easier route to engaging the poor if they don't have to recreate the wheel along the way.

Christian Initiatives

Denominational and independent mission organizations abound and are easily accessible for those who desire to pursue maximum funding through traditional agencies working among the poor. No further mention, therefore, needs to be made of those options in this section. I would instead direct your attention to more specific possibilities for personal and corporate application of my appeal for increased giving to and involvement with the poor.

I would begin by pointing to the important effort in stewardship education represented by Ronald Sider's *Rich Christians in an Age of Hunger,* first published in 1977.[1] Beginning from a biblical base and moving into an analysis of social justice issues, international economic policy, and the injustices that are dramatized in an age of globalization, his book offers an up-to-date prophetic challenge for wealthy believers. He urges them—that is, he urges *us*—to pursue more redemptive stewardship practices for the sake of the world's poor.

Rich Christians, revised several times since its first printing, provides a worthy introduction to a broad range of complex issues that Western Christians need to be familiar with if they want to be good stewards in our era of world history. Sider's book offers a readable exposure to a variety of far-reaching subjects that have adverse impact on under-resourced peoples all over the world. Detailed alternatives are articulated in this seminal work, calling for practical solutions that can be applied at a personal or corporate level. Sider's suggestions include encouragement for Christians to consider embracing a "graduated tithe" as their income grows. He also favors communal living alternatives that can increase our experience of covenant unity even as they reduce our expenditures.

These communal models will require changes in local church structures so that there is more opportunity to "watch over one another" as we try to live in ways that please Jesus and that manifest our determination

---

1   Ronald J. Sider, *Rich Christians in an Age of Hunger: A Biblical Study* (Downers Grove, IL: InterVarsity, 1977). Published most recently as *Rich Christians in an Age of Hunger: Moving from Affluence to Generosity* (Nashville: W Publishing Group, 2005).

to confront rather than conform to our surrounding culture. In few areas is the relational support and personal accountability Sider recommends more necessary than in the arena of financial stewardship lived out in the context of a society mesmerized by materialism. His appeal for widespread Christian commitment to simplified lifestyles is perhaps his most practical suggestion. Over the nearly three decades since *Rich Christians* appeared, other Christian leaders, such as John Stott, Richard Foster, Os Guinness, Tom Sine, and Ralph Winter[2] have joined Sider in the call for limiting our lifestyle choices for the sake of the poor. Their books can be accessed by reference to the bibliography that follows.

As these influential authors provoke our thinking and call us back to a biblical basis for social involvement and ministry to those in need, others have become *visible activists* for Christ's sake and *viable advocates* for the poor. Two recent examples may be seen in the generous intentions and global goals set by the successful authors Bruce Wilkinson and Rick Warren. Wilkinson wrote the popular book, *The Prayer of Jabez,* and Warren produced the even more widely acclaimed "Purpose Driven" series of books. One of these, *The Purpose Driven Life,* has proven to be the most popular hardback book in history, selling more than thirty million copies.[3] Both men have a declared passion to use their fortunes to help relieve suffering in Africa.

Already Wilkinson's grandiose plans for Swaziland have faltered.[4] Time will tell whether Warren's even more comprehensive "P.E.A.C.E. Plan" will prove effective. That plan is designed to create a movement of local churches mobilized through small group initiatives to address the

---

2   Both Ralph and Roberta Winter have published articles on this issue in *Mission Frontiers* magazine. For examples, see Dr. Winter's "Commitment to a Wartime Lifestyle," September–October 1994, available at http://www.missionfrontiers. org/1994/0910/so948.htm; and his wife's "The Non-essentials of Life," May–June 1992, available at http://www.missionfrontiers.org/1992/0506/mj922.htm.

3   Lisa Miller, "The Giving Back Awards: 15 People Who Make America Great," *Newsweek*, July 3, 2006, http://www.msnbc.msn. com/id/13530551/site/newsweek/?page=5.

4   Michael M. Phillips, "Unanswered Prayers in Swaziland: U.S. Preacher Sees His Dream Vanish," *The Wall Street Journal*, December 19, 2005.

world's five most significant needs. Those needs, presented in the order of Warren's acrostic, are planting churches among unevangelized and unreached peoples, equipping leaders, assisting the poor, caring for the sick, and educating the emerging generation.[5] I applaud Warren's visionary ideas and I believe we need more Christians to come forward with God-sized strategies intended to make a real difference in the world. But such programs, born with high *expectation*, should be managed with great care in their *execution*—being implemented in close cooperation with indigenous leaders. This is a priority Westerners too often disregard.

Warren's model readily reflects the biblical vision and the economic values of the Scriptures, an all too rare offering even from the Christian community. Leadership and largess are equal components of his *modus operandi*. He and his wife are excellent examples of serious stewardship, having committed themselves, in spite of their financial windfall, not to change their lifestyle. They are reimbursing Saddleback for the salary the church has paid Warren for twenty-four years of ministry. They have established three foundations to steward *The Purpose Driven Life* sales proceeds—none of which they are taking for personal use. And the Warrens are now "reverse tithers," giving away 90 percent of their income and keeping just 10 percent for themselves. Two principles Warren believes God wants him to live out simultaneously in light of his book's success are the stewardship of *affluence* and the stewardship of *influence*.[6] Warren's P.E.A.C.E. Plan deserves our careful consideration.

When we think of other advocates for the poor, few have been as tireless as U2 rock star, Bono, who has championed innovative efforts like Jubilee 2000, Live Aid, Live 8, the ONE Campaign, and the Micah Network (with special emphasis on the Micah Challenge). These diverse efforts at relieving poverty and curbing injustice have been important

---

5   See details of Warren's strategy at http://www.thepeaceplan.com/ and Berit Kjos, "Warren's P.E.A.C.E. Plan and UN Goals—Part 1," August 2005, Kjos Ministries website, http://www.crossroad.to/articles2/05/peace-un.htm.

6   James A. Smith Sr., "Legislators Welcome Rick Warren in Session's Final Week," *Florida Baptist Witness*, May 6, 2004, http://www.floridabaptistwitness.com/2523.article.

because they bridge the usual chasm between the Christian c
and secularly motivated social activists. They have also attr∤
celebrities to serve as spokespersons for needy people who have no
voice. Each of these programs merits our investigation, a process easily
accomplished via the Internet. Such global initiatives represent a significant new step in mobilizing activist Christians in a growing call for
debt relief for the world's poorest nations, for environmental awareness,
for increased government funding for the world's most impoverished
countries, and for more volunteerism. Results have been mixed: elicit-
ing tantalizing promises readily enough, but promises that too often fail
to be fulfilled. While these efforts have successfully secured dramatic
commitments for increased government aid for fighting poverty and for
combating the global AIDS pandemic, many of the pledges made, even
those endorsed by presidents and prime ministers in very public forums,
have remained largely unfunded. The reality is that many rich Western
nations have been disingenuous, agreeing in principle "to give" at higher
levels but proceeding "not to give" in actual practice.

The UN's Millennium Development Goals

The Christian emphasis on detailed strategic alternatives for increasing aid and for encouraging systemic reforms in international finance is
mirrored (and largely exceeded) by the secular agenda promoted most
prominently by the United Nations. In its attempt to establish and support a global strategy for economic reform and relief of extreme poverty, the UN has declared a comprehensive plan under the aegis of the
Millennium Project. The plan details specific Millennial Development
Goals (MDGs). These objectives, endorsed by all heads of state, were established in September 2000 and include targets to be pursued until 2025
(with bench mark goals to be evaluated in 2015). The UN's MDGs are
aimed at eight specific issues: eradicating extreme poverty and hunger;
achieving universal primary education; promoting gender equality; reducing child and maternal mortality; reversing the spread of HIV/AIDS
and malaria; reducing by half the proportion of people without access to

safe drinking water; ensuring environmental sustainability; and developing a global partnership for development, with targets for aid, trade, and debt relief.

These goals are comprehensive, complex, expensive, and altogether dependent on a level of international cooperation and funding never before achieved in the history of humankind. Columbia professor Jeffrey Sachs, author of the popular book *The End of Poverty*, is a special adviser to Kofi Annin and director of the Millennium Project. He was the chief architect for this far-reaching UN program. Sachs has proposed that ending extreme poverty (defined to include 1.1 billion people living on less than one dollar a day) is a plausible possibility if that end is pursued through a combination of government funding and private philanthropy.[7] Thus this specific objective is an important part of the MDG agenda.

In September 2005, five years into the UN's anticipated reform period, progress on the MDGs was evaluated and seen as woefully inadequate. In an address to the Executive Board of the United Nations Development Program, incoming administrator, Kemal Dervis said:

> At the beginning of my tenure, ten years before the 2015 [benchmark] deadline, I would like to express my strong belief that the Millennium Development Goals are technically and economically attainable. There is sometimes some doubt expressed on this, but I think that *from a technical and economic point of view, they can be attained.* Success does however require the resources proposed in Monterrey, accelerated capacity and institution building in the less developed countries and a more equitable growth pattern also in the emerging market economies.

---

7 Jeffrey D. Sachs, *The End of Poverty: Economic Possibilities for Our Time* (New York: Penguin Press, 2005), 24–25. Sachs' conception of ending extreme poverty aims also at developing sufficient fiscal momentum to offer the poor opportunities to begin climbing the ladder of progressive economic development. Collective action through effective government provision of health care, education, and infrastructure underpins the goal of providing such opportunities; and these, he asserts, must be largely funded through private and public foreign assistance in order for poor national economies to be stimulated to grow.

*But if we continue with a business-as-usual approach which
lacks a real sense of urgency, then we won't make it.*[8]

Dervis could have said, more simply, that if the rich nations of the
world keep refusing to fund the MDG agenda they have pledged to support, then UN efforts are doomed to failure.

Opportunities Lost for Lack of Interest

Requisite funding is an obvious and essential element in all plans
for relieving the pain of extreme poverty. But an adequate flow of resources is difficult to obtain and even more difficult to sustain. Over the
last thirty years, leaders like Sider and Stott could address the need for
increased support for the poor and the priority for Christians to be active
in promoting social justice. But they could not dictate a transformation in
attitudes among churches, mission agencies, or individual Christians regarding their giving habits or their activism. Their efforts, consequently,
did not achieve the hoped-for result. There has been no groundswell in
the sense of moral responsibility among believers to bear the burdens
of the poor. This is true in spite of tireless efforts by Stott and Sider to
sponsor meetings and to publish materials that show the way to greater
generosity within the Christian community. Apathy has been the general
rule and outraged action has been the rare exception. In the face of urg-
ings to the contrary, individual contributions among American Christians
steadily declined from 1968 to 2001—a period in which per capita income increased almost every year.[9] Far too many Christians have simply
decided consistently "not to give."

Reflecting a similar limitation, UN delegates and conferees promoting relief and development plans during this same time frame have had
no real influence over the funding decisions of participant governments

---

8   Speech available at http://www.undp.org/dpa/statements/kd/2005/kdEB060905.shtml
(italics added).

9   Ronald J. Sider, *Rich Christians in an Age of Hunger: Moving from Affluence to
Generosity* (Nashville: W Publishing Group, 2005), 200.

and wealthy philanthropists who could (and who may yet) support the UN's complex programs aimed at eradicating poverty and relieving global suffering. There are rare exceptions to this general dearth of giving. In 1997, for example, media mogul Ted Turner pledged to give $1 billion to the UN over ten years in equal annual installments of $100 million.[10] He has made good on that promise. But such examples of private philanthropy are unusual.

More common are the instances where governments of wealthy Western nations have been miserly. In the context of multiple international meetings attended by some of the world's most powerful government leaders and in a variety of written international agreements signed by heads of state, significant commitments for increased aid have been made and then repeatedly and routinely ignored. Most prominent in this regard is the pledge on the part of richer governments to allocate 0.7 percent of their gross national product to eradicating global poverty. This pledge was first put forward in UN sponsored meetings in 1970.[11] Yet only four nations have fulfilled this promise over the intervening thirty-six years. Denmark, Norway, Sweden, and the Netherlands seem to offer uniquely laudable examples to other rich nations by their compliance with this internationally recognized minimal standard of generosity. But all four of these nations were already exceeding the 0.7 percent official developmental assistance (ODA) goal in 1970, and all four have gradually decreased their support as a percentage of GNP over the decade from 1993 to 2003. In their cases, compliance with the 0.7 percent standard actually represents a *reduction* in proportional allocations for the poor.

The United States is, incidentally, at the bottom of the list of industrialized donor nations if we focus on ODA measured as a percentage of GNP. Like the four nations noted above, America is also moving backwards in its allocation percentage in spite of having repeatedly promised

---

10 See the United Nations Foundation website, www.unfoundation.org, and specifical-lyhttp://www.unfoundation.org/about/chairman_message.asp.

11 Anup Shah, "The US and Foreign Aid Assistance," http://www.globalissues.org/TradeRelated/Debt/USAid.asp#RichNationsAgreedatUNto07ofGNPToAid

more aid to the world's poorest nations. The United States offered only 0.14 percent of its GNP for ODA in 2003, down from 0.15 percent in 1993.[12] Sachs suggests, "Not one in a million U.S. citizens even knows about this pledge [of support for the poor]. . . . Spin as we might in the United States about generosity, poor countries are fully aware of what we are *not* doing."[13]

But this is only one reflection of empty promises coming from Western governments regarding support of the world's poor. One of the most famous commitments of the past century was the international community's 1978 pledge of "Health for All by the Year 2000." This was only one of many lofty end-of-the-century milestones UN planners were fond of proclaiming as the new millennium approached. But aiming at and hitting such strategic targets are vastly different undertakings. Rhetoric has all too often exceeded reality in terms of fulfillment of such pledges. Despite the goal of improving health dramatically over the last two decades of the twentieth century, "The world arrived in 2000 with [an out-of-control] AIDS pandemic, resurgent TB and malaria, and billions of the world's poor without reliable, or sometimes any, access to essential health services. At the World Summit for Children in 1990, the world also pledged universal access to primary education by the year 2000, yet 130 million or more primary-aged children were not in school by then."[14]

Recent history has proven that the UN cannot deliver on promises that member governments refuse to pay for. Expecting "more bricks" while providing "less straw" is a strategy with biblical precedent, but it is not one that holds much promise for the poor. Western governments need to rethink their funding commitments and reform these unjust practices.

Another example can be observed with respect to US promises made in 2002. In March of that year, President Bush spoke at an international UN conference convened in Monterey, Mexico. There he pledged

---

12 Sider, *Rich Christians*, 32–33.

13 Sachs, *The End of Poverty*, 340.

14 Ibid., 213.

to dramatically increase America's funding for development assistance. His commitment involved establishing a new "Millennium Challenge Account" (MCA) that was intended to demonstrate his administration's desire to "lead by example" in addressing the global needs of the poor. The plan promised $5 billion in new aid over the ensuing three fiscal years, money to be added in excess of existing US commitments.[15] As of July 2006, only nine countries have been approved for grants under the program. No funds at all flowed from this promising proposal until Madagascar received the first grant of $109 million in April 2005—representing an amount well under Bush's stated goal of $5 billion and at a date well past the third anniversary of his pledge. By now the promised support under the MCA proposal should have already been paid in full! Institutional requirements for poor countries to qualify for MCA funding have, however, been onerous, imposing, and hard to meet. Consequently, after four years only $2.06 billion in funds have been committed under the MCA strategy.[16]

It is no wonder leaders from developing nations no longer hold their breath when representatives from rich nations speak about forthcoming grants in aid. John Stott has wisely said that "there is a great need today for more righteous indignation, anger, [even] outrage, over . . . evils which are an offense to God."[17] Presumably this stream of broken promises to the poor fits the category of such societal evils that Stott believes do, in fact, offend God. He comments on the point specifically, saying the primary Christian principle to be applied today is "distributive justice."[18] Not only has little outrage been expressed by US citizens over our government's failure to perform on its promises to the poor, our populace has largely failed even to take notice. Being now informed, the question is whether we will care enough to become advocates seeking

---

15 Ibid., 336–37.

16 Statistical summary available at http://www.cgdev.org/doc/MCA/Compacts.sector. GAO.pdf.

17 John Stott, *Decisive Issues Facing Christians Today* (Old Tappan, NJ: Fleming H. Revell Company, 1990), 369.

18 Ibid., 139.

justice for the poor. The UN's MDGs are ostensibly intended to make amends for the empty promises of the past, but hopes already begin to wane as time passes and programs routinely continue to go unfunded or underfunded.

The Problem of Broken Faith in Broker Bankers

Part of the problem involved with getting funds to the poor stems from the common use of the International Monetary Fund (IMF) and the World Bank as the primary institutional brokers for global economic assistance. These institutions were created after World War II to maintain order in the global monetary and foreign exchange systems and as an effort to provide sound fiscal advice and development loans to Third World nations. Intended to serve the world's poorer countries, the IMF and the World Bank have instead been dominated by the rich nations that fund them. They have created an international lending environment that is unjust, one that requires more in debt service from the poorest nations than those same countries receive in economic assistance. The net flow of money has been *out of* the Third World instead of *into* it ($43 billion in 1987 alone, according to the World Bank).[19] Intimidating and sometimes unsympathetic, these organizations, intended be a remedy for poverty in the modern world, have often proved instead to be disappointingly difficult to access.

Nobel laureate and Columbia University professor Joseph Stiglitz insists these institutions too often employ a "one size fits all strategy in diverse and complex international settings."[20] Sachs asserts, "When impoverished countries have pleaded with the rich world for help, they have been sent to the world's money doctor, the IMF. The main IMF prescription has been budgetary belt tightening for patients much too

---

19 Ibid., 137.

20 Joseph E. Stiglitz, *Globalization and Its Discontents* (New York: W. W. Norton, 2002), 34.

poor to own belts."[21] The result is the proliferation of global distributive injustice, a reality that dramatizes the divide between the rich and the poor, making it abundantly clear to under-resourced peoples that equal worth is not easily experienced if one does not enjoy the advantages of equal wealth.

Stiglitz speaks as an inside critic, having worked for the World Bank as its chief economist for three years (1997–2000). Reflecting on the status quo, he says, "The IMF is a political institution. . . . It has served the interest of the more advanced industrial countries rather than the developing world. . . . The IMF's standard operating procedure is a new form of colonialism. . . . The Fund casts itself as the monopoly supplier of 'sound advice' . . . the font of wisdom, the purveyor of orthodoxy too subtle to be grasped in the developing world."[22]

The practices and procedures of these institutions will need to be reformed if relief is ever to come to the poor. That is why "debt relief" activism is on the increase and why acquiescence to present global structural realities is no longer an option. Should we fail in achieving reform in the global economic systems as a whole, Stiglitz suggests we may, in the end, merely "replace old dictatorships of national elites with new dictatorships of international finance."[23] The Christian commitment to support economic justice must find its way into the Christian agenda if we are to meaningfully engage the poor and help them find viable solutions to their unenviable problems.

Making Excuses for Minimizing Aid

Sachs makes it abundantly clear that, notwithstanding the slow response of rich nations and the relatively minimal response of wealthy individuals (he does not mention the indifference of the church and the

---

21 Sachs, *The End of Poverty*, 74.

22 Stiglitz, *Globalization*, 30–31, 89.

23 Ibid., 247.

mission community, though we should), "Targeted investments backed by donor aid lie at the heart of breaking the [world's] poverty trap."[24] He goes on to state, "Ending poverty by 2025 will require a 'global compact' between rich and poor countries. . . . The rich countries will need to move beyond the platitudes of helping the poor, and follow through on their promises to deliver more" aid and development resources.[25]

Stiglitz concurs, suggesting in his book *Globalization and Its Discontents* that present realities dictate the need for more aid. "[Even] relatively small amounts of money could make an enormous difference. . . . The evidence is that aid given selectively can have significant impact both in promoting growth and in reducing poverty."[26] Aid flows, however, have never been massive nor scaled in any way commensurate to the levels needed to spur economic growth within impoverished nations.[27] These secular economists agree that more aid should be made more accessible in more places more often if we hope to make a dent in the global poverty juggernaut.

Unfortunately, the secular development community seems to have developed its own "standard litany of excuses used to justify the status quo,"[28] just as Western Christians have developed a system of missiological defenses that argue against giving to help the poor. Sachs says, "Opponents of foreign assistance today claim *erroneously* that it does more harm than good."[29] He cites Africa as an example and notes, "The mantra of excuses for limiting aid . . . include the assertion that Africa's poor are so [negligibly] educated as to be beyond outside help; that they are subject to corrupt governments that prevent effective intervention; that African morals are so broken that AIDS cannot be contained or con-

---

24 Sachs, *The End of Poverty*, 260.

25 Ibid., 266.

26 Stiglitz, *Globalization*, 242–43.

27 Sachs, *The End of Poverty*, 336.

28 Ibid., 268.

29 Ibid., 361 (italics added).

trolled; and that modern African values and its underdeveloped institutions defy all hopes of successful relief."[30]

Sachs classifies all these excuses as myths that have been repeated publicly for so long, or whispered in private so often, that they have been accepted as truths by the public and the development community. His perspective on the issue can be summarized succinctly, "The biggest problem today is not that poorly governed countries [in need of aid] get too much help, but that well-governed [poor] countries get far too little."[31] This is often the case simply because rich nations largely ignore their public pledges of assistance and underfund initiatives that might actually relieve suffering.

"Planners" and "Searchers" Look for Answers

Not all secular leaders agree with Sachs' proposed supersized solutions to global poverty. New York University economics professor William Easterly, another former World Bank executive, offers a wildly divergent alternative in his book, *The White Man's Burden: Why the West's Efforts to Aid the Rest Have Done So Much Ill and So Little Good.* Disapproving of the top-down macro-planning techniques of UN strategists like Sachs, Easterly promotes bottom-up alternatives on a micro-enterprise scale. He suggests that grandiose plans "shaped at the top are not connected with reality at the bottom."[32] We should, therefore, avoid the oversized schemes of "planners" like Sachs, favoring instead the more practical interventions proposed by localized workers he calls "searchers."

Planners attempt to implement grand, comprehensive, and utopian schemes to address issues like poverty reduction, health care, or education accessibility on a national level. *Searchers* identify specific prob-

---

30 Ibid., 309.

31 Ibid., 269.

32 William Easterly, *The White Man's Burden: Why the West's Efforts to Aid the Rest Have Done So Much Ill and So Little Good* (New York: Penguin Press, 2006), 17.

lems solvable at a local level, such as lack of water in a given village, the presence of guinea worms in a regionalized population, or insufficient university options in an urban setting. Searchers are seeking practical ways to resolve problems locally. The difference in approach can be described as supply-side versus demand-side responses to the issues of poverty and economic growth.[33]

Easterly also promotes what he calls "piecemeal reforms" that have proven to be effective in actual practice and recommends support of such programs initiated by indigenous leaders on the ground or by outsiders who reside on site, rather than in far-removed ivory towers.[34] Results are dramatically different when aid comes through a demand-side process in which the specific forms of assistance received are shaped by requests from personnel on site. Aid offered in this manner is more helpful than resources that are merely a reflection of the inventories easily available to NGOs and governments for distribution. Easterly's emphasis is on delivering what localized leaders need, not what distant donors want to provide. He says, "Only insiders have enough information to find solutions, and most [effective] solutions are homegrown."[35]

Piecemeal efforts could include micro-enterprise loans, support for local schools, and marketing programs for distributing and selling inexpensive products or imported medicines to the very poor. There is no common theme among the options Easterly favors that would shape a centralized planning approach generating megaprojects like the UN's MDGs because, as he repeatedly stresses, he believes that no such formula really works. Abandoning the search for a magic wand or a silver bullet to end extreme poverty, Easterly points us toward contextual relevance, localized oversight, indigenous accountability, grass-roots initiatives, and small-scale projects as the more promising keys to reducing the burden of poverty in a world overcome with overwhelming need.

---

33 Ibid., 5–6; consult these pages for an extended description of the differences between "planners" and "searchers."

34 Ibid., 15.

35 Ibid., 6.

gh Sachs, Stiglitz, and Easterly disagree on which global strat-
___ might offer a viable approach to dealing with global poverty, all three offer tacit support from a secular perspective for the primary thesis of this book. The world's problem of extreme poverty will not be solved without an exponential expansion of generosity. "Funding plans cannot realistically expect the poor to suddenly pick up the full tab for expanded projects" they need.[36] Large-scale donor financing (including a heavy dose of private philanthropy) will be required for decades to come. In surprising concert with my argument in chapter 8, Sachs writes, "Such payments are not a welfare handout, but . . . actually an investment that [can break] the poverty trap once and for all."[37]

Our efforts to relieve poverty and to bring more effective change to the world's most under-resourced peoples hinge on the singularly important decision as to whether individuals, governments, or international coalitions like the UN (and I would add churches and mission agencies) will ultimately decide whether "to give or not to give" in the face of enormous need. Short of an affirmative answer on this most important question, we are left sadly with only an "irresolute resolve"—a recognized need to express generosity in support of the world's needy people that gets consistently ignored in actual practice. We cannot force conviction on others, but we can set our own course. In the end we are all left to address that dilemma, personally determining what is right for "me and my house." My recommendation is that we aim to give more and to get more personally involved with the poor wherever we can do so in ways that relieve their burdens, that minister hope in the midst of their hardships, and that reinforce our covenant relationship with them as children of God.

---

36 Sachs, *The End of Poverty*, 276.

37 Ibid., 246.

CHAPTER SIXTEEN

Three Guiding Lights for a World Bereft of Giving

Ronald Sider and John Stott have worked as tirelessly as anyone in the Western world to reinforce the call for repentance among rich Christians in a world facing injustice and extreme poverty. Stott offers keen insight into the priority that *simplicity* and *generosity* should have as we deal with poverty in the modern world. These are, in effect, the first two of three guiding lights that should help us discern our way through the dilemmas that stewardship of material wealth create for so many.

Simplicity, Stott says, "is first cousin to contentment. It concentrates on what we need, and measures this by what we use. It rejoices in the Creator's gifts, but hates waste, greed and clutter. It says with the book of Proverbs 'give me neither poverty nor riches, but give me only my daily bread,' for to have either too much or too little may lead me to disowning or dishonoring God (30:8 ff). It wants to be free from anything and everything that distracts from the loving service of God and others."[1] By pursuing simplicity in our lifestyles, we increase the store of resources we have to give and we look for reasonable ways to share our riches in the context of covenant relationships.

Simplified Living and Maximized Giving

As I mentioned in the last chapter, other evangelical leaders have joined Sider and Stott in calling for a return to simple lifestyle choices as an important first step toward a saner expression of stewardship than Westerners tend to manifest in their passionate pursuit of consumption. The modern Christian emphasis on simplicity began in 1974, when delegates gathered at the initial Lausanne Congress on Global Evangelism. These men and women from all over the world showed the same sensible and biblically based spirit of concern that Stott and Sider promote by asserting as part of the Lausanne Covenant: "All of us are shocked by the poverty of millions and disturbed by the injustices which cause it. Those of us who live in affluent circumstances accept our duty to develop a simple life-style in order to contribute more generously to both relief and evangelism."[2]

Pursuing the issue with relentless focus, Stott and Sider went beyond their subsequent publishing efforts and organized a follow-up consultation in 1980. That gathering included eighty-five delegates from twenty-seven countries (half from the Third World) who convened to promote the actual practice of simplified living in keeping with the Lausanne Covenant resolution. Their interest was generated by a concern that "nothing that has happened in the six years since the Lausanne Congress has lessened the sense of 'shock' which poverty and injustice,

---

1   John Stott, *Decisive Issues Facing Christians Today* (Old Tappan, NJ: Fleming H. Revell Company, 1990), 247.

2   From paragraph 9, "The Urgency of the Evangelistic Task," of the Lausanne Covenant. Available at http://www.lausanne.org/Brix?pageID=12891.

the Covenant said, gave to the participants. So there is a critical need for Evangelical Christians to take part in the international justice debate."[3]

The lack of progress since the first Lausanne meetings was rooted in an absence of practical application based on the original covenant acknowledgment of shocking poverty present in many parts of the world. Well-intentioned as the covenant pronouncement had been, little action had grown out of it. So as John Stott helped organize the follow-up meeting he noted, "We become personally culpable when we acquiesce in the status quo by doing nothing."[4] Gathering leaders to address the issues of global poverty and economic injustice was a means to take responsibility for and to challenge afresh the apathy of Christians around the world. Those participating in the "International Consultation on Simple Lifestyle" desired to make sure that practical changes were actually occurring as a consequence of the concerns expressed in 1974 over the plight of the poor. The culmination of this gathering in 1980 was Lausanne Occasional Paper 20, "An Evangelical Commitment to Simple Life-style." This paper added a number of additional resolutions shaped by the participants in the consultation to encourage a greater Christian response regarding the shocking scourge of poverty. The hope was to encourage concrete responses *in deed* to match the concerns already expressed *in word.*

Chief among the new resolutions was the consultation's repetition of the earlier call for Christians to live more simply and a new recognition of the need to become more involved in political action. The former concern remained a central aspect of the delegates' solidarity with the poor and was stated more comprehensively than in the 1974 Lausanne Covenant.

We intend to reexamine our income and expenditure, in order to manage on less and give away more. We lay down no rules or regulations, for either ourselves or others. Yet we resolve

---

3   From section 6, "International Development" of Lausanne Occasional Paper 20: "An Evangelical Commitment to Simple Life-style," exposition and commentary by Alan Nichols. Available at http://www.lausanne.org/Brix?pageID=14737.

4   Ibid., section 7, "Justice and Politics."

to renounce waste and oppose extravagance in personal living, clothing and housing, travel and church buildings. We also accept the distinction between necessities and luxuries, creative hobbies and empty status symbols, modesty and vanity, occasional celebrations and normal routine, and between the service of God and slavery to fashion. Where to draw the line requires conscientious thought and decision by us, together with members of our family. Those of us who belong to the West need the help of our Third World brothers and sisters in evaluating our standards of spending. Those of us who live in the Third World acknowledge that we too are exposed to the temptation to covetousness. So we need each other's understanding, encouragement and prayers.[5]

The consultation delegates went further to declare that being in relationship with the poor should become an essential element of their strategy as well. Their resolution in this regard could be viewed as a harbinger of my own call in this book for a return to more "covenantal approaches" to our practice of Christian stewardship. They said, "We resolve to get to know poor and oppressed people, to learn issues of injustice from them, to seek to relieve their suffering, and to include them regularly in our prayers.[6]

Addressing Systemic Injustice

The new emphasis on political action offered an important admission that Christian social concern must go beyond individual efforts to relieve poverty, because "Personal commitment to change our life-style without political action to change systems of injustice lacks effectiveness. Personal commitment needs social action to authenticate it."[7] The consultation's concluding paper quoted Ron Sider:

---

5   Ibid., section 5, "Personal Life-Style."

6   Ibid., section 3, "Poverty and Wealth."

7   Ibid., section 7, "Justice and Politics."

One of the most urgent agenda items for the church in the industrialized nations is to help our people begin honestly to explore to what extent our abundance depends on international economic structures that are unjust. To what extent do current patterns of international trade and the operations of the International Monetary Fund contribute to affluence in some nations and poverty in others? Unless we grapple with that systemic question, our discussion of simple life-style has not gone beyond Christmas baskets and superficial charity which at times can even be, consciously or unconsciously, a philanthropic smoke screen diverting the oppressed from the structural causes of their poverty and our affluence.[8]

The issue of systemic injustice, the need for radical political change, and the serious call for major societal reforms was so intensely a part of the discussion during the consultation that participants actually addressed the merits of seeking political redress through civil disobedience (which was affirmed "when obedience to God demands it") and even through violent revolution (which was not embraced).[9] A spirit of Christian activism was definitely in the air, but it proved to be neither contagious nor compelling in its impact among the broader global Christian community. Simplified lifestyles did not become the rage and Western giving declined rather than increasing over the two decades that followed. Paraphrasing G. K. Chesterton, simplicity, as a Christian ideal, has not been tried and found wanting—it has been found difficult and left untried.[10]

Why the mediocre response to so passionate an appeal by credible Christian reformers? American Baptist stewardship consultant, Ronald E. Vallet, offers a possible explanation when he suggests that many evangelicals have simply lost their focus. He notes that a clear vision no lon-

---

8   Ibid., section 2, "Stewardship."

9   Ibid., section 7, "Justice and Politics."

10 Chesterton's exact quote: "The Christian ideal has not been tried and found wanting; it has been found difficult and left untried." Available at http://www.quotedb.com/quotes/493.

for many American churches, and the nature of their mission
e fuzzy. "The church lives in a visionless vacuum" that fails
both to move hearts and to motivate action on stewardship issues.[11]

Vallet concludes that the church won't be able to turn the world
upside down again until pastors and members "are driven by the im-
peratives of the gospel" and begin to live once more as an alternative
community sharing in covenant and intent on serving God's purposes on
earth.[12] His writings, along with those of other contemporary leaders like
Os Guiness and Miroslav Volf, offer attempts to refocus today's churches with respect to a renewed stewardship vision. Adopting a simplified
lifestyle is part of a personal strategy that allows godly contentment to
constrain our consumptive appetites so that we are able to live on less
and give more.

Being Rich and Ready to Share

Generosity, Stott's second guiding light, invites us to use the surplus
that simple living generates to add one kind of wealth to another. Citing
1 Timothy 6:17–18, Stott points us to the words of Paul: "Command
those who are rich . . . to be rich. More precisely, 'Command those who
are rich in this present world . . . to be rich in good deeds.' . . . Tell them
'to do good, to be rich in good deeds, and to *be generous and willing to
share*.' Then they will be imitating our generous God 'who richly provides us with everything for our enjoyment.'"[13]

Yale Divinity School professor Miroslav Volf captures the essence
of generosity in a fresh way. He writes in *Free of Charge: Giving and
Forgiving in a Culture Stripped of Grace* about what he calls "the law
of the flow." "God gives so that we can exist and flourish, but not only

---

11 Ronald E. Vallet, *Stepping Stones of the Steward: A Faith Journey through Jesus'
Parables*, 2nd ed. (Manlius, NY: REV/Rose Publishing, 1994), 167.

12 Ronald E. Vallet, *The Steward Living in Covenant: A New Perspective on Old
Testament Stories* (Manlius, NY: REV/Rose Publishing, 2001), 226.

13 Stott, *Decisive Issues*, 245–46 (italics added).

for that. God gives so that we can help others exist and flourish as well. God's gifts aim at making us into generous givers, not just fortunate receivers."[14] We are therefore to be available to God as his instruments for blessing others.

> We are not simply final destinations in the flow of God's gifts. Rather, we find ourselves midstream, so to speak. [God's] gifts flow to us, and they flow from us. . . . If the flow were to stop, we would only be receivers, not givers. We would then be unlike what is most divine in God [the Pure Giver], and we would be no givers at all. . . . But we were created to be and to act like God. And so the flow of God's gifts shouldn't stop as soon as it reaches us. . . . Indeed giving to others is the very purpose for which God gave us the gifts. To pass them on . . . is the thing to which God's gifts oblige us.[15]

Volf supports my contention expressed earlier in this book that we are to be channels of God's material grace flowing to others—we are to be rivers, not reservoirs. We cannot, with good conscience before God, do with God's gifts what we please. Volf says, "[Gifts] come to us with a name and address other than our own . . . [and] some of them belong to my neighbor in need."[16] If I block the flow, I fail God; but I also fail the intended needy recipient God had in mind for me to bless. I was trusted to serve and I need not fear loss in doing my part as a generous giver. If God is the third party in the relationship between givers and recipients, givers will always prosper. That's the "law of the flow"! And it's the key to remaining generous. "If you give what you were given to give, more will be given."[17]

Volf offers a warning we all would do well to heed. "Part of growing up is learning the art of giving. If we fail to learn this art, we will live

---

14 Miroslav Volf, *Free of Charge: Giving and Forgiving in a Culture Stripped of Grace* (Grand Rapids: Zondervan, 2005), 47.

15 Ibid., 49–50.

16 Ibid., 60.

17 Ibid., 79.

unfulfilled lives, and in the end, chains of bondage will replace the bonds [of material blessing] that [were meant to] keep our communities together."[18] Remember how Paul, in Philippians 4:15, makes the "matter of giving and receiving" an integral part of fellowship. If we believe in the concept of covenant relationships; if we are truly concerned about our neighbors in need and the deprived members of God's extended global family; if we are committed to justice for the poor; and if we believe that God expects us to exercise reasonable stewardship in managing the material resources he entrusts to us; we can't afford—indeed the poor cannot afford—to be satisfied with the status quo. We cannot accept the level of our present efforts to bring meaningful relief to those in need, and we cannot be lulled to sleep by the language and logic that has so easily excused our passivity in the face of extreme poverty. As Stott has written so poignantly, "Apathy is the acceptance of the unacceptable; leadership begins with a decisive refusal to do so.[19]

Our articulation of the issues involved with giving wisely and well must therefore be amended to meet the challenges we face in responding with meaningful action. That is why I am asserting the need for Western Christians to abandon dependency concerns and the self-supporting paradigm in order to release God's people to give more freely again. We must embrace more broadly the call to simplicity. We must embrace more faithfully the call to generosity. And I would add a third "guiding light" for the desperate journey of the poor through the world of disparate wealth. Christians must embrace more creatively the commitment to *sustainability* as a key issue in attempting to help those who lack the most basic resources. Because 2.7 billion people live on less than $2 a day, even modest decisions by rich Christians to give a little can make a big difference to those in need.

---

18 Ibid., 17.

19 Stott, *Decisive Issues*, 369.

Redefining Sustainability

By now it should be clear that unanimity and personal popularity were not my goals in writing this book. My goal was to inspire renewed debate on an issue too easily deemed settled by materially satisfied (even satiated) believers. I also hoped to prompt a level of generosity that could be a means to the end of generating *sustainable impact* in terms of genuine and lasting relief for the world's poor. So, while I expect that Christians may be guided to vastly differing approaches to dealing with global poverty, just as we saw in the previous chapter that Sachs and Easterly have landed in divergent places working on the problem within their secular arenas, I also expect that generosity will be a common denominator at the heart of any solution Western Christians pursue in their attempts to offer relief to under-resourced people. Looking for options that allow us to decide simply "not to give" is an indefensible practice in the face of the growing and persistent problem of global poverty.

I used the phrase "sustainable impact" in the preceding paragraph intentionally. I meant for that phrase to indicate my sense of the goal we should have in mind as we work to relieve poverty. Sustainability has become a widely accepted benchmark when we are considering decisions about giving. Well it should be. But sustainability traditionally has been understood to indicate our estimate of how ready the recipients of aid may be to assume total responsibility for maintaining, operating, and improving the initiatives supported by our investments. Projects have been considered sustainable only if they can be continued without an ongoing infusion of outside resources. If it appears they cannot, the concern for sustainability tends to dictate a choice "not to give" in the first place.

The rationale behind this traditional understanding is governed by a focus on "inputs." Specifically, we want to know how soon indigenous leaders can assume full responsibility for shared projects so that we can suspend our inputs—our ongoing financial investments—altogether. This focus on inputs drives us toward the historical emphasis on the self-supporting paradigm and dramatizes the dependency issue. This version of sustainability is, in effect, borrowed from the business world, and it presumes that financial inputs should always generate disproportionate financial outputs. That is, investments should create reasonable returns (reflected as profits—outputs that exceed inputs by an observable margin). Profits should be sufficient to allow recipients of our investments to support the ongoing project costs without continued assistance. With adequate profitability, the start-up projects we invest in become sustainable enterprises. Thus sustainability has always been tied to profitability.

If our investment fails to generate such anticipated returns—that is, if no profit margin is produced or a net loss occurs—then our giving is expected only to create dependency. Under such circumstances conventional wisdom dictates that giving should be curtailed. So goes the traditional argument with our standard language and logic. We associate inputs with outputs, and measure outputs in terms of dollars, because "cash return on investment" is the logical metric used to measure success. This is standard marketplace wisdom. Business experience teaches us that a profit stream is necessary if a venture is to continue indefinitely, if it is to be sustainable. Profit makes the business world go round. That truism has largely been imported to the mission arena, and is accepted as a relief and development reality as well.

But Jim Collins, Stanford professor and author of two best-selling books focused on organizational excellence (*Built to Last* and *Good to Great*), has recently questioned this theory for its applicability in the social sector. His newly formulated conclusions assert, in part, that imposing a "profit metric" as a measure of success in social sector enterprises is unfair and unhelpful. Money, he suggests, is not a reasonable outcome metric for most nonprofit entities, because social sector agendas cannot be easily valued by using a "pricing system." Profitability as a means of evaluation "ties perfectly to the economic core in all businesses . . . [but] the same idea does not translate into the social sector."[20] Instead, Collins proposes that nonprofit organizations should look for nonmonetary outcomes to evaluate their effectiveness.

---

20 Jim Collins, *Good to Great and the Social Sectors: A Monograph to Accompany Good to Great* (Boulder, CO: Jim Collins, 2005), 18–19.

I believe that new quantitative and even qualitative metrics need to be discovered for nonprofit entities and that they should be used to assess sustainability for ministry projects aimed at helping the poor. Let me illustrate by extending this idea into the medical mission arena. Imagine what would change if we shifted our evaluation of success in medical missions from a focus on profitability based on "inputs" (measured in terms of return on dollars invested) to "outputs" (measured in terms of improved community health—the outcomes presumably desired). This approach to analysis would move us from a traditional concern for profitability (measured by a monetary metric) to other measurable, but nonmonetary, results. Our focus could be redirected so that we monitor the desired long-term "sustainable impacts" we want to see rather than focusing on sustainable net income.

If, in our example, we are starting a village clinic in central Africa, and after two years the clinic is treating five hundred patients per month (using indigenous doctors and nurses), we may be winning even if the clinic is losing money. If our outcome metrics are designed to look for a drop in infant mortality rates in the area, or for a reduction in malaria cases, or for the increased distribution and effective use of antiretroviral medicines by AIDS patients, then significant progress may be occurring even if financial profits are not. Maybe we could track the number of people receiving AIDS prevention education and monitor the reduction in new AIDS cases recorded at the clinic. Are not positive metrics in these reflections of improved health care a demonstration of a "sustainable impact" being achieved? If the community is too poor, however, to afford funding the clinic's staff salaries, the cost of building and equipping the clinic facility, or the expenses associated with funding the ongoing acquisition of medical supplies and payments for operating costs—the project may well be still succeeding in terms of "sustainable impact." Breaking the scourge of poor health may be a more valuable outcome than breaking even or making a profit.

If we Westerners were to "begin with the end in mind," focusing on desired nonfiscal outputs, could we not start our investments among the poor (making inputs) with a commitment to remain involved in this way as coworkers-in-covenant? This would mean helping to fund the effort and remaining dedicated to sharing the financial costs of the project, in cooperation with our national brothers and sisters, as long as the desired outcomes (in nonmonetary terms) are being achieved. Approaching shared goals in this fashion, and being freed from the traditional concern over dependency that often dictates an early departure from project sponsorship, I believe the nature of our relationship with the poor can be altered in fundamental and positive ways.

This could allow us to define sustainability in the way Roosevelt once dared to define the Lend-Lease program for arming America's World War II allies: by "eliminating the dollar sign" from our analysis of outcomes. I believe we could adopt a *faith approach* to ministry that would be more pleasing to the Lord than the predominantly *fiscal approach* we have traditionally used. Our goal could become investing cash more freely—without seeking a return in kind. We could then support relief and development among the poor while keeping our focus on nonmonetary outcomes as a measure of success and sustainability. I am convinced that the kingdom would be better advanced, as ministry is offered in Jesus' name with good and lasting effect, if this were our approach. Redefining "sustainable impact" among the poor this way could allow us to apply more consistently the biblical texts that call us to bear the burdens of needy neighbors and to extend grace to the "least of these."

So I propose that we allow *impact* to replace *income* as our evaluation criterion. Let's call projects "sustainable" because they are generating a "kingdom profit," whether they generate a "cash profit" or not. If the local economy can support the ongoing effort in the end, that is well and good. But in many contexts poverty is so entrenched that quick fixes born of small investments over short periods of time are not going to turn the tide. Poverty as an economic condition may still prevail, even as the desired results of Western generosity are proving sustainable in terms of the nonmonetary outcomes delivered.

Collins adds another important insight about social sector realities that we do well not to miss. He suggests, "Nonprofit funding tends to favor [programs], not building great organizations . . . [a decision] that is highly dysfunctional [because] to make the greatest impact on society requires first and foremost a great organization, not a single great program."[21] Collins goes so far as to suggest that designated gifts are often counterproductive if "sustainable impact" is our objective. This is because they take ministry leaders away from what they do best and redirect their energies to the goals of the donor's bequest. He advises leaders in nonprofit organizations to "reject resources that drive them away from the center of their [core competencies]."[22] This is never an easy choice for those who depend upon donations for survival to make. So Collins urges would-be donors to address this issue on their end of the giving and receiving continuum. He suggests that supporters who want to generate maximum results with their contributions should "give [unrestricted] resources that enable the institution's leaders *to do their best work the best way they know how.* Get out of their way and let them build [maximum momentum] and great organizations!"[23]

These ideas represent radical shifts in the language and logic of sustainability as we apply that term in relief, development, and mission settings. I believe such changes in our philosophy of philanthropy are long overdue. And so are the levels of repentance and leadership that are needed to support the kinds of fundamental reform in Western funding this book has proposed.

Finding the Courage to Lead

I must therefore be honest to say that combating poverty will require a rare sort of commitment if we are to change the status quo. The battle for lasting relief will take relentless leadership, because victory will require mobilization of millions of the nonpoor who will choose to give and to go where the pockets of poverty are most extreme and who will remain there

---

21 Ibid., 24.

22 Ibid., 23.

23 Ibid., 25 (italics in original).

long-term in order to reverse the tide of intolerable conditions. Millions of Christians will need to get actively involved in easing the suffering of those who live in conditions of extreme need and to bring reform to the unjust systems that perpetuate indefensible disparities of wealth and health. But the millions needed to stem the tide of global poverty will make the decision to enter the battle one soldier at a time. It will do no good for them to *enlist* if they will not *persist* to the end of the struggle.

The role of a reformer requires perseverance perhaps more than any other quality. This is the capacity to stick with a task, to simultaneously maintain direction and momentum, and to face obstacles optimistically as opportunities. It is not so much pigheadedness as it is the insight to know that the battle must be relentlessly pressed if victory is to be won. Perseverance in a leader, says Stott, is "the ability to 'turn stumbling blocks into stepping stones.' . . . A would-be social reformer must possess, in the first place, the virtues of a fanatic without his vices. He must be palpably single-minded and unself-seeking. He must be strong enough to face opposition and ridicule, staunch enough to endure obstruction and delay."[24]

Abolitionist leader William Wilberforce is a prime example of a reformer utterly devoted to his goal. In England's House of Commons in 1789, Wilberforce said of the slave trade: "So enormous, so dreadful, so irremediable did its wickedness appear that my own mind was completely made up for Abolition. . . . Let the consequences be what they would, I from this time determined that I would never rest until I had effected its [end]."[25] So at Wilberforce's initiative abolition bills and foreign slave trade legislation were repeatedly debated in the Commons for more than a decade. Yet every initiative failed. The Foreign Slave Trade Bill was not passed until 1806 and the Abolition of the Slave Trade Act until 1807. This part of the campaign, ending slave trade within the empire, had taken eighteen years.

But Wilberforce was not finished. He next began to direct his energies to actually abolishing the institution of slavery itself and securing the

---

24 Stott, *Decisive Issues*, 373.

25 Ibid., 374.

emancipation of slaves in the United Kingdom. In 1823 the Anti-Slavery Society was formed. In 1825 ill health compelled Wilberforce to resign his post at age sixty-six and to continue his campaign from outside the government. In 1831 he sent a personal message to spur the Anti-Slavery Society on in its efforts. The message said: "Our motto must continue to be *perseverance* . . . the Almighty will crown our efforts with success" if we stay the course.[26] And so God did. In July of 1833 the Abolition of Slavery Bill was finally passed in the House of Commons, more than forty years after Wilberforce began his battle against slavery. He was then seventy-four. Three days later he died, having literally persevered until the end of his days.

In 1957, William Proxmire, a Democrat from Wisconsin, was elected to assume the Senate seat vacated by the infamous Joseph McCarthy after his death. Proxmire offers an equally inspirational American example of perseverance. Following the end of World War II and with memories of the Holocaust still fresh, the UN passed the Genocide Convention in 1948. The Convention was inspired and enacted because of the tireless efforts of a Russian-born Jew of Polish descent named Rafael Lemkin. An international attorney who had himself survived the Holocaust, Lemkin had coined the word for this heinous crime. "Genocide" became the internationally accepted term to denote a virulent form of violence. It includes "acts intended to destroy, in whole or in part, a national, ethnical, racial or religious group." The UN resolution was a pledge that this great evil, and the crimes against humanity which often accompany it, would never be repeated in world history.

President Harry S. Truman signed the Convention on behalf of the United States when it was passed by the UN in 1948. But the Senate stubbornly refused to endorse the treaty. In 1967, after a decade in office, a constituent convinced Proxmire that steadfast disregard for the Genocide Convention was an act of moral cowardice on America's part. So the senator pledged to speak in favor of the Convention, committing to do so *every day* that Congress was in session until the Convention was

---

26 Ibid.

ratified. He made good on that pledge for a period of nearly twenty years. After 3,211 consecutive speeches calling for formal US ratification of the UN Genocide Convention, such an endorsement was finally passed and then signed into law by President Ronald Reagan on November 4, 1988.[27] Wilberforce and Proxmire show us the kind of perseverance that counts in leading people toward significant reform.

As we have seen, endorsing change is only a step in the right direction. Faithfully implementing actual reform is a harder issue. So the need for committed leadership in battling global poverty and promoting economic justice is a critical concern. Radical transformation in the giving patterns of rich Christians will require leaders with the indomitable will of a Wilberforce and the enduring persistence of a Proxmire. As one writer said in paying tribute to Proxmire after his death, to secure and sustain the attention of the masses on issues of social justice, we will always need "someone who will not be silenced, will not be beaten, will not be discouraged, and who will make the world stand up, take notice, and pay heed to the victims."[28]

The ranks of those committed to leading the body of Christ to a place of restored generosity and remedial justice are thin. But there is a plenty of room for you to take your place in this battle. For those who care to enlist, there is a unique role for each of us to play. There may yet be many questions to be answered along your way to this battlefield. But few questions are of more importance in the initial stages of deciding your part in ending poverty than the one I have posed here again and again. Faced squarely with the choice, you must determine whether you are inclined "to give or not to give" of your own resources and energies. All your other decisions in dealing with disparate wealth will flow from this one!

---

27 The Genocide Convention Implementation Act was popularly called the Proxmire Act. The text of the law can be viewed at http://www4.law.cornell. edu/uscode/html/uscode18/usc_sec_18_00001091----000-.html.

28 David Schraub, "The Debate Link" Internet blog, December 16, 2005, http://dsadevil. blogspot.com/2005/12/tribute-to-senator-william-proxmire.html.

CHAPTER SEVENTEEN

The Devil's Cunning

John Nevius wrote a disclaimer of sorts for his 1885 work, *Methods of Mission Work,* which introduced his thoughts on the three-self formulations of mission theory. I want to use the concluding thoughts he offered *then* as a template for my own reflections *now* as I close this review of issues touching on missions and money. In stating what I regard as serious objections to current missiological methods, I recognize that I may come into immediate conflict with the opinions of my colleagues. With that possibility in full view, I have attempted to write as a concerned seeker earnestly desiring to discern the path God would have Westerners walk as careful stewards in a world characterized by uneven material blessing.

In former years I believed in and worked under, to a considerable extent, the traditional interpretations of the three-self formula and the assumption that I need not challenge the lifestyle choices missionaries make since their decisions along that line are so intensely personal. What I have written admittedly alters that stance. I do offer specific challenges for my readers, and calls to action that I hope will be given due consideration. If my words are taken by some to be unduly harsh, I would ask that they be received primarily as a confession of my own previous error, and only secondarily as faultfinding with others. Foreigners going to many cultures with the intention of devoting themselves to business or diplomacy have made their mistakes over the years; it is not strange, but instead to be expected, that we missionaries should make ours as well. This book is my appeal for Western mission leaders to acknowledge potential errors in our past so that we (and the world's poor) might profit by our repentance in the future.

I am aware that it is possible to state facts in such a way that the impression given will be a false one and the conclusions arrived at misleading in the judgment of many. In speaking of the issues raised here in one setting of Westerners and nationals together in a common audience, I was accused by some of the Westerners of unfairly slanting these reflections on the three-self paradigm. That criticism motivated me to keep reflecting on these matters, to be more careful in my choice of language and logic to express my concerns, and to refine my conclusions for the sake of clarity. I have tried to be just in the consequent examination of the facts; but beauty, in this regard—as with so many aspects of life and ministry—is probably to be found in the eye of the beholder.

Those reluctant to reconsider their established convictions surely will have the most difficulty dealing with what I have presented here. In that sense, refining my argument is not likely to have removed the irritation I expect some Westerners to feel as they consider this contemporary challenge to the conceptual sacred cow that the three-self paradigm has become. My readers will have to judge for themselves whether I have succeeded in my earnest endeavor not only to offer fresh perspectives and to draw honest inferences from them, but to present them in such a way that the impression is made, at least, of an attempt to be honest and just in my analysis—even if such analysis is not always affirmed.

Guided by a Presuppositional Bias or a Biblical Basis?

I am concerned that we stop accepting settled missions principles that are of doubtful value, especially if it seems they have uncertain scriptural merit. Our current understanding of the three-self paradigm fits that category in my judgment, being drawn as it is from experience and supported generally only by anecdotal reflection masquerading as sacerdotal reasoning. *Proponents of the three-self paradigm rely too much on presuppositional biases and too little on biblical principles to be left unchallenged.*

Dietrich Bonhoeffer aptly warned his fellow Germans to remain focused on the Word of God as they formulated their convictions in response to the menace of Nazism. We are not faced with so great an evil here, but we still dare not leave the Bible out of our thinking as we decide whether "to give or not to give" in support of mission outreach to the poor. Bonhoeffer wrote, "How often we hear innumerable arguments 'from life' and 'from experience' put forward as the basis for the most crucial decisions, but the argument of Scripture is missing. [Adding] this authority would perhaps point in exactly the opposite direction."[1] So it does.

I believe that insisting on biblical support for the proper use of money in mission will force us to change our direction dramatically. We have been so indoctrinated into the school of thought that effectively urges us "to buy and to keep" that little support is needed anymore to defend the notion that we are better serving God and the kingdom when we choose "not to give." At times the argument against giving generously is put forward with no defense at all—being asserted as a foregone conclusion.

Let me illustrate this point with a quote from the November–December 2004 issue of *Mission Frontiers* magazine. In an article entitled "How to Kill a Church-Planting Movement," Southern Baptist church planting expert David Garrison enumerates "seven deadly sins" that he contends will murder our efforts to multiply churches in unreached cultures. His insights are drawn from his book entitled *Church Planting Movements:*

---

1   Dietrich Bonhoeffer, *Dietrich Bonhoeffer Works Volume 5: Life Together and Prayerbook of the Bible,* ed. Geffrey B. Kelly, trans. Daniel W. Bloesch and James H. Burtness (Minneapolis: Augsburg Fortress, 1996), 63.

How God Is Redeeming a Lost World. Garrison identifies the "Devil's Candy" as the fifth deadly sin and writes:

> To a hungry child the sweet taste of candy is irresistible, but that sugary burst of energy is no substitute for the kind of good nutrition required for long-term growth. In the same way there are sweet Christian virtues that Satan uses to seduce us away from a Church Planting Movement.
>
> The Devil's Candy is deceptive because it refers to good things that have real value, but if these good things keep us from our vision of churches planting churches, then they become a detour that we can ill afford.
>
> One example of the Devil's Candy is money. Money, though not inherently evil, is also not essential to Church Planting Movements, but it can produce a quick burst of energy. When a missionary's hunger to see quick results prompts him to hire pastors and to construct church buildings with foreign funding, he has bit the Devil's Candy! Building a movement on foreign funds is like running a machine with an extension cord that stretches across the ocean. When the movement reaches the end of the cord's length, it will abruptly stop. A Church Planting Movement must have an internal engine and internal fuel if it is going to flourish."[2]

Examining this assertion, I stumble badly over the complete absence of documentation or doctrinal reference to support Garrison's view. Aside from a passing reference in another paragraph to Roland Allen's often-cited book, *The Spontaneous Expansion of the Church,* absolutely no support is offered for Garrison's claims. Even the customary anecdotal defense is omitted, ostensibly because the point is so unassailable as to be self-evident. It is not! Let me offer three objections that will illustrate why we need to argue against the point he is trying to make.

---

2   David Garrison, "How to Kill a Church-Planting Movement," *Mission Frontiers: The Bulletin of the U.S. Center for World Mission,* Pasadena, CA (November–December 2004): 16. Available at http://www.missionfrontiers.org/archive.htm.

The Devil's Candy Is the Wrong Concern

First, every expeditionary army in reality must have a resource pipe-line that runs unhindered from the base of operations to the front lines. The logistics of extending supply lines can be a nightmare—but extend they must! Failure on this point has contributed to the defeat of some of history's greatest generals, including the likes of Cornwallis, Lee, and Rommel. Sustaining long supply lines is a fact of life for all armies that fight on a global scale. This necessity is also a reality for God's mission-ary forces, the men and women who fill the ranks of the elite corps of the church militant.

Garrison and other missiologists concerned about dependency find it absurd to presume that long supply lines should be needed to sustain emerging indigenous churches and leaders in the unreached cultures of the world. But they would not debate the need to solve the logistical problems involved with maintaining those same long supply lines in sup-port of Western missionaries resident on those same fields. They know that keeping an army of mission workers on the field takes money, practi-cal support, and transportation systems that reach around the world and certainly across ocean barriers. If supply lines are roughly equivalent to Garrison's "extension cord" metaphor, he has no problem with supplies reaching missionaries sent from North America or Europe.

The inherent contradiction in Garrison's premise is immediately observable. His problem is not with the length of the supply line; we build global delivery systems every day in the modern world. He is re-ally struggling with the possibility that indigenous leaders and emerging churches among unreached peoples might benefit from our extension cords. I must ask the obvious question: *Why shouldn't the same cord that supplies Westerners also supply national Christians who fill the frontline ranks in kingdom warfare and who serve in the same trenches?* Isn't this exactly the outcome God had in mind when the Holy Spirit inspired Paul to write, "God is able to make all grace abound to you, so that in all things at all times, having all that you need, you will abound in every good work. . . . You will be made rich in every way so that you can be generous on every occasion" (2 Corinthians 9:8, 11 NIV)?

The truth is that Satan is succeeding not when we deliver "foreign funds" to far away and needy people—he is succeeding when we refuse to do so! In this debate we should be more concerned about the *Devil's Cunning* than the *Devil's Candy*. We have not been seduced when we move in the spirit of the "sweet Christian virtue" to give, but rather when we allow such virtues to be recast as vices. When we see generosity as a hindrance and selfishness as a help to the cause of Christ, we have truly been led astray. The seduction is complete when our misunderstanding and misapplication of a century-old mission perspective convinces us that we are doing the right thing when we cut God's supply line to the impoverished parts of the world, where people are suffering as much from a famine of the Word as they are from a life-threatening lack of food. Enemy armies always gain an advantage when friendly supply lines break down. Yet that is the very end that Garrison and others who fear dependency seem to promote.

Second, we must consider from where the power energizing Garrison's extension cord is presumed to originate. It seems that he imagines the power is coming from a Western source. It is not! Rooting our rationale in the text of Scripture, God is the one who gives people the power to make wealth (Deuteronomy 8:18). Every good thing bestowed and every perfect gift that anyone, anywhere enjoys comes from above, from the Father (James 1:17). If there is a power cord—sticking with Garrison's analogy—it may well pass through a Western nation as it winds its way throughout the world, but its source is not to be found on our side of the ocean! The cord comes from heaven and its source is God, the sustainer of all life in all regions of the globe. If the cord is first entrusted to a Western locale, we dare not presume the Father intended to supply our need and neglect human beings elsewhere. Psalm 67, specifically verses 2 and 7, makes the point unmistakably: God blesses us for the express purpose that his ways may be known throughout the earth, that his salvation may reach to the nations, and that all the ends of the earth might reverence him.

The Devil's Candy indeed! This is an unfortunate term for the supply of God's supernatural resources meant to sustain his children all around the world. God calls the extraordinary provision he makes available from altogether unexpected sources "manna from heaven." It only becomes the Devil's Candy when Western stewards become rich fools and robbers, presuming "to buy and to keep" to themselves the riches meant to be shared with others. In the end, hoarding our surpluses will not help the needy. Neither will holding back resources bring blessing to us.

Third, Garrison asserts that "a Church Planting Movement must have an internal engine and internal fuel if it is going to flourish." God forbid that any Christian working to share the gospel of Christ cross-culturally should expect, hope for, or be satisfied with a ministry that is capable of flourishing on the strength of an "internal engine and internal fuel." Only in the name of Jesus, only in the power of the Holy Spirit, and only with the contributions of Christians from other cultures will we ever hope to see a church planting movement sustained in each of the world's unreached contexts. Indigenous communities should provide all that they can to advance the gospel locally. Many do so with greater sacrifice than we are apt to acknowledge. But they need not stand alone.

Balancing My Response to an Imbalanced Position

To balance my concerns about this aspect of Garrison's report on church planting movements, let me say that I find much in his book (which greatly expands on the article cited above) that I agree with heartily. His reports from around the world about massive kingdom expansion occurring through church planting movements are thrilling! I want to carefully note that he backs off the seemingly strident denunciation of giving that this article portrays in his book's expanded treatment of the subject of giving. In an appendix, rather than in the main text of his book, Garrison specifically says that we should feel free to give to pioneer missionary efforts among truly unreached people because the lost will not pay for their own evangelization. He also acknowledges that it is appropriate to give in support of Bible translation and distribution, to gospel literature production and distribution, to radio broadcasts and other media ministries, to church planting training centers, and to leadership development processes. Acceptable, too, are contributions in support of the poor and the needy and in response to chaotic events like natural disasters, wars, and famines. In Garrison's view, what we assiduously are to avoid is giving for pastors' salaries and for church facilities.[3]

I am arguing that even these last two ministry opportunities are not inappropriate if our giving is done with no strings attached and in contexts where we are in covenant relationships with leaders whose churches are self-governing and self-propagating. Funding fellow soldiers' salaries is as important and legitimate a use of "allied funds" as is logistical support and ammunition.

Even as I try to soften the tone of my effort to take Garrison's characterization of the "Devil's Candy" to task, I must nonetheless insist that we contend with the simplistic statements that his book and articles extracted from the book, like this one in *Mission Frontiers* magazine, make about giving. Taking issue with these perspectives is important because the obviously hard-and-fast conclusions they represent will lead a casual reader to exactly the wrong application in actual practice. Too many people who read Garrison's article will not read his book in its entirety. And most who read the book will not take time to read the appendix that balances his position on finances. Left unchallenged, writers like Garrison will, therefore, simply end up encouraging people to believe they are doing the right thing when they choose "not to give." Too many Western Christians have already decided that not giving is the appropriate posture to strike in the interest of promoting self-support and avoiding dependency dynamics. It is time to challenge this conviction and to make a major midcourse correction in the direction of generous giving.

Encouraging poor nationals to become financially independent so they can stand alone in the battle is simply not a necessary goal if we share wisely and readily with those in need. I join D. G. Moses and the believers gathered at the Willingen Conference more than fifty years ago in declaring that statements made in support of self-reliance, like those

---

3   David Garrison, *Church Planting Movements: How God Is Redeeming a Lost World* (Midlothian, VA: WIGTake Resources, 2004), 266–67.

made by Garrison's article (more than by his book), reflect a "dangerous narrowness of view" regarding self-sufficiency and autonomy. The conclusions such statements encourage are inherently unhealthy and at times overtly unbiblical. Let me be clear in pressing my argument. *I am not appealing for authors like Garrison to choose more careful verbiage in expressing the traditional view; I am calling for a complete reformation of perspective. The issues I am contending with are not semantic concerns—they are strategic ones.*

I am convinced the time has come to openly challenge our settled conclusions about missions giving and to slaughter the sacred cow represented by the self-supporting paradigm. My readers will have to decide whether or not to join me in this sacrifice. Putting this outdated dogma to death is an effort to effect timely change in a world that is rife with opportunities for those who are rich in material resources and willing to share more readily.

I am not recommending that my readers throw caution to the wind as they reflect on these matters. I do encourage them, however, to be intent on catching the wind of the Spirit as they make decisions about how to respond to the paradigm shift I am promoting. We might at least consider that any gentle blowing of the Spirit discerned here could be a harbinger of winds of coming change—winds that are intended by God to move us in a new direction as we navigate the world of mission opportunities that lies before us.

I expect the pictures painted here generally to be hard for Western missionaries to appreciate immediately. It would be easy for many to pass the images by, looking elsewhere in God's gallery for perspectives that are less controversial and less unsettling. Options abound that would likely leave ministry colleagues more comfortable, less burdened, and freer to continue with the status quo than mine do. Perhaps the preference to remain on familiar ground is to be expected from those who rest in a secure position on the more advantaged end of the economic continuum. But if the insightful comments of the mission statesmen noted above (and not necessarily my own offerings) are even nearly correct in their critique of Western missionary practice, we dare not refuse at least some serious reflection on the pictures they paint for our period of world history.

The remedies I suggest here are not intended to be quick fixes or easy solutions to the problems posed by disparate Western prosperity. They are, rather, a proposal of principles that I believe could support better mission practice as we struggle continually with the dilemmas inherent in deciding whether "to give or not to give" in support of world mission. I hope my reflections will stimulate my ministry associates and other missionaries to examine their hearts afresh, search the Scriptures again, and seek counsel from national partners about how we might become more effective in our task—learning to live as righteous rich people among the impoverished unreached while aspiring to some measure of usefulness, as our national neighbors care to define our usefulness.

I am not offering dogma here. I am making proposals for creative alternatives to missiological perspectives that have gone largely unchallenged for too long a time. I am also appealing for more dialogue on these issues. In that respect, I hope I have succeeded in providing grist for the mill of corporate and personal reflection and interaction. It is my sincere prayer that the Spirit of God might use this effort to make better missionaries of us all.

The Sins of Sodom Revisited

I also pray that others will be helped, by God's grace, to discern more prudently what it means to be truly faithful stewards as well as truly generous givers. That goal is more important than we realize when we stop to reflect on God's consistent judgment inflicted upon nations that fail to show mercy to the oppressed. Such was the basis for prophetic denouncements penned by Amos and Isaiah against the pagan nations surrounding Israel. An absence of compassion was the root of the demise of Nebuchadnezzar and even some of Israel's own kings.

Few recognize that selfishness, as well as homosexual sin, led to the destruction of Sodom and Gomorrah. Listen to the haunting words of

Ezekiel 16:49–50: "Now this was the sin of your sister Sodom: She and her daughters were *arrogant, overfed and unconcerned; they did not help the poor and the needy*. They were haughty and did detestable things before me. Therefore I did away with them as you have seen" (NIV emphasis added). This great prophet captures God's concern for social justice just as forcefully as Moses did in Genesis 19 when he focused attention on Sodom's sexual perversion. In the twenty-first century, Western cultures struggle mightily to avoid repeating both of these serious sins. Perhaps our "advanced" societies have not become greatly more civilized in the modern era after all.

My point here is that we must find a way to give more freely and more abundantly if we desire to please God. If we err in the matter of our giving, we should choose to err on the side of generosity. We may have a sense that we are approaching an acceptable level of giving when our generosity begins to be a bit painful personally. Otto A. Piper, the late professor of New Testament theology at Princeton Seminary, wrote, "We refuse to act as God's agents [of grace] when the portion of our money which we destine for others is so small that we do not feel the pinch when we give."[4] C. S. Lewis put it in a similar vein as he too argued for his contemporaries in the body of Christ to give more:

> I do not believe one can settle how much we ought to give. I am afraid the only safe rule is to give more than we can spare. In other words, if our expenditure on comforts, luxuries and amusements, etc., is up to the standard common among those with the same income as our own, we are probably giving away too little. If our charities do not at all pinch or hamper us, I should say they are too small. There ought to be things we should like to do and cannot do because our charitable expenditure excludes them.[5]

---

4   Otto A. Piper, *The Christian Meaning of Money* (Englewood Cliffs, NJ: Prentice-Hall, 1965), 70.

5   Os Guinness, *Doing Well and Doing Good: Money, Giving, and Caring in a Free Society* (Colorado Springs: NavPress, 2001), 252.

So I end this chapter where I began this book, by calling for Western Christians to aim at a legacy of largess—not a rich fool's bargain that settles for self-indulgence and an ever-increasing store of resources. I have asserted that the traditional dictates of the three-self paradigm have made that goal harder to pursue practically and generous giving harder to promote persistently than God intended. I hope others who agree will join me in encouraging a rebirth of a spirit of extravagant giving among Western believers.

I also hope I have made it easier for others to discern what it means to steward our resources well as we try to do the right thing in twenty-first century missions. In the final analysis, I believe "the right thing" means doing more, not less; giving more, not less; and caring more, not less, as we demonstrate, by personal example, the hilarious joy to be found in incarnating the generous heart of the Father in the context of people who have yet to meet him.

In the days of service left to each of us on this earth, we will no doubt continue to face the difficulties imposed by disparate wealth, debilitating poverty, and diverse opinions about what Jesus wants us to do in funding God's global mission. We will be forced repeatedly to make personal decisions whether "to buy and to keep" or to share our resources in support of ministries targeting people groups that are both impoverished and unreached. May more of us choose to bring joy to the Father's heart by sharing his burden for the world as eagerly as we welcome the blessing of the wealth he has entrusted to us.

For my part, I urge us to give more wisely by returning to the dictates of Social Calvinism, to minister more consistently within the context of truly covenantal relationships, and to share more generously whether we are guided by a strategy like my Missionary Marshall Plan or by some other equally useful agenda. Nothing less will suffice if we expect to hear the Lord's accolade, "Well done, good and faithful servant!" when we face Jesus in the fullness of the kingdom and review with him our decisions about whether it was better in our lifetime "to give or not to give."

"Buffetting" Western Givers

In my preface to this book, I wrote, "Even in past mission consultations shaped specifically to address the dependency issue forthrightly, it seems to me that most of the potentially powerful punches, the ones that might hit us squarely and get our attention in forceful ways, have too often been pulled. My hope is that this book will correct this error. My readers will need, therefore, to brace themselves and be prepared to take a few carefully placed blows intentionally targeted to strike at the heart of traditional perspectives on this subject. I hope to stretch them beyond the comfort zones defined by current missiological convictions on this subject."

I trust that by now readers will find the buffeting they have endured to have been an effective wake-up call to their sense of personal responsibility to encourage more frequent decisions "to give" in support of lost and needy people around the world. The word *buffet* means to drive home or force with, or as if with, repeated blows. Synonyms include the verbs "pound," "pummel," or "beat." No doubt some will think I have pressed my assault on the established arguments against giving too far and too forcefully. Others may conclude that they are giving adequately already; such donors will likely dismiss my concerns out of hand. But I believe some will take my exhortation toward greater generosity more seriously.

I have tried to be wise in choosing where to aim each point I have made in promoting a change in our Western ways of thinking about giving. I did this hoping to provoke rather than alienate readers who may find themselves on the other side of this debate. But presenting a case against a position so pervasively accepted as that represented by the three-self paradigm is no easy matter. Established perspectives are not easily dislodged and replaced by fresh challenges or by unconventional suggestions about how a problem might be approached. Like a rusty nut that is stuck fast but needs to be removed from an old, weathered bolt, as time passes more elbow grease is required to break the grip of the old connection.

I was musing about my effort to "buffet" Western givers as I worked with my editor on finishing the manuscript for this book. During that time, I was astounded to hear reports from all the major media outlets focusing global attention for several days on a single Western giver. All the media hype was aimed at reporting the largest personal gift in US history, as seventy-five-year-old Warren Buffett gave away $37 billion of his vast fortune. The media frenzy that followed this amazingly benevolent act was intensified because of the irony associated with the recipient of Buffett's generosity. Buffett, the world's second-richest man, effectively gave custody of most of his billions to a foundation operated by the world's wealthiest man, fifty-year-old Bill Gates, and his wife, Melinda.

The magnitude of this enormous contribution is hard to grasp. To put the gift into *financial perspective*, it represents nearly twice the combined giving of the three most generous US philanthropists of the last two centuries. In current dollars, Andrew Carnegie, John D. Rockefeller,

and John D. Rockefeller Jr. gave away a combined total of $1
to various charities. To put the gift into *global perspective*, Bu
nual infusion of stock will also double the annual distribution of grants
from the Gates Foundation from approximately $1.5 billion to over $3
billion per year. This amount is roughly equal to the entire annual UN
budget! It is thirty times the budget for the World Bank and forty times
the total yearly budget for the International Red Cross!

To put the gift into *spiritual perspective*, I believe it demonstrates
the reality that the kingdom principles articulated by Jesus are at work,
moving hearts to be generous, even among nonbelievers—whether or
not they recognize Jesus as Lord. I have read nothing indicating that
either Buffett or the Gates are motivated in their philanthropy by a faith
perspective, though Melinda Gates is reported to identify openly as a
member of the Catholic Church. Still, God's Word and kingdom realities are at work in their lives! The principles I have in mind are drawn
from the following verses included in passages where Jesus is speaking
specifically of financial stewardship:

1. "From everyone who has been given much, much will be re-
    quired" (Luke 12:48).

2. "I tell you that to everyone who has, more shall be given" (Luke
    19:26).

3. "Whoever can be trusted with very little can also be trusted with
    much" (Luke 16:10 NIV).

Both Buffett and the Gates have stated publicly that their giving is
governed by a sense of responsibility to "give back to society" a measure
of the vast wealth their success has afforded them. Expressed in biblical
language, we could say they are acting generously because they know
intuitively that *to whom much has been given, much is required*. I credit
the hand of God, reflecting the first kingdom principle noted above, with
the direct (if unseen and unacknowledged) influence that is guiding these
wealthy individuals' altruism. No doubt some Christians will think this is
going too far, presuming a godly influence that these donors might deny.
But remember that one way we can see the kingdom advancing is when

we are able to observe biblical principles impacting society even when conversions have not yet occurred. I think Buffett's gift is an example of Andrew Walls' "Gospel Test" that we should not miss.

Secular observers surely haven't lost sight of this extraordinary generosity! One foreign secular news outlet, Radio Singapore International, put it this way:

> Philanthropy is one thing. But to give huge sums of money, not peanuts, to an entity that is not going to perpetuate your name—what does one call that? "Generosity" seems apt, but it seems insufficient. "Selflessness"—a total lack of ego—would better fit the bill, but that too seems insufficient. I know of only one word that would suffice, and that is "charity." To give with no expectation of return; to give for the love of giving; to give with no desire to perpetuate your name—that's true charity.[1]

It would be a shame if the world can see the remarkable selflessness of this act of benevolence and Christians refused to acknowledge the supernatural source of so great a spirit of charity.

I also recognize, in Buffett's recent donation, the effect of the second principle in the Scriptures noted above. How better to explain the decision of the second-richest man in the world to entrust the greater portion of his wealth to the benevolent direction of the richest man in the world? To secularly minded observers, the irony of this act obscures the biblical explanation found in the simple promise of God to bless faithful financial stewardship—*to everyone who has, more shall be given*. So the Gates, who have given $30 billion of their own resources to the foundation that bears their name, are entrusted with even more wealth to manage because Buffett has recognized their philanthropic reliability and wisdom. Put in biblical terms, *having been faithful with very little* (a hard phrase to use for a multibillion dollar trust!), Buffett assumes the Gates *can also be trusted with much*. Thus his decision reflects the third

---

1 "Warren Buffet's [*sic*] Staggering Gift," Radio Singapore International, July 5, 2006, http://www.rsi.sg/english/callfromamerica/view/20060705142413/1/.html.

scriptural principle noted above. God is amazing in his influence and wisdom!

In an interview in *FORTUNE* magazine, Buffett was asked why he decided to give the lion's share of his resources to a foundation already so well-endowed—rather than adding to the resources of the Susan Thompson Buffett Foundation, the charity he and his wife established many years ago and which was renamed for her after her death in 2004. Buffett explained, in no uncertain terms, his decision to trust the Gates because of their proven faithfulness:

> The short answer is that I came to realize that there was a terrific foundation that was already scaled-up—that wouldn't have to go through the real grind of getting to a megasize like the Buffett Foundation would—and that could productively use my money now.
>
> The longer answer is that over the years I had gotten to know Bill and Melinda Gates well . . . [and I] had grown to admire what they were doing with their foundation. . . . I'm getting two people enormously successful at something, where I've had a chance to see what they've done, where I know they will keep doing it—where they've done it with their own money, so they're not living in some fantasy world—and where in general I agree with their reasoning. . . .
>
> What can be more logical, in whatever you want done, than finding someone better equipped than you are to do it? Who wouldn't select Tiger Woods to take his place in a high-stakes golf game? That's how I feel about this decision about my money.[2]

What was the impact on the Gates when this enormous trust was placed in them? Not surprisingly, they responded soberly by saying, "We are awed by our friend Warren Buffett's decision to use his fortune to

---

2 Carol J. Loomis, "A Conversation with Warren Buffett," *FORTUNE*, June 25, 2006, http://money.cnn.com/2006/06/25/magazines/fortune/charity2.fortune/index.htm.

address the world's most challenging inequities, and we are humbled that he has chosen to direct a large portion of it to the Bill & Melinda Gates Foundation. . . . As we move forward with the work, we do so with a profound sense of responsibility. Working with Warren and with our partners around the world, we have a tremendous opportunity to make a positive difference in people's lives."[3]

Most of the funds distributed by the Gates Foundation are presently spent on medical projects, including AIDS research, inoculation programs for poor children, and other health and education related causes. Seventy percent of the foundation's grants go to international projects. Though I cannot personally endorse all the recipients of the Gates Foundation's generosity (Planned Parenthood is one major beneficiary), it is immediately obvious that a great deal of good is being done worldwide because of Bill and Melinda Gates' established benevolence. Their previous giving patterns will likely be maintained since Buffett's gift was made with the hope that the expansion of the Gates Foundation's formulation of grants would be "one of depth, rather than breadth."[4]

My purpose in writing this book has been in part to demonstrate that more could and should be done to release resources from the West to the rest of the world in an effort to relieve suffering and to advance the gospel in our time. The extraordinary generosity of these two families alone has the potential to make an enormously healing and helpful impact on the world in the twenty-first century. I am praying that the "Buffetting effect" of this gift will be like a major earthquake in the Christian community, one with aftershocks that will reverberate in a way that will shake many more billions of dollars in gifts from the pockets of wealthy Westerners. Buffett's example should be an immediate challenge to all Western believers to reconsider their level of stewardship.

---

3   Bill and Melinda Gates, "Statement on Warren Buffett's Announcement," Bill & Melinda Gates Foundation website, June 25, 2006, http://www.gatesfoundation.org/AboutUs/Announcements/Announce-060625.htm.

4   Letter from Warren Buffet to Bill and Melinda Gates, communicating the terms of his donation, June 26, 2006. Available at http://berkshirehathaway.com/donate/bmgfltr.pdf.

He did, after all, dispose of 85 percent of his accumulated fortune in this unprecedented gift.

Together, the Gates and Warren Buffett will now be able to take amazing steps toward meeting the world's most serious material needs—food, clean water, and health care. Who ever would have imagined that only two families could provide so great a store of resources for humanitarian purposes?

In focusing on Buffett's stunning generosity, I don't want to appear as if I am fawning over this unprecedented philanthropic event. I simply see an element of divine timing in the Lord's making so significant an example of extraordinary giving available as my book goes to press. Presumably we should follow God's example and take note of the charitable instincts of nonbelievers in instances like this. Consider the evidence for this suggestion found in the story of the Roman centurion, Cornelius, as his conversion to faith in Jesus was drawing near.

> Now there was a man at Caesarea named Cornelius, a centurion of what was called the Italian cohort, *a devout man and one who feared God with all his household, and gave many alms to the Jewish people and prayed to God continually.* About the ninth hour of the day he clearly saw in a vision an angel of God who had just come in and said to him, "Cornelius!" And fixing his gaze on him and being much alarmed, he said, "What is it, Lord?" And he said to him, *"Your prayers and alms have ascended as a memorial before God."* (Acts 10:1–4, italics added)

I see no reason why we should assume that God has taken any less notice of Warren Buffett's extreme generosity than he did the unexpected almsgiving of Cornelius. Perhaps heaven has a memorial to mark this twenty-first century gift just as it did the one Luke describes in the first century! In making this point, I am not suggesting a special *heavenly reward* is somehow associated with this gift (or with any other act of unselfishness for that matter). It simply seems to me that this text indicates there is somehow a special *heavenly regard* for the heartfelt generosity of nonbelievers. (Acts 11:13–14 seems to make it clear that Cornelius was not a believer when the Lord affirmed heaven's recognition of his almsgiving.) Still, God rejoiced over the centurion's generosity. If God is also rejoicing over Buffett's unprecedented gift in our day, so should we!

In my opinion, we Christians are remiss if we fail to take some special note of Buffett's contribution, offering at least our acknowledgment of his largess in the same spirit of appreciation that God exhibited in the first century for a nonbeliever's selfless decision to give in service of the interests of others. I don't think that Buffett's gift makes him a saint! But I do think that too many commentators (some of them evangelicals) have been uncharitable in reporting his charitable intent. All Americans, and especially we Christians, can afford to be more generous in our praise!

Buffett's eternal destiny obviously cannot be determined apart from his ultimate decision to acknowledge Jesus as Lord and Savior, as did Cornelius. It is not, after all, as if Buffett could "buy his way into heaven" as some have misunderstood his comments accompanying the announcement of this contribution to indicate. Buffett told the crowd at the New York Public Library (cite of his announcement regarding his unprecedented contribution), "There is more than one way to get to heaven, but this is a great way."[5] Evangelicals and non-evangelicals alike were quick to pounce on Buffett's apparently poor theology of salvation, assuming he believed that his gift had secured him a place with God after death.

One Internet blog wrote on this question under the unkind title, "Is Warren Buffett Going to Hell?"[6] Buffett quickly responded in his own defense, clarifying his position in an open letter to offended Fordham University theology professor, Richard Dillon. Dillon had publicly taken

5   Thomas Hargrove, "The Week in Review," Scripps Howard News Service, June 30, 2006, http://www.shns.com/shns/g_index2.cfm?action=detail&pk=WEEKINREVIEW-06-30-06.

6   "A DealBreaker Investigative Report: Is Warren Buffett Going To Hell?" DealBreaker.com, http://www.dealbreaker.com/2006/07/dealbreaker_exclusive_will_war.html.

the billionaire-turned-philanthropist to task for presuming his gift had reserved a place for him with God for eternity. Buffett wrote:

> For years when people have asked me about various techniques of investing . . . I reply "There's more than one way to get to heaven" to indicate that various methods can produce good results.
>
> Similarly at the New York Public Library, the discussion was about an individual giving to someone else's foundation. I said I thought it was a good idea to let someone who was better at the process than I make the donations, and I had chosen Bill and Melinda Gates to do so. I then added "But there is more than one way to get to heaven" indicating that others might well choose different people to carry out their philanthropic work.
>
> In my view, it would be crazy to think that entrance into heaven—if there is such a place—would depend on giving away surplus wealth which in no way affects the well-being of the giver.[7]

In my opinion, it is a shame that people in general and Christians in particular are so ready to judge, to find fault, and to communicate disfavor rather than delight when a person acts in so unselfish a manner as Buffett has unquestionably done on this occasion. Unfortunately, Buffett's gift was met with broad cynicism as well as with praise in the media. He was criticized for giving to the wrong causes (a concern I share to some degree), for taking advantage of his gift to avoid estate taxes, for making a public display of his generosity, for retaining too much of his massive resources (the $7 billion Buffett maintained as a personal fortune roughly equals Rupert Murdoch's accumulated net worth),[8] and for practicing "reckless benevolence." Why can we not simply affirm

---

7   "Warren Buffett Responds to 'Is Warren Buffett Going To Hell?'" DealBreaker.com, http://www.dealbreaker.com/warren_buffett/.

8   David Nason, "Hardly Too Little, but Way Too Late to Earn Adulation," The Australian, July 3, 2006, http://www.theaustralian.news.com.au/story/0,20867,19660792-643,00.html.

the obvious generosity exhibited in this charitable act and pray for other magnanimous decisions to follow this one—and for more Americans of means to be challenged by the example?

After all, the charitable intention of just these two wealthiest of American families demonstrates exactly the point I am endeavoring to make. Western wealth is held too much in reserve when global need is so apparent. According to *Forbes* magazine, the United States has another 313 billionaires who could follow Buffett's example of extravagant giving at some level if they were moved to do so.[9] More than four million more rich Americans have a net worth in excess of $1 million.[10] How much in untapped resources is available for the world's poor if we think of the assets held privately by this large group representing the wealthiest people in our country? Truly America is uniquely poised to serve the kingdom of God and the lost world as the War Chest for World Missions!

But most of my readers are likely to be among the portion of more ordinary believers who already give regularly and sacrificially in smaller amounts to see the kingdom advanced worldwide. Recognition and affirmation is due to you, too, for your commitment to unusual faithfulness in giving! Be encouraged that God's kingdom counts as most precious not the gifts of billions of dollars made from huge stores of wealth but the smallest ones made from the most meager reserves. In Mark 12:41–44 Jesus affirmed his appreciation of small gifts made by the poor, a reflection of the issue of proportional sacrifice discussed in chapter 14. The kingdom rejoices over gifts measured in widow's mites, mustard seeds, and little jars of oil—the most noteworthy examples of charity from a heavenly perspective.

May I urge you to be praying for more Christians to follow your example (and Warren Buffett's) by embracing a new level of generos-

---

9 "Forbes 400: Record 313 US Billionaires," *CNNMoney.com,* September 23, 2004, http://money.cnn.com/2004/09/23/news/newsmakers/forbes_400/.

10 Jeffrey D. Sachs, The End of Poverty: Economic Possibilities for Our Time (New York: Penguin Books, 2005), 364.

ity expressed toward lost and needy people all over the world? Ask the Lord to use Buffett's donation as a first fruits expression of a harvest of giving that might begin to flow in your lifetime and mine to transform the world, spiritually and practically. May we find our way back to a twenty-first century application of the first century spirit of generosity and mutual concern that allowed Luke to observe in the first church ever planted, "The congregation of those who believed were of one heart and soul; and not one of them claimed that anything belonging to him was his own, but all things were common property to them. . . . There was not a needy person among them" (Acts 4:32, 34).

As we pray for God to raise up an army of extravagant givers, we might also pray for Warren Buffett and Bill and Melinda Gates to be reached with the gospel personally so that their administration of future gifts might be even more directly guided by the hand and the wisdom of God. Ask the Lord to put committed Christians in influential places on each of their staff teams. It might even be appropriate to write letters of affirmation and appreciation for their good intentions and their extraordinary example of generosity. We should be "Buffetted" and benefited greatly by such worthy examples of men and women who are making the better choice when faced with the decision "to give or not to give"!

BIBLIOGRAPHY

Aldrich, Joseph C. *Lifestyle Evangelism: Crossing Cultural Boundaries to Reach the Unbelieving World.* Portland: Multnomah, 1981.

Allen, Roland. *Missionary Methods: St. Paul's or Ours?* Grand Rapids: Eerdmans, 1962.

Anderson, Rufus T. *Foreign Missions: Their Relations and Claims.* New York: C. Scribner & Co., 1869.

Apter, David E. *Rethinking Development: Modernization, Dependency, and Postmodern Politics.* Newbury Park, CA: Sage Publications, Inc., 1987.

Barnhouse, Donald Grey. *The Invisible War: The Panorama of the Continuing Conflict between Good and Evil.* Grand Rapids: Zondervan, 1965.

Bauckham, Richard. *The Bible in Politics: How to Read the Bible Politically.* Louisville: Westminster/John Knox Press, 1989.

Beaver, Pierce R. *To Advance the Gospel: A Collection of the Writings of Rufus Anderson.* Grand Rapids: Eerdmans, 1967.

Bennett, Chuck, and Glenn Schwartz. "Two Christian Leaders Discuss Dependency." *Mission Frontiers: The Bulletin of the U.S. Center for World Mission*, Pasadena, CA (January–February 1997): 25. Available at http://www.missionfrontiers.org/1997/0102/jf9712.htm.

Beyerhaus, Peter, and Henry Lefever, *The Responsible Church and the Foreign Mission.* London: World Dominion Press, 1964.

Blue, Ron. *Master Your Money: A Step-by-step Plan for Financial Freedom.* Nashville: Thomas Nelson, 1986.

Blue, Ron, with Jodie Berndt. *Generous Living: Finding Contentment through Giving.* Grand Rapids: Zondervan, 1997.

Bonhoeffer, Dietrich. *Dietrich Bonhoeffer Works Volume 5: Life Together and Prayerbook of the Bible.* Edited by Geffrey B. Kelly. Translated by Daniel W. Bloesch and James H. Burtness. Minneapolis: Augsburg Fortress, 1996.

Bonk, Jonathan J. *Missions and Money: Affluence as a Western Missionary Problem.* Maryknoll, NY: Orbis Books, 1991.

Bosch, David J. *Transforming Mission: Paradigm Shifts in Theology of Mission.* Maryknoll, NY: Orbis Books, 1991.

Bounds, E. M. *Winning the Invisible War.* Pittsburgh: Whitaker House, 1984.

Burkett, Larry. *Debt-Free Living.* Chicago: Moody, 1989.

———. *What Ever Happened to the American Dream.* Chicago: Moody, 1993.

———. *Your Finances in Changing Times.* Chicago: Moody, 1975.

Camps, A., L. A. Hoedemaker, M. R. Spindler, and F. J. Verstraelen, eds. *Missiology: An Ecumenical Introduction.* Grand Rapids: Eerdmans, 1995.

Collins, James C., and Jerry I. Porras. *Built to Last: Successful Habits of Visionary Companies.* New York: HarperBusiness, 1994.

Collins, Jim. *Good to Great: Why Some Companies Make the Leap . . . and Others Don't.* New York: HarperBusiness, 2001.

———. *Good to Great and the Social Sectors: A Monograph to Accompany Good to Great.* Boulder, CO: Jim Collins, 2005.

Crosson, Russ. *Money and Your Marriage.* Dallas: Word, 1989.

Dayton, Howard L. Jr. *Your Money: Frustration or Freedom?* Wheaton: Tyndale, 1971.

Diamond, Sara. *Not by Politics Alone: The Enduring Influence of the Christian Right.* New York: The Guilford Press, 1998.

Easterly, William. *The White Man's Burden: Why the West's Efforts to Aid the Rest Have Done So Much Ill and So Little Good.* New York: Penguin Press, 2006.

Egger, Robert, and Howard Yoon. *Begging for Change.* New York: Harper Business, 2004.

Ely, Richard. *Social Aspects of Christianity.* New York: T. Y. Crowell, 1889.

Escobar, Samuel. *The New Global Mission: The Gospel from Everywhere to Everyone.* Downers Grove, IL: InterVarsity, 2003.

Foster, Richard J. *Freedom of Simplicity.* New York: Harper Collins Publishers, 1981.

―――. *Money, Sex and Power: The Challenge of the Disciplined Life.* San Francisco: Harper & Row, 1985.

Garrison, David. *Church Planting Movements: How God Is Redeeming a Lost World.* Midlothian, VA: WIGTake Resources, 2004.

―――. "How to Kill a Church-Planting Movement." *Mission Frontiers: The Bulletin of the U.S. Center for World Mission*, Pasadena, CA (November–December 2004). Available at http://www.missionfrontiers.org/archive.htm.

Guinness, Os. *Doing Well and Doing Good: Money, Giving, and Caring in a Free Society.* Colorado Springs: NavPress, 2001.

Hesselgrave, David J. *Communicating Christ Cross-Culturally: An Introduction to Missionary Communication.* Grand Rapids: Zondervan, 1991.

Hiebert, Frances F., and Paul G. Hiebert. *Case Studies in Missions.* Grand Rapids: Baker, 1987.

Hiebert, Paul G. *Anthropological Reflections on Missiological Issues.* Grand Rapids: Baker, 1994.

Hughes, Philip E. *Commentary on the Second Epistle to the Corinthians, The New International Commentary on the New Testament.* F. F. Bruce, General Editor. Grand Rapids: Eerdmans, 1962.

Johnston, Douglas M. Jr. "Religion and Foreign Policy." Chapter 6 in *Forgiveness and Reconciliation: Religion, Public Policy and Conflict*

Transformation. Raymond G. Helmick, SJ, and Rodney L. Peterson, eds. Philadelphia: Templeton Foundation Press, 2001.

Johnstone, Patrick. *The Church Is Bigger Than You Think.* Great Britain: Christian Focus Publications/WEC, 1998.

Jones, E. Stanley. *The Unshakable Kingdom and the Unchanging Person.* Nashville: Abingdon, 1972.

Kirk, J. Andrew. *What Is Mission? Theological Explorations.* Minneapolis: Augsburg Fortress, 2000.

Kornfield, William J. "What Hath Our Western Money and Our Western Gospel Wrought?" *Mission Frontiers: The Bulletin of the U.S. Center for World Mission,* Pasadena, CA (January–February 1997). Available at http://www.missionfrontiers.org/1997/0102/jf9710.htm.

Koyama, Kosuke. *Three Mile an Hour God: Biblical Reflections.* Maryknoll, NY: Orbis Books, 1980.

Kraft, Charles H. *Defeating Dark Angels: Breaking Demonic Oppression in the Believer's Life.* Ann Arbor, MI: Servant Publications, 1992.

Kraft, Charles H., and Tom N. Wisley, eds. *Readings in Dynamic Indigeneity.* Pasadena, CA: William Carey Library, 1979.

Lewis, C. S. *A Grief Observed.* New York: Harper Collins Publishers, Inc., 2001.

MacGregor, Malcom. *Your Money Matters.* Minneapolis: Bethany, 1977.

McGavran, Donald A. *Understanding Church Growth.* Grand Rapids: Eerdmans, 1970.

Miley, George. *Loving the Church . . . Blessing the Nations: Pursuing the Role of Local Churches in Global Mission.* Tyrone, GA: Authentic Publishing, 2003.

Miller, C. John. *Powerful Evangelism for the Powerless.* Phillipsburg, NJ: Presbyterian and Reformed Publishing Company, 1980.

Miller, Darrow L. *Discipling Nations: The Power of Truth to Transform Cultures.* Seattle: YWAM Publishing, 2001.

Murphy, Ed. *The Handbook for Spiritual Warfare.* Nashville: Thomas Nelson Publishers, 1992.

Myers, Bryant L. *Walking with the Poor: Principles and Practices of Transformational Development.* Maryknoll, NY: Orbis Books, 1999.

Neely, Alan. *Christian Mission: A Case Study Approach.* Maryknoll, NY: Orbis Books, 1997.

Nevius, John L. *Methods of Mission Work.* New York: Foreign Mission Library, 1895.

Olasky, Marvin N. *The Tragedy of American Compassion.* Washington, DC: Regnery Gateway, 1992.

————. *Renewing American Compassion.* New York: Free Press, 1996.

————.*Compassionate Conservatism.* New York: Free Press, 2000.

Otis, George Jr. *The Last of the Giants.* Tarrytown, NY: Fleming H. Revell Company, 1991.

Ott, Craig. "Let the Buyer Beware." *Mission Frontiers: The Bulletin of the U.S. Center for World Mission*, Pasadena, CA (September–October 1994). Available at http://www.missionfrontiers.org/1994/0910/so947.htm.

Padilla, C. René. *Mission Between the Times: Essays on the Kingdom.* Grand Rapids: Eerdmans, 1985.

Perkins, John. *Let Justice Roll Down.* Ventura, CA: Gospel Light, 1976.

————. *With Justice for All.* Ventura, CA: Regal Books, 1982.

————. *Beyond Charity: The Call to Christian Community Development.* Grand Rapids: Baker, 1993.

Peterlin, Davorin. "The Wrong Kind of Missionary: A Semi-Autobiographic Outcry." *Mission Studies* 12, no. 2 (1995): 164–74.

Petersen, Jim. *Church Without Walls.* Colorado Springs: NavPress, 1992.

Piper, John. *Let the Nations Be Glad.* Grand Rapids: Baker, 1993.

Piper, Otto A. *The Christian Meaning of Money.* Englewood Cliffs, NJ: Prentice-Hall, 1965.

Ramachandra, Vinoth. *The Recovery of Mission: Beyond the Pluralist Paradigm*, Grand Rapids: Eerdmans, 1996.

Remenyi, Joseph V. *Where Credit Is Due: Income Generating Programs for the Poor in Developing Countries.* London: Intermediate Technology Productions, 1991.

Rickett, Daniel. *Building Strategic Relationships: A Practical Guide to Partnering with Non-Western Missions.* Pleasant Hill, CA: Partners International, 2000.

Robb, John D., and James A. Hill. *The Peacemaking Power of Prayer.* Nashville: Broadman & Holman Publishers, 2000.

Ronsvalle, John L., and Sylvia Ronsvalle. *The State of Church Giving through 2000.* Champaign, IL: Empty Tomb, 2002.

Rowell, John. *Magnify Your Vision for the Small Church.* Atlanta: Northside Community Church, 1999.

Sachs, Jeffrey D. *The End of Poverty: Economic Possibilities for Our Time.* New York: Penguin Press, 2005.

Samuel, Vinay, and Chris Sugden, eds. *Mission as Transformation.* Carlisle, CA: Regnum Books International, 1999.

Schwartz, Glenn J. "A Champion for Self Reliance: An Interview with Glenn Schwartz." *Mission Frontiers: The Bulletin of the U.S. Center for World Mission,* Pasadena, CA (January–February 1997). Available at http://www.missionfrontiers.org/1997/0102/jf979.htm.

———. "Guideposts for Giving." *Mission Frontiers: The Bulletin of the U.S. Center for World Mission,* Pasadena, CA (September 2001). Available at http://www.missionfrontiers.org/2001/03/200103.htm.

Scott, Lindy. *Economic Koinonia Within the Body of Christ.* Mexico City, Mexico: Editorial Kyrios, 1980.

Sen, A. K. *Development as Freedom.* New York: Anchor Books, 1999.

Sharpe, Robert F. *The Planned Giving Idea: Creative Ways to Increase the Income of Your Institution.* Nashville: Thomas Nelson, 1978.

Shenk, Wilbert R. "Henry Venn 1796–1873 Anglican (CMJ)." *Occasional Bulletin of Missionary Research* 1, no. 2 (April 1977).

———. *Henry Venn—Missionary Statesman.* Maryknoll, NY: Orbis Books, 1983.

Sherman, Dean. *Spiritual Warfare for Every Christian.* Seattle: YWAM Publishing, 1990.

Sider, Ronald J., ed. *Living More Simply: Biblical Principles and Practical Models.* Downers Grove, IL: InterVarsity, 1980.

————. *Just Generosity: A New Vision for Overcoming Poverty in America.* Grand Rapids: Baker, 1999.

————. *Rich Christians in an Age of Hunger: Moving from Affluence to Generosity.* Nashville: W Publishing Group, 2005.

————. *The Scandal of the Evangelical Conscience: Why Are Christians Living Just Like the Rest of the World?* Grand Rapids: Baker, 2005.

Silvoso, Ed. *That None Should Perish: How to Reach Entire Cities for Christ Through Prayer Evangelism.* Ventura, CA: Regal Books, 1994.

Sine, Christine, and Tom Sine. *Living on Purpose: Finding God's Best for Your Life.* Grand Rapids: Baker, 2002.

Sine, Tom. *The Mustard Seed Conspiracy: You Can Make a Difference in Tomorrow's Troubled World.* Waco: Word, 1981.

————. *Mustard Seed vs. McWorld: Reinventing Life and Faith for the Future.* Grand Rapids: Baker, 1999.

Starcher, Rich. "Supporting National Church Leaders." *Africa Alive: A Publication of the EFCM Africa Office.* February–March 2000.

Stiglitz, Joseph E. *Globalization and Its Discontents.* New York: W. W. Norton, 2002.

Stott, John. *Decisive Issues Facing Christians Today.* Old Tappan, NJ: Fleming H. Revell Company, 1990.

Taylor, William D., ed. *Global Missiology for the 21st Century: The Iguassu Dialogue.* Grand Rapids: Baker, 2000.

Thomas, Norman E., ed., *Classic Texts in Mission and World Christianity.* Maryknoll, NY: Orbis Books, 1995.

Tippett, A. R. *Verdict Theology in Missionary Theory.* Pasadena, CA: William Carey Library, 1973.

Townsend, Peter. *Poverty in the United Kingdom: A Survey of Household Resources and Standards of Living.* Harmondsworth, UK: Penguin Books, 1979.

Truman, Harry S., *Memoirs by Harry S. Truman: Two Years of Trial and Hope.* Garden City, NY: Doubleday & Company, Inc., 1956.

Vallet, Ronald E. *Stepping Stones of the Steward: A Faith Journey through Jesus' Parables.* 2nd ed. Manlius, NY: REV/Rose Publishing, 1994.

————. *The Steward Living in Covenant: A New Perspective on Old Testament Stories.* Manlius, NY: REV/Rose Publishing, 2001.

Vincent, Marvin R. *Word Studies in the New Testament.* Mclean, VA: MacDonald Publishing Company, n.d.

Volf, Miroslav. *Exclusion and Embrace: A Theological Exploration of Identity, Otherness and Reconciliation.* Nashville: Abingdon, 1996.

————. *Free of Charge: Giving and Forgiving in a Culture Stripped of Grace.* Grand Rapids: Zondervan, 2005.

Wagner, C. Peter. *Warfare Prayer: How to Seek God's Power and Protection in the Battle to Build His Kingdom.* Ventura, CA: Regal Books, 1992.

Warren, Max. *To Apply the Gospel: Selections from the Writings of Henry Venn.* Grand Rapids: Eerdmans, 1971.

Walls, Andrew F. *The Cross-Cultural Process in Christian History: Studies in the Transmission and Appropriation of Faith.* Maryknoll, NY: Orbis Books, 2002.

Wuest, Kenneth S. *Wuest's Word Studies from the Greek New Testament, Volume One.* Grand Rapids: Eerdmans, 1973.

Yohannan, K. P. *Revolution in World Missions.* Carrollton, TX: Gospel for Asia, 2003.